SPOILED SILK

Spoiled Silk

The Red Mayor
and the
Great Paterson Textile Strike

GEORGE WILLIAM SHEA

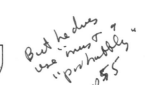

Fordham University Press
New York
2001

Library of Congress Cataloging-in-Publication Data

Shea, George William.
    Spoiled silk : the Red mayor and the great Paterson textile strike / George William Shea.—1st ed.
        p.   cm.
    Includes index.
    ISBN 0-8232-2133-4 (hardcover) — ISBN 0-8232-2134-2 (pbk.)
    1. Brueckmann, William.   2. Brueckmann, Katherine.   3. Socialists—United States—Biography.   4. Mayors—New Jersey—Haledon—Biography.   5. Silk Workers' Strike, Peterson, N.J., 1913. I. Title

HX84.B726 S54   2001
331.892′87739′0974923—dc21   2001033828

Printed in the United States of America
01   02   03   04   05   5   4   3   2   1
First Edition

This book is dedicated to my grandparents:
William Brueckmann, Katherine Ruhren, Sadie Long,
and George Shea

CONTENTS

....

Preface   ix

1.   Like Just Yesterday   1

2.   The Cedar Cliff Hotel   20

3.   The Business and the Party   28

4.   Stubborn Dutchman   36

5.   Strike in the Paterson Mills   49

6.   The Haledon Meetings Begin   56

7.   Desperation Takes Hold   68

8.   The IWW on Trial   72

9.   A Question of How You See It   79

10.   The Strike Ends   89

11.   Family Matters, Party Matters   101

12.   The War   114

13.   Good Times   120

14.   Loss   128

15.   A Visit to Morrissee Avenue   134

16.   Bad Times   141

17.   Just Not in Him   152

18.   I Had a Son   160

19.   New Family   167

20.   Sunday Walks, Sunday Mass   175

CONTENTS

21. Retired Now 184

22. Things Run Down 194

23. The Last Walk 198

Index 203

PREFACE

·······················

PEOPLE KNOW RELATIVELY LITTLE about the radical left movement that flourished in the United States in the early part of the twentieth century. Most identify it with romantic figures like John Reed, the journalist who left the United States to join the revolutionaries in Russia who were forming the Soviet state, or with the bitter strikes and union actions that frequently resulted in violence. With the advent of the Cold War, the far left was so thoroughly discredited and demonized that few saw beyond the caricature of leftist politicians and thinkers, let alone understood the vision of men and women who had embraced the Marxist social agenda in the United States in earlier years.

Few socialists were in fact either romantic intellectuals or violent subversives and spies. They were, on the whole, quite average citizens. Many were recent immigrants who were, with difficulty, carving out a life for themselves and their families in America. They had relatively little interest in the international Marxist movement. They had been attracted to the socialist dream in Europe while living under regimes that, in many cases, denied them economic opportunity and access to significant political power. Many of them felt, rightly or wrongly, that they were being denied these things in their adopted country as well and that the solution to the problem, here as in Europe, was the establishment of a socialist system.

My maternal grandparents, William and Katherine Brueckmann, were two such people. As this memoir will tell, they came to the United States from the Rhineland at the end of the nineteenth century. Because they were weavers, they settled in Paterson, New Jersey, then a major center of textile manufacturing. They raised a family there and became deeply involved in socialist politics. William Brueckmann became the mayor of the neighboring suburb of Haledon and played an important role in the famous silk strike of 1913, in which the Socialists joined with Big Bill Haywood's Industrial Workers of the World to champion the workers' cause.

The events of that famous strike make for an exciting story, but the strike itself failed. Its failure was, in a way, symptomatic of the broader failure that the left would suffer in the coming decades, a failure precipitated by nativism and xenophobia during the First World War, hastened by the prosperity of the twenties, and sealed at last by the attacks of the extreme right during the Cold War.

The story of William and Katherine Brueckmann is the story of two new U.S. citizens who had no taste whatever for violence or subversion but who embraced a political and social agenda that they believed would improve the lives of their fellow citizens. They hoped that they could, through democratic means, change their new country for the better. They struggled to do this and failed. Eventually, in order to survive, they were forced, in their actions at least, to compromise and to accept the capitalist system of the United States. Like many people who make such compromises, they never quite abandoned the idea, however, and imagined, even after having achieved considerable financial success, that they were still socialists at heart.

In telling their story, I have decided not to confine myself to their public life. That public life is, of course, both stirring and significant, but the effect it had on their private life is perhaps even more interesting. And so the second part of this book tells the story of how their political disappointments and compromises changed their family and their community. This part of the story must be a two-fold tale—one that describes the effect of their disappointments on their private lives and one that examines as well the contradictions and problems of the society they had somewhat grudgingly accepted, problems that contributed, it seems to me, to their tragedy.

And it was a tragedy. Here were, after all, two basically good people, dedicated to a vision of a better society, each unhappily subject to weaknesses of character, which were aggravated and magnified by the turmoil and frustration that engulfed them. For him the weakness was a certain rigidity of mind, a stubbornness, and an insensitivity to the weaknesses of others; for her it was an excess need to love and be loved, along with a tendency to enfold and overprotect and, perhaps, to forgive too easily.

But their story is not just a personal tragedy. It raises, I think, larger social and ethical issues that still haunt the U.S. culture, its economic life, and its political system. In the twenties, William and Katherine Brueckmann accepted a society that was based on the idea that happiness lay largely in the acquisition and consumption of goods and in the gratification of physical needs. They entered a period of good times that, but for a brief hiatus in the thirties, still endures, informed by the politics of pleasure and haunted by its dark offspring—substance abuse, waste, and pollution, not to speak of self-indulgent greed and deteriorating public manners and taste. Their story is then, it seems to me, a grim reminder of the dark underside of the hedonistic ethical paradigm that informed the system with which they made their compromise. The sadness that marked their later life is the sadness that has, in one way or another, visited all too many U.S. families in recent decades. In short, the story of their lives is, sadly, a sign of things to come and of an ethical paradox that still plagues us.

In writing this story, I was blessed in several ways. The accounts of the Brueckmann's public life had, of course, to be carefully researched and drawn from a close reading of newspaper accounts and public records like the minutes of the Council of the Borough of Haledon. These documents were always very graciously made available to me. Beyond that, since I continued to live in Haledon until well into the eighties, I was able to conduct many oral interviews with neighbors who recalled the events of the period that I was treating. These people were very helpful, and I am most grateful to them. I also came into possession of the autobiography of August Ruhren, my grandmother's brother, *The Wandering of a Proletarian*, which, along with his German poems, helped me a great deal in understanding and reconstructing the early period of the family's life in the United States. Above all, of course, I am in debt to my grandparents themselves, with whom I spent a great deal of time as a child and a young man. My grandmother was a great storyteller, and the accounts of her evening storytelling are not fiction. Nor are the references to the long walks in the woods or shared reading sessions with my grandfather. I remember almost everything they told me and can still hear the sound of their voices—her soft, sly laughter, his stern *Junge* or *Unsinn* or the resigned "It's no use talking."

I cannot, of course, claim that every word they speak in this story is verbatim. I have tried, however, to capture their thoughts and views as best I could, not making things up, but when needed, putting into their mouths the words I believe they would have spoken—a writer's trick as old at least as Thucydides. Where I am just imagining their thoughts and words, I try to make that clear to the reader, and beg the reader and my grandparents to forgive any false impression I may create.

As the reader will find in the story that follows, my grandfather distrusted storytelling and storytellers. Indeed he said to me one day, "In time they will run out of stories to tell." He was wrong, of course. He did not realize that his life and the life of Katherine Ruhren, his wife, gave the lie to that curious notion.

New York, January 1998

SPOILED SILK

1 Like Just Yesterday

. . . .

"IT SEEMS LIKE JUST YESTERDAY we came to America," my grand-mother often said to me. I sat with her then on winter nights at the front of the old house on Zabriskie Street, watching the shadows cast by the rotating wheel in the make-believe fireplace and listening to her stories of what she called "the old country" and of her fabulous journey from it to the United States. Her old country was, I came to understand, the Rhineland and the old German town of Krefeld where, in the 1870s, she had been born into a family of weavers, whose fortunes rose and fell with the fortunes of that trade. Her father worked in plush, a special skill, she explained to me, and he had passed on much of what he knew to his children—to Katie, my grandmother, to her brothers, August and Joe, and to her two sisters, Anna and Christine. The family needed the children's hands to work the looms and so, in spite of their success in elementary school, my grandmother and her sisters and brothers never went to high school.

But they loved storytelling, the Ruhren family. I suppose that's why I was treated to those evenings of remembering, to Uncle Joe's funny tall tales at parties, and to the pleasure even now, at the turn of the century, of reading Uncle August's autobiography, which he wrote in the mid-1940s and called *The Wanderings of a Proletarian*. It's from that little book of August's that many of the facts about the Ruhren family's early days and their trip to the United States must come, for, as much as I enjoyed those evenings with my grandmother, I must confess that many of her own tales have fled from my memory. I can remember that she told me about wearing wooden shoes as a child and about being struck on the knuckles when she made mis-takes in school. I remember too her stories of the voyage on the *Maasdam*, of how its screw broke in mid-ocean and how it had to be towed back to Plymouth for repairs. But it is to August's book that I must turn for most of the details about the family's life in Germany and their emigration to the United States.

Times turned bad in Germany in the early 1890s and life grew difficult even for weavers in plush. What was more, the young men faced service in the army, something they resented and had no taste for. So, by ones and twos and threes they left Krefeld, the men first, the women after them, often pretending that they were going to the United States just for a visit but determined, even as they boarded the Rhine steamer for Rotterdam, that the land across the sea would be their new home. It was, they had been told, a place of great promise.

The promise often seemed far off to them. August writes vividly of the ship and the steerage and the rolling sea. There were sixty men in his cabin, each carrying just a single suitcase and the plate and blanket he had been issued at the top of the gangplank. Days when they could walk on the deck above were not so bad, but when a storm arose and there was no going up "to feed the fishes," as they said, then the cabin was truly a prison that rang with the noise of rolling pipes beneath their bunks and with the very distant sound of the band that played above them in first class. In later years on those story-telling nights my grandmother, Katie, laughed over the story of her brother Joe's shooting herring bones off his fork and into the beards of the Hasidic Jews who shared his steerage cabin on the *Maasdam*. They were still barely out of childhood then, and the laughter must have made up for the distance between them and the promise of the new country.

My grandfather, William Brueckmann, was a stern man—especially compared to his future brother-in-law—with a round German face, bright blue eyes, and a long handlebar mustache. When I was a boy, I listened to the stories of his early life on the walks we took together on Sunday mornings. He had grown up in the countryside near Krefeld and had shown extraordinary promise as a student. I still have his report cards from the high school in Elberfeld. He was always the first in his class, and he told me often about how his teacher came to his father's house and begged to be allowed to send his prize pupil to the university. It was impossible, of course. The Brueckmanns too were weavers, and my grandfather's hands were needed at the looms. And so to work he went, taking solace as a young man in the *Turnverein* (gymnastic society), where he excelled at acrobatics, in the long walks in the country on Sundays, for he loved nature, and in the socialist tracts that held out promise of a better life to come. He too, however, felt the effects of the worsening German economy and dreaded the inevitable service in the kaiser's army, and so he too took the Rhine boat and sailed across the ocean to the land where the promises might come true.

My grandparents were not allowed off the ship in Hoboken where the first- and second-class passengers disembarked. If there were family members there to meet them, they could only shout greetings from the pier, for the immigrants had, of course, to call at Castle Garden, where they were examined and asked how much money they had. August could remember admitting that he had only $1.26, and when he was told it would not take him very far, he had to explain hurriedly in his broken English that his father would be waiting for him. So the clerk smiled and let him pass. My grandfather, on the other hand, remembered being complimented as he passed through immigration for his already impressive command of English. "You'll make something of yourself here," the clerk who read over his papers said, and my grandfather replied, he told me, that making something of himself was just what he intended. He did not add when he told the story that he had in fact made something of himself, but I was certain that he expected me to make that judgment for myself. He had by then been mayor of our town for ten years, longer than anyone either before or after him. But I am ahead of myself.

On the streets of Manhattan, the immigrants changed their money, if they had not already done so, often stuffing it into their shoes for safekeeping, for they had been warned that the sharp New York stevedores preyed upon greenhorns. For the Brueckmanns at least the warnings turned out to be true, and my grandfather loved telling the story of his encounter with a gang of stevedores outside a pier on West Street on the day of his arrival in the United States. It happened just after he and his father and his brother Paul had changed their money in a bank near Castle Garden. They were making their way north and caught sight of a group of longshoremen, seven or eight of them, singing and laughing, obviously drunk. As the Brueckmanns drew closer, my grandfather saw that the men were passing bottles of beer around and challenging one another to take longer and longer draughts. Now and then one man would push another against the wall of the pier, and then the two of them would fall to the ground and begin to punch one another. One man with a round face and a red beard was louder than the rest. He kept a large bottle in his hand all the time, and when he tossed his head back and drank, the other men would turn to him, clap their hands, and chant, "More! More!

More! More!" Then he would laugh, spitting out what he could not swallow and, shaking the bottle, spray his friends with the foaming beer.

As my grandfather and his father and brother drew closer, the man with the red beard took the bottle from his lips and stared at them. Then, taking one of his friends aside, he whispered something in his ear. He was whispering, my grandfather realized, about them; he could tell from the way the man kept glancing in their direction. This frightened my grandfather because he understood that he and Paul and his father would be no match for the stevedores, who could easily steal everything they had. As they drew opposite the door of the pier, my grandfather saw the man with the red beard make a sign to his friends, who stopped their drinking and formed two groups. Four men remained near the door of the pier; the others moved slowly toward the curb along which the Brueckmanns were walking. Then suddenly the man with the red beard began to shout at a smaller man beside him. The little man looked frightened and backed away from him, but the bearded man came after him, pushing his shoulders, first one, then the other, with his open hand until the little man was at the edge of the water. The little man looked down anxiously at the river and began to plead with the bearded man, who continued to push him. The men who had walked to the curb began to call to the bearded man, but he ignored them, pushing now with all his strength, so that the little man, who was tottering at the very edge of the river, cried out in terror and, gesturing frantically toward my grandfather, called for help.

My grandfather calculated that the drop to the water was more then twenty feet and realized that if the man fell he might drown. But the bearded man seemed unconcerned, for he pushed his victim to the very edge and began to force him over it. As the little man let out one last hysterical scream, my grandfather dashed from his father's side to the spot where the two men were struggling. Too late. Before he could reach them, the bearded man thrust the little man headfirst into the water below. My grandfather stopped and scanned the small waves breaking against the pilings of the pier. Bits of wood and rotten vegetables bobbed on its surface, and then, in a moment, the face of the little man appeared among them, streaked by his wet hair and grinning a clown's grin.

As the little man began to swim toward one of the pilings the man with the red beard came toward my grandfather. "Hey, Dutchman," he called, "want to swim? You a good swimmer, Dutchman?"

My grandfather said nothing. He kept following the swimmer with his eyes, confused now to hear the man laughing as he headed back through the water to a piling from which a ladder hung. When he turned back toward his father and brother, he saw that the men at the curb were now standing around them, and his fear grew greater. The man with the red beard came even closer to him now and said, "Hey, Dutchman, where are you goin'?"

My grandfather looked the man in the eye and said, "We go to New Jersey on the ferry. Then to Paterson."

"No," the bearded man cried, putting his face even closer to my grandfather's, "You don't want to go to Paterson. Paterson's no good, you hear? You want to stay here in New York."

My grandfather looked over the man's shoulder and saw that the men at the curb were not allowing his father and brother to pass.

"You got money, Dutchman?" the man with the red beard was shouting, waving his bottle of beer at him. "Money from the old country, hey? How much money, Dutchman? *Wie viel Geld*, hey?"

Below them, the little man in the water had reached the ladder and was beginning to climb up to the pier. He was singing now, in a high voice like a woman's voice, some song in English that my grandfather could not understand. "We go to Paterson," my grandfather said to the bearded man. "So kindly let us pass, I ask you."

"Listen, Dutchman," the bearded man said, stepping closer again, "Tell me this. Are you a citizen? Are you a citizen, hey? No, you're not. Well, I'm a citizen of this country, and you greenhorns better show me a little respect, you hear? You better show a little respect for citizens if you want to stay in this country, greenhorn, in these United States of America, greenhorn, you hear?"

The man who had fallen into the water had now made it to the top of the ladder and was scrambling back onto the pier. My grandfather could still hear his singing echoing inside the pier's vast shed, and he heard as well a woman's voice, a husky voice deeper than that of the little man, shouting angrily.

"Girls," the bearded man said, taking a long swallow from his bottle and smiling slyly. "*Fräuleins*, Dutchman. You like that?"

"I asked you nicely," my grandfather said. "I asked you nicely. Now let me pass."

"*Geld*, Dutchman?" the bearded man said. "*Geld*? We got *Fräu-leins, ja*. We got schnapps. Inside. Come on."

Over the man's shoulder my grandfather could see that one of the men at the curb was pushing his brother Paul, and so he put his suitcase down and looked steadily at the bearded man. "You let my father and brother pass," he said slowly. "You let them pass over there and then I have schnapps with you." My grandfather watched as the bearded man turned and stared for a moment at his brother and father. Several horse-drawn carts rattled along past them. The bearded man watched as they went by. Then, after another drink, he shouted to his friends, "Hey, Sammy, hey, Sammy, you listen to me. Let those two go. This greenhorn wants a drink. Come over here and let those two go."

My grandfather watched as the men around his father and brother hesitated. Then the man called Sammy turned and signaled to the others to follow. Slowly they moved away and sauntered back to where my grandfather and the bearded man were standing. Paul, clearly confused and afraid, looked over at my grandfather, and my grandfather, fearing what might happen if they hesitated, motioned to him to lead his father away. At first Paul refused to move, but my grandfather motioned even more forcefully, and so, reluctantly, Paul took his father's arm and led him slowly past the pier and along the water's edge, looking back again and again until they passed behind a line of wagons that stood just beyond the pier.

When the man called Sammy and his friends reached the place where my grandfather and the bearded man were standing, they picked up the bottles of beer they had left behind and began to drink again. The bearded man drank too, opening a new bottle and throwing his head back for a long swallow. Then the other men chanted, "More! More! More! More!" as he drank, and my grandfather began to think that they would forget about him and that, if he watched carefully, he might find a time to run away and rejoin his father and brother who would, he guessed, be waiting for him farther up the street.

Inside the pier the high voice of the little man and the husky voice of the woman continued their strange duet. The bearded man laughed at the sound, burped, and wiped his lips with the back of his hand. "So, greenhorn," he said, turning to my grandfather, "you come with us now. You come inside." He took my grandfather's shoulder and pushed him toward the door of the pier. My grandfather took several steps and then stopped as he remembered the suitcase he had been carrying, but when he turned to find it, he saw that one of the other men had already picked it up and was carrying it into the pier behind them.

The bearded man pushed my grandfather forward again until they reached the entrance of the pier. Beyond it, the vast dark shed stretched for a great distance before my grandfather's eyes, which, accustomed as they were to the bright sunlight, could make out almost nothing in the darkness. Through the wide bays on the left side of the pier he was able to see the rusty hull of an old freighter. Between the ship and the door stood piles of what seemed to be crates and barrels upon whose sides he made out, little by little, the names of places—Plymouth, Rotterdam, Hamburg. As his eyes grew accustomed to the darkness, he could make out chains and hooks hanging from the ceiling above him.

The air on the pier was heavy with the smell of the droppings of the cart horses. Beneath him, my grandfather could hear the lapping of waves against the pilings, and high up in the pier's rafters he could hear the cooing of many pigeons. The bearded man led him around a pile of barrels, and suddenly the face of a woman appeared. It was like a white rose that had begun to wilt, mottled, with brown spots here and there, its skin as limp as the dyed red curls that hung beside its cheeks. It was the face of the woman whose husky voice he had heard. She was still shouting angrily at the little man who had been pushed into the river and who stood behind her now, removing his wet clothes. He was being helped by a second woman, a younger girl who accompanied her work with a cooing that echoed the cooing of the pigeons above.

"So, Hildy," the bearded man shouted. "See what I have for you. A nice greenhorn."

The woman turned and looked at my grandfather, straightening her silk blouse and red skirt. "What do I care about greenhorns?" she shouted. "What do I need greenhorns for? Don't I have enough trouble trying to make you drunks do your jobs?"

My grandfather watched as the bearded man raised his hand in front of the woman's face and moved his thumb and forefinger together. "*Geld*, Hildy," he said. "*Geld*. Just from the boat. A greenhorn."

But Hildy was angry. She clamped her teeth firmly shut and hissed at the bearded man through them. "*Geld?*" she cried. "What *Geld?* You think you got the kaiser here? Look at this boy," she said, taking my grandfather by the arm. "Look at this poor little Dutchman. Scared to death he is."

"Why should he be scared?" the bearded man laughed. "Me and Sammy here, we treat greenhorns good. Schnapps, *Fräuleins.* Right, Sammy?"

"Of course he's scared," Hildy said, making my grandfather sit down on one of the barrels beside her. "It's only natural he's scared, the way you drunks behave."

"It's a free country," the bearded man said.

"I'll 'free country' you," Hildy said, getting up from the barrel and shaking her fist at the bearded man's face. "I'll 'free country' you. I'm here to get a day's work out of you, you and Sammy and the rest of these drunks. And I can't get it. Free country, is it? Free country to loaf and play your rummy games, as far as I can see."

"He wants some schnapps, Hildy, some schnapps." The bearded man made the gesture for money with his fingers.

Behind them the little man who had climbed out of the river, nearly naked now, was drying himself off with a piece of burlap. The younger woman shook with laughter as she watched him. Hildy turned to her suddenly. "Annie," she shouted, "get that rummy some clothes, will you?"

"We work hard for you," the man called Sammy shouted at Hildy.

"You work hard, my ass," Hildy shouted back. "Free country to loaf and drink in, that's all you want. And I'm the one has to answer to Mr. Vander Jagt. I never know when he's going to come through that door asking me for the count of the wagons. And what am I supposed to say when he sees you all drunk and the goods not piled right and you sitting with this German kid right off the boat?"

"Vander Jagt's a rummy too," the man called Sammy said. "The only difference is Vander Jagt's a rich rummy and we're poor rummies."

"Vander Jagt owns the company," Hildy said. "That's what counts here."

"You don't owe anything to the company, Hildy," the bearded man said. "Look, this little greenhorn's got some money, and I got him in here with a nice little dodge."

"I don't care what he's got and what he hasn't got," Hildy shouted, placing herself between my grandfather and the bearded man. "All I know is that I'm sick of you rummies and your games. So I'm telling you now to put down the beer bottle and get some dry clothes for Kelly over there and get back to work, or I'll tell Vander Jagt about all this, and he'll throw you all off the pier. Who'll pay for the beer and the schnapps then, I wonder? Who'll pay then?"

The bearded man came forward suddenly and put his face close to Hildy's. "Fat whore," he said.

Hildy slapped his face and turned to the man called Sammy. "Give me the boy's suitcase," she demanded.

Sammy pushed the case across the floor with his foot.

"Pick it up," Hildy said to my grandfather, "and follow me." My grandfather got up and picked up the suitcase.

"Do what Mama Hildy says," the bearded man called after my grandfather as he followed the woman to the door. "Mama Hildy, take good care of your little Dutchman." He stepped toward them and called out louder, "Watch out for Mama Hildy, greenhorn. Watch out good. What you find under that skirt, dirty business, I'm telling you. You watch out good."

My grandfather did not look back. He walked slowly to the door behind Hildy, hearing the cooing of the pigeons in the rafters and the lapping of the water beneath the pier. A wagon had just been drawn up in front of the pier, and the horse drawing it stood at the door, pawing the cobbles and shaking its head. He was surprised by its sudden appearance. It seemed larger than the horses he had seen as a boy. "It's just a horse," Hildy said, pushing him by it. "Dumb Germans," she muttered. "Why we let them in I'll never know." Then she pointed my grandfather toward the street and said, "Get going now before they come out here again."

My grandfather did not hesitate. He stepped out onto the paved area in front of the pier and walked to the curb. He could not see clearly in the bright sunlight, but he moved quickly just the same, turning north when he reached the street and walking in the direction he had seen his father and brother go. After a block he began to run, catching his feet on the uneven cobbles and hearing his heart pounding against the walls of his chest.

In a few minutes, he reached the Erie Railroad Ferry Terminal at Chambers Street where he found his father and brother waiting for him. He ran up to them, and they took him by the arm and questioned him about what had happened. *"Nichts,"* "Nothing," he replied, reaching into his pocket to make sure that the money his father had given him was still there. When he found it, he smiled. *"Alles gut,"* "Everything's all right," he said, and taking Paul's arm, he led them both into the ferry terminal. There they purchased tickets and boarded a ferryboat to Jersey City.

I need nothing in August's book to make that ferry ride vivid for me, for half of a century later, I made the same trip hundreds of times, commuting back and forth to high school by train and ferry. I too knew those wide boats and their tall black funnels, the sounds of docking, the lowering of the gangway, and the rush of people into the old wooden station with its interior balconies along which self-important railroad men strode unsmiling above the crowds of passengers below. To that shed of a place, my grandfather, his father, and his brother came too in the early 1890s and, passing through the old terminal, made their way to the trains, surprised to find no distinction of classes but just row after row of upholstered seats on which even they were permitted to sit. The promise came, in that moment, a little closer.

They traveled across the meadowlands and the newly blooming suburbs of northern New Jersey, through Passaic and Clifton, to the Silk City. Where else would a weaver go but to Paterson? There, dozens of red brick mills huddled beneath the Great Falls in that archetypal industrial city whose dream was the dream of Alexander Hamilton himself—to create the U.S. industrial society, to start it here where the obliging Passaic fell into its gorge offering the promise of its cheap power to any entrepreneur bold enough to respond. The city's founders had soon after started the Society for Useful Manufactures, invited eager businessmen, and finally welcomed the immigrant workers, Irish and Germans, Jews and Italians, skilled and unskilled, to their riverside city. And the factories shot up—Colt's firearms, Roger's steam locomotives, machine works, and above all, textiles, the weaving of linen and woolen clothing, of intricate lace and labels and plush. Soon the dye houses came too, the dank, foul-smelling halls in which the products of the weavers were bathed in a new brilliance. I can still remember the childhood sensations, the clattering of the looms through mill windows in the summertime and the acrid smell of the dyes that hung in the air on hot July days.

Almost no one visits Paterson now. Alexander Hamilton's dream faded; the city did not keep its promise. So I will have to make you see it, make you see something of what those two brave families, the Ruhrens and the Brueckmanns, saw when they arrived at the Erie station on Market Street. The Preakness Hills, part of the Ramapo chain, stretch to the west and north of the city. I know those hills in my leg muscles, having pumped an old prewar bicycle up and down them. Tree-covered even now, they are watered by streams that flow into the Passaic, which rises far to the west and south. The hills cradle the river for a while and then hurl it from their heights just above Paterson. In its narrow gorge, the river is all turmoil for a short distance, and then it bends slowly to the east and south, holding the city in that bend. Paterson itself is more or less flat after the river's fall, with lots of space for mills along the banks of the Passaic as it bends and lots of space for houses in the flat land it encircles. The rich mill owners and middle-class managers built their houses on that flat land, which is called the Eastside, but the immigrants had to settle on the hills, the Irish in Dublin on the slopes of Garrett Mountain, the Germans and Italians in Totowa and on Temple Hill.

My grandparents and their families were among the most fortunate of the immigrants in Paterson. Since they were weavers, they were considerably better off than others who had no special skill. Many of the Irish had to take jobs as cigar makers or as what my grandfather called "ditchdiggers," and this was true of many of the Italians as well. But life, even for the weavers, was not easy. Hours in the mills were long—fifty-five hours a week—and workers never knew from day to day whether they might be laid off without warning. Things got so bad for Uncle August that he was forced at one point to move his family as far away as Easton, Pennsylvania, to find work.

August's problems were complicated by the fact that he, like many of the newly arrived Germans, held radical socialist views. On top of that, he was also an outspoken man. He tells of being chosen at one mill to speak with the foreman about an increase in pay. He asked for a 40 percent increase for the workers and, by hollering at the foreman, got them between 10 and 22. The following week, however, he found that he was being given old and unworkable warps upon which he could make little money, and so he gave the foreman a piece of his mind and quit. He went to work at a mill called "The

Slaughterhouse" then, a place where the foremen extorted money from the workers and fired anyone who refused to pay up. In the end, he and many of his family and friends found that they had to move from mill to mill, never knowing where the next month's rent money would come from, never settling into a job but always moving, moving from broadsilk weaving to velvet, from twisting at a ribbon mill to warping, the youngest forced at times to work on the carts, loading and unloading goods until they nearly collapsed of fatigue.

They were angry, these men. What they had fled in the old country took hold of them again, here, in the land of promise. Their anger sharpened their determination, however, and they joined not only the *Singerbünde* (singing societies) and the *Turnvereine* but drifted as well into the meetings run by Socialists and radical labor agitators where they heard the angry slogans that were current then: "Why should we have to work fifty or sixty hours a week just to survive, weaving silk for the wives of men who have never done an honest day's work?" "What we make should be ours." "The workers must unite!" "All for one and one for all!"

My grandfather, William Brueckmann, joined the party too. He had, after all, vowed to make something of himself, and he was determined to do that even if it meant having to change the system, which he quickly saw as rotten. He had come, as August had, with his father and brother and had, like August, spent the first months in a boardinghouse in the Totowa section of Paterson. The men's lives were lonely and tedious then—long hours of work in the mills, dismal places to live. Even if they rented a small flat, it would contain little furniture, and their free time would be spent boiling laundry, often ruining it, cooking badly, and drinking too much. There could be no entertainment beyond the occasional glass of beer, for all of the extra money had to be saved to provide for the passage of the women and younger brothers who had stayed behind in the old country.

I think my grandfather was shrewder than most. He had a keen sense of the importance of money in this new country, and he held his tongue in the mills rather than risking the loss of his job. He worked very hard and saved even harder, denying himself even the smallest pleasures. His half-sister Frieda told me many years later, not long before she died, that he had thirty thousand dollars in the bank before he was forty years old. And then there was the Party. He realized, you see, that losing your temper in the mill and hollering at

the boss was worse than useless. Workers had to organize, my grandfather understood that. "All for one and one for all!" It was the system, he decided, that didn't work in this supposed promised land,
and so this young weaver who had almost gone to university in the
old country understood quickly that there was only one way to fix the
system: get into politics. That's why he became a socialist and, as he
put more and more money in the bank, he began to attend meetings
regularly and began to be known. He made his voice heard. He told
me of this on our Sunday walks, told me how he had bought books
of speeches in English and painstakingly copied them out word for
word so that he could speak in public and not sound like a greenhorn,
told me of how he learned parliamentary procedure so that he would
not be made a jackass of, so that, in the end, he could run a meeting
himself.

When Bill Brueckmann met Katie Ruhren and her brother August,
the Ruhrens lived in a large house on the Pompton Road just before
the border between Manchester and Wayne Townships. The house,
which stands there still, I believe, is now in the Borough of Haledon,
but that town had not yet been incorporated in the nineties. The
Ruhrens moved there after August married a girl he had met when
he sailed from Rotterdam and who had later turned up in one of the
mills where he worked. August and his bride took the top floor of the
house, and the rest of the family lived below them, Katie among
them.

Katie was the eldest girl and had a soft and beautiful face that
turned my grandfather's head at once. She was seventeen when she
arrived in the United States, and her two sisters, Christine and Anna,
were several years younger. They all worked in the mills, walking, my
grandmother told me, two and a half miles down the hill to Paterson
every morning, starting out at six, no matter what the weather, crossing the Passaic River at the foot of the hill and walking the final few
blocks through the Riverside section to the mill. Six days a week they
did this, trudging back up the hill in the evenings regardless of the
weather, in summer heat, with temperatures below zero, in torrential
rain and driving snow. My grandfather told me one day about the
worst of the snowstorms in those early years in the United States. It
seems that it had begun to snow one winter afternoon while the
workers were still in the mills, at first just a light snow, but in a short
time a heavy driven storm of flakes so thick that you couldn't see the

street from the mill windows. By four-thirty the sun had disappeared and the snow was still falling. It lay two feet deep in most places, but where the wind swept it up, it formed drifts taller than a man. My grandfather and his father and brother trudged home through the drifts and collapsed in front of the coal stove, exhausted even by the short climb to Totowa. Later, as they ate their supper, they learned from the Swiss family who lived below them that the snowfall was in fact a blizzard and that many workers were finding it impossible to get home from the mills. Many had fallen in the snow and had had to be carried into nearby houses where, half-frozen, they had been given schnapps and wrapped in blankets.

My grandfather knew that Katie and her family had to walk all the way from Riverside up the hill to Haledon and then, even worse, up the hill beyond Haledon to their house on Pompton Road. The walk was almost four miles long, all of it uphill, with many stretches of road where there were no houses at all. My grandfather got up from the table when he had finished his supper and put on his overcoat. He said nothing, but his mother, who knew how things were between him and Katie, suspected what he meant to do and pleaded with him not to go out. My grandfather shook his head. Leaving the house, he trudged along Totowa Avenue, across Hamburg Avenue and then over to North Fourth Street. In places the snow reached his waist and he had great difficulty moving through it, but, warmed by the supper he had just eaten, he forced his way to the Haledon Avenue hill up which Katie and her family had to make their way home.

There were few people on the streets. Only occasionally did he pass a man coming in the opposite direction, lifting his knees high to get through the snow and breathing too hard to call out a greeting. For long periods my grandfather saw no one at all, and he began to be afraid. Suppose he fell? Suppose he passed out from the exertion and the cold? He stopped to rest, and the sight of candles in the windows of a nearby house gave him the courage to push on toward the top of the hill.

Now he saw absolutely no one, and he could hear no sounds except for the wind in the trees and the whipping of the snow against the houses along the road. With his heart pounding even faster against the walls of his chest, he made his way slowly up the steepest section of the hill, trying in vain to make out the tracks of others who might have passed along the road earlier. As the icy flakes drove against his face, he felt anger welling up inside him, anger with the driven snow and with the stupid fury of nature. He loved nature, it was true, but this? Still he plodded forward, picturing Katie lost somewhere in the blizzard ahead of him. Quite exhausted now, he fell several times in the snow and began to lose his sense of direction until at last he found the trolley tracks in Haledon, where the last car had cleared some of the deep snow away. He stood there, where the two avenues crossed, at the foot of the last hill, and in desperation called out, "Katie," and again, "Katie," shouting her name over and over into the wind and the driven snow.

My grandfather stood at the crossroads for about ten minutes, cupping his hands around his lips from time to time and calling out Katie's name and the names of her sisters and brothers. No one replied at first, but then, as he sank to his knees, he saw two figures coming toward him through sheets of driven snow. He thought at first that they were animals, but as they drew nearer he saw that they were in fact two men crawling on their hands and knees. Moving slowly toward them, he grasped the first man by the arm. The two men looked up at him then, and he saw that they were Katie's father and her brother Joe. "Katie," my grandfather shouted at them. "Katie. Where is she?"

Ruhren put his face close to my grandfather's face and stared at him in confusion.

"Katie," my grandfather shouted again. "Where is Katie?"

"Not with us," Ruhren said slowly. "Not with us."

My grandfather saw at once that Katie's father had been drinking and that it was no use questioning him any further. He turned to Joe and asked again, "Where is Katie, Joe? Where is she?"

Joe bit his lip nervously and turned his head. "Down there," he said, turning back to my grandfather again. "Behind us down there."

My grandfather pushed them both aside and started walking again, this time back down along the trolley tracks toward Paterson. The snow, even thicker now, was being driven straight into his eyes. Had he not been able to feel the trolley tracks with his foot as he went he would not have been able to find his way. Step by step, with the snow at times almost as high as his shoulders, he pushed his way along the avenue. The tears that ran from his eyes had become ice on his cheeks now, and his body was trembling in the icy wind. Now his feet were no longer just cold but painful as well, and with each step, the pain moved up through his legs and knees. Soon he found himself shouting out as he stumbled on, shouting to drive away the pain. Several times he felt the temptation to lie down in the soft snow, but he had heard stories in the old country of men who had lain down in snowstorms and, sleeping, had frozen to death. And so, again and again, he forced himself to stand up and move forward. He passed through the center of Haledon, scarcely seeing it, for there were no longer any lights in the houses and no sound but that of the snow.

After a half hour of walking, he guessed that he ought to be somewhere near Burhans Lane, the narrow street that ran between Haledon and Paterson, and, feeling that he could walk no further, that he would have to rest, he allowed himself to sit down beside a high snowdrift. As he sat there, scraping the ice from his cheeks, he saw a faint light moving along the avenue toward him. My grandfather stared at it as it drew closer. Then, when it was no more than twenty feet away, he was able to make out the figure of a man holding a lantern. He tried to struggle to his feet then but found that he was not strong enough and had to call out for help.

The man came over to the snowdrift, and my grandfather saw that he was an older man with a wrinkled German face. "Ach, Junge," the man said, guessing that my grandfather was German himself, "Hier muss Man nicht schlaffen. Hier wirst du sterben." "No one should sleep here. Here you will die." The older man helped my grandfather to his feet and led him slowly back along the tracks in the direction from which he had come. When they had walked fifty yards or so, he pushed my grandfather to the left and led him slowly around several high drifts of snow. Then both of them stopped in front of a building that stood right on the avenue, and the man, when he found the door, opened it and pushed my grandfather inside.

My grandfather found himself inside a small tavern. Along the left wall ran a long wooden bar, and behind it stood a fat bartender with a smiling Irish face. "That looks like a stiff one, Max," the bartender called as they stepped inside. "Where did you find him?"

"Ja," Max replied, "Out on the tracks half-dead. Some schnapps for him. A good double schnapps." Turning from the bar, he made my grandfather sit down beside his wife at a table across the room. The man's wife took his hands and rubbed them as the bartender brought him the double schnapps.

"No night for a stroll," the bartender said as he put the glass down.

My grandfather said nothing. He picked the glass up with both of his hands and moved it slowly to his lips. The schnapps was like fire in his mouth, but he drank it down in one swallow nevertheless. It tore at his cold throat as it went down and made him think of a piece of silk being torn in the mill, but when it reached his stomach, it made him feel better at once. Then turning to Max's wife, he said, "Three German girls, three sisters, two tall and one shorter. Three girls. I was looking for them but I couldn't find them." My grandfather felt as though he were going to fall asleep now. "Katie," he said, "Katie Ruhren and her sisters. I couldn't find them."

As his eyes began to close, he found that he could scarcely make out the woman's face, but he heard her say, as if from a great distance, "They were here, *Junge*. Yes, here. No need to worry. I saw them. Katie was the tallest one. Yes, they were here. They had a drink, and then a lady from Burhans Lane took them to her house around the corner. So you better go to sleep now. In the morning you can find them.

In time, of course, the snow would melt. Spring would come, then summer and the Sundays when, if the weather was fine, the Ruhrens would throw parties at the house on the hill to Pompton, retreating to August's carefully tended garden. An acre of land stretched behind the house, and on it they could hold parties to which dozens of guests might be invited. They had clambakes and drank beer. They consumed tons of wurst and potato salad and drank more beer. The laughter never ceased until, later in the evenings, they remembered the old country and sang its songs: *"Du, du, liebst mir in Herzen, du, du. . . ."* It was here that my grandfather had first met my grandmother. And he courted her at that house on the hill to Pompton too. On Sunday mornings, he would walk me by the place and tell me about it. "When I was courting your grandmother . . . ," he would begin and then tell again their stiff and proper romancing, her laughter and his seriousness as he wove his love into the vision he had of making something of himself.

Did they go to church on those Sundays? Certainly not. Both families, the Ruhrens and the Brueckmanns, were, of course, Catholics by birth. My grandmother was proud of having made her First Communion and still recalled the feel of her first pair of leather shoes, which had been purchased for the event. But they had all drifted away from the Church. Somehow they had imbibed in the old coun-

William Brueckmann (circa 1900).   *Katherine Ruhren Brueckmann*
                                      (circa 1900).

try a new radical spirit that trusted nature and work but had conceived a deep distrust of the clergy. My grandfather admitted that he
had two cousins who had become Jesuits, but they were spoken of, if
at all, in dark terms. Weaknesses were hinted at, drink and laziness.
For my grandmother, priests were always unnatural. They didn't
work hard enough to suit her, and worse still, they did not marry.

In fact, the Ruhrens enjoyed telling derogatory stories about
priests. August allowed himself to be talked into a church wedding
by his wife but saved his self-esteem by writing of how the priest
made him pay an extra five dollars to have the bans read on only one
Sunday instead of three. I would bet anything that it was his last visit
to a church. My grandparents, when they married in 1899, took their
oaths before a justice of the peace. No, my grandfather wanted nothing to do with the priests, whom he saw as the lackeys of the mill
owners, men who kept the workers in line by threatening them with

hellfire. He had read and was still reading socialist pamphlets. The message of Karl Marx was clear: religion in all its forms was a relic from the past, an obstacle that had to be eliminated if the workers' paradise was to become a reality. So Katie had no church wedding, but the picnic afterward must have been grand.

2   The Cedar Cliff Hotel

AFTER THEY WERE MARRIED, my grandparents took rooms on Doremus Street on the edge of the Totowa section of Paterson and near the boundary between the city and the small town that would become Haledon, the same town in which Katie's parents' house was located. My grandfather had been watching the building that had been going on in Haledon, and it struck him that it was on its way to being a prosperous place, a good place in which to settle and perhaps, in time, to start a business.

I'd better tell you about Haledon. It lies to the north of Temple Hill and the Totowa section of Paterson, half way up the Preakness Hills at the level from which, farther to the east, the Great Falls descend. It is set in a shallow valley between two spurs of the hills. The valley itself is traversed by a small stream on one side of which rises the western ridge line that includes High Mountain and Pennyroyal Mountain and on the other side a lower ridge line called the Goffle. The stream has its source several miles to the north, not far from Franklin Lake, and wanders through the valley, bending to the west as it leaves Haledon to meet the Passaic about a mile or so above the falls. The early Dutch settlers in the area had called the stream the *Krakeel Val* or Quarrelsome Brook, a good name, for it is a particularly stony and noisy little stream. In several places along its course, dams had been built creating small lakes. The biggest one—at least until the Haledon reservoir was built—was situated at the northern end of Haledon and was called the *Valdamm*, a word that I think came into English as Oldham, now the brook's and the pond's official name. *Valdamm* may also be the origin of the name Haledon; at least I've never heard any other plausible explanation of the name. In fact the brook was never called anything in my day but Molly Ann's Brook, these words themselves being a corruption, I am told, of Molly's Jahn's Brook, whoever Molly's Jahn may have been. The double apostrophes cried out for simplification, and so Molly Ann's Brook it became.

The long valley through which Molly Ann's Brook flows came in time to be shared by two of the towns that were carved out of the original Manchester Township, Haledon and beyond it, North Haledon. An old stone house still stands in Haledon, witness to the presence there of a farming family even in colonial times. In the course of the nineteenth century a number of affluent families settled on the two ridges to the east and west, among them that of Garrett A. Hobart, who was vice-president under McKinley and who had a farm on Pompton Road just beyond the Ruhren's house. The houses that dominated the town in its earliest years were the two giant Victorians owned by the Goodbody family that stood on high ground beside the main street that is now called Belmont Avenue. It ran straight north out of Haledon and into what would become North Haledon, a place that, when I was growing up, had only a handful of houses and a few dozen small farms.

The valley was a good place to live. Nestled as it was between the ridges on either side, it presented a small, secure prospect that a child could easily assimilate and manage. It was like a walled place. In the middle of the night, I can remember, when the raucous fire siren called out to the volunteer firemen, its sound echoed against the hill walls all around us, a reminder that we were settled in a place with the welcoming feeling of a small warm room. To the south spread an open view, and so, by climbing just a little way up the ridge to the west, one could look out over the entire city of Paterson and then lift one's eyes and see, even farther to the east, the towers of New York City on the horizon.

What Bill Brueckmann saw when he looked out his Doremus Street window toward Haledon was a place on the brink of a big change. The change would come because the trolley car had come—up Temple hill, along West Street and the Paterson Hamburg Turnpike, until, at the top of the hill, it turned north and made its way along Belmont Avenue. What was about to be the Borough of Haledon was also about to become a trolley suburb. The farmland was being surveyed and divided. I still have the deed for the old house on Zabriskie Street where, in the evenings, my grandmother told me her tales of the old country. The deed speaks even now of men with rods and chains establishing the property lines, measuring the distance from an elm tree, long gone now, and marking down what was to become the troublesome Hoxie and Beam Line, over which property owners would argue for generations to come.

The trolley made it inevitable that a town would grow up where the farms had been. The valley was, after all, a pleasant place. Cedar trees and hemlocks grew in abundance, as did oaks and maples, chestnuts and elms. The soil was rich and the water table high, permitting the easy digging of wells. And so the land sold fast and well, and substantial houses began to rise, Victorians in clapboard and brick with broad verandas and smaller cottages with tiny porches in front and neat gardens behind. My grandfather noted all this from his window and noted as well that a number of mills were being built, a ribbon mill and a mill for weaving ornate silk labels. Before long they were joined by a finishing company and a dye house, and the sky over Haledon was loud in the morning and at noon and at five in the afternoon with the cry of steam whistles, calling recent immigrants to work or sending them home to supper. Some took the trolley, but some wanted to live in Haledon itself, and so boardinghouses were built too.

My grandparents both continued to work in the mills after they were married. It meant that they were able to put more money "on the bank" as my grandmother said. It was the German-American bank, of course, and the Brueckmanns' balance there grew and grew, so that, when the opportunity came to go into business, they were ready with the cash required to get started. My grandfather, who was still a staunch socialist, recognized that the workers needed organization, but he also recognized that they needed a place to live and eat and drink, and so he bought the Cedar Cliff Hotel, the largest boardinghouse and restaurant in town. Three thousand dollars for the whole thing—the building and the bar and all the glassware and china. A dozen boarders and thirty more for lunch every day. It was a good business. The trolley stopped at the door, and the sound of carpenters' hammers almost never ceased on either side of Belmont Avenue as the houses and the shops and the new mills took shape.

The old building, located just beyond the bend in the avenue at the point at which it heads dead north, survived well into the 1990s and enjoyed a special vogue in the middle of the century because it was visited from time to time by its then owner's cousin, the well-known comedian Lou Costello. But those days were in the distant future when, not long after their marriage, in the century's first decade, my grandparents took over the building and the business. The building was a barn of a place, three stories high, with a bar and large hall on the first floor, rooms for the family on the second, and the boarders' quarters under the eaves on the third. My grandparents had to run the whole place themselves, with only the help of my grandfather's half-sister Frieda, who came to live with them when her parents died.

My grandfather tended bar from noon until at least midnight, and my grandmother and Frieda tended to the boarders' rooms and prepared the lunch each day for forty workers. My grandmother told me, on those storytelling evenings, of how she would get up before six in the morning and walk up the hill for several miles to purchase vegetables at a farm along the turnpike to Preakness. She enjoyed the walk, the smell of the cedars in the summer, the calls of the jays and robins. When she returned, she and Frieda would drag out the galvanized tubs in the kitchen, heat the water, and boil the bed linens. They had to be done almost daily, you see, because many of the men were dirty, and lice bred fast. The men were alone and miserable and often drunk, and my grandmother despaired of keeping the place as clean as she wanted it. One night she thought she had found a leak in the water pipes, but when her husband came and smelled the water running down into the second floor, he knew at once that it was urine. An inebriated boarder on the third floor had not made it to the bathroom.

Life grew even harder when the first baby came, a boy, called William for his father, who took heart at the boy's birth. This was the future, the promise that had beckoned from across the sea. All the opportunities that he had never had would fall to this child. No teacher would beg to send his son to the university and go away disappointed. Bill Brueckmann would send him himself and, as he often said, "No mistake about it." Oh yes, Bill Brueckmann looked extra sharp now, worked harder than ever. The glasses in the barroom sparkled as they never had before. He stayed open a little later now and made more money. There was the boy to think about.

His own elation over the birth of his son was the antithesis of what the men in his barroom felt. Their discouragement was written plain and clear on their faces. It fueled their thirst in the evenings and filled my grandfather's cash box. In the summer when the heat grew unbearable, their desperation grew even worse, and they longed to be back in the old country. They asked themselves then why they had come. The wages were not as good as they had expected, and they were forced to live in squalor, some in the crowded boardinghouses, others in dirty rented rooms in Riverside or Temple Hill. If they had children of their own, they worried about them constantly, wanting to give them an education but knowing that if someone in the family grew ill, the children too would have to be sent to the mill to make ends meet. Sometimes the children would see friends working and making money, and so they would leave school and give up hope of a better life, surrendering themselves to the mill owners and their foremen, who drove them harder and harder until the young people too grew ill or died. In August when the smell of manure drifted in from the avenue and the nights were filled with the endless chirping of the cicadas, as men drank and wept, even my grandfather began to feel the weight of their sorrow. For most of them, things seemed always to take a natural course to sickness and dying and despair, like the dust settling on the bar. Very little seemed to take hold. Their efforts were like the sunlight falling through the winter trees. Wasted. Was it the system, he wondered, or was it something even deeper than that? My grandmother's stories held no answer to those questions, but at times, she admitted, the crushing work and the desperation around them seemed about to get the better of them.

But the boy, Billy, played with their big dog Rover beside the back pump. The child had his bath in the kitchen in one of the galvanized tubs, a thin blond figure in the old photos, staring out at me with a whimsical, puzzled look. And sometimes there were gay evenings too. The *Turnverein* rented the big hall once a week, and my grandmother would bring Billy in to watch their marvelous acrobatics before he went to bed. Sometimes there were parties, even costume parties. There are their faces staring wide-eyed in yet another snapshot—my grandfather, Bill Brueckmann himself, dressed as a pirate in cut-off trousers with a checkered sash around his waist and white muslin wrapped around the calves of his legs. He has a kerchief around his neck, and a velvet vest gives a dash of color to his swashbuckling image. My grandmother stands beside him dressed as a schoolboy in a pair of her husband's old pants that reach to her armpits. Her sister Christine is also there with her husband, a Swiss weaver named John Lischer. Christine wears a short gingham dress and long underwear with lace at the ankles, and John is a clown, in a suit of red and yellow material with a star-shaped collar and large buttons. His cone-shaped hat is made of the same material, and he stretches his pants out sideways until they are as wide as they are long. They all look a bit astonished to be dressed that way, to be at a masquerade at all. Bittersweet. I can almost hear the fiddler playing my grandmother's favorite song, "When a Gypsy Makes His Violin Cry." Chinese lanterns bob above their heads, and just behind them a man wearing a donkey's head dances with a woman with painted oriental eyes. It is all make-believe. "*Unsinn*," my grandfather no doubt said when his wife tied the kerchief around his neck. It was his strongest judgment: "nonsense." He reserved it for everything that was childish and unreal.

The barroom in the mornings was real—salesmen having their schnapps and taking orders, my grandfather washing glasses or balancing the books. And the barroom at night was even more real. The later the hour, the more despondent the customers would grow, spending more and more on drink. Fights broke out, and my grandfather would have to take out the policeman's nightstick that always lay ready under the bar and, making his way through the smoke and confusion, order the drunks to leave the premises. There were times when the fights got so bad that he would have to call on a few of his close German friends to help him remove the rowdiest drinkers. Other times he simply had to close the bar and, locking the front door, climb to the bedroom where he would find his wife exhausted and already asleep. How distant the promise seemed then. How long ago the afternoons when he and Katie had lain in the grass together on the hills beyond Haledon.

The worst night was the night my mother was born. My grandmother never wearied of telling the story, embellishing it a little, adding, I always suspected, a few details she could not possibly have known herself. She was, after all, up in the bedroom in labor. When she recounted the events of that night, she dwelled on her own pain for a while, telling me of how Frieda had tied sheets to the end of the brass bed so that she could pull on them when the pains grew severe. Below, in the barroom, my grandfather had taken the nightstick out early that night and had laid it on the bar. He knew the baby was coming. "Some peace and quiet tonight, please, gentlemen," he had said.

By eleven thirty that night, most of the customers had gone home, many out of respect for my grandmother, whose cries they could sometimes hear, but at one of the rear tables, six big Germans sat playing pinochle. One was very drunk, and he suddenly began to holler that he could fight any man in the place and beat him too. He was obviously losing money at cards and wanted to hit somebody to make himself feel better. Two more card players, who were also very drunk, got to their feet and faced the man who had issued the first challenge. They were grinning and rubbing the palms of their hands with their knuckles. My grandfather picked up the nightstick and strode to the end of the bar, but before he could get around it, the fight had broken out. The three men were punching one another, and some of their friends had risen to their feet. My grandfather saw now that they were all even drunker than he had imagined, and so he motioned to the other customers in the barroom to come and help him. As he did so, he could hear his wife screaming upstairs. The pains, it seemed, were getting worse.

"Gentlemen," he said when he reached the brawling Germans, "I ask you to stop this and get out of my place." He turned and looked behind him. Three other men, who had been sitting at the bar, were still about ten feet away. All six of the Germans were swinging their fists now, hollering even louder than before. Lifting the nightstick, my grandfather hit one of them on the back of the head. "Out of my place," he shouted, raising the stick to hit a second man. "Out of my place." But then, as the first man he had struck fell to the floor, the others stopped fighting with one another and, turning to him, stared at him for a moment with their mouths open. When they realized what had happened, they rushed at him. Two of them twisted the nightstick from his hand and a third began to punch him in the stomach and chest. He heard the nightstick roll across the floor and, turning his head, saw the other customers running for the door. One man, as he escaped, threw a stein of beer at one of the Germans, and it hit the man on the head, drawing blood.

My grandfather turned around again just in time to see a fist coming toward his face. He tried to turn away but could not, because two of the drunks were holding him tightly now. The fist struck him on the cheekbone, nearly causing him to lose consciousness. He felt blood running down his face and then the agonizing drumming of fists against his stomach. Above him he could still hear his wife screaming, far away, it seemed now, and he could also hear the Germans shouting as they punched him again and again, "*Papa Brueckmann, gut! Papa Brueckmann, besser!*" "Papa Brueckmann, good! Papa Brueckmann, better!" Then he passed out.

The drunks poured a pitcher of beer over his head but failed to revive him. They dragged him outside and, laughing hysterically, stretched him across the trolley tracks. Then, falling over one another, they stumbled away, calling as they went, *"Papa Brueckmann, Papa Brueckmann, der Strassenbahnwagen kommt!"* "Papa Brueckmann, Papa Brueckmann, the trolley is coming!"

My grandfather lay unconscious on the tracks for a few minutes until the vibration of the approaching trolley awakened him. As he slowly regained consciousness, he heard the trolley drawing near and then his wife's screams above him and then another sound—the crying of a baby. He got to his feet, went back into the empty barroom and, wiping his face with a towel, climbed the stairs to the second floor. At the top of the stairs, Frieda met him and told him that his wife had given birth to a baby girl.

3 The Business and the Party

··

MY GRANDFATHER SOLD the hotel. He did it not so much because of his own difficulties in keeping order but because he didn't want his children growing up above a barroom. The boy was nearly five years old and took in most of what he saw around him. The girl was an infant, it was true, but my grandfather adored her and couldn't stand the idea that she would grow up surrounded by people and things that were sordid and uncouth. The baby had been named Helen, but my grandfather called her Kitty until the day he died. For him, she would always be an exquisite pet.

One night the volunteer fire department, of which my grandfather was now a member, gave a ball at which he told my grandmother about his plans to give up the hotel. Many shops had been opened in Haledon in recent years, and now that the borough had been incorporated, it was not unlikely that even more businesses would be started. He explained to his wife that the town had no newsdealer and nowhere to buy tobacco and stationary and candy. Suppose they opened a shop to sell all of these, adding perhaps a small ice-cream parlor? After all, they had good experience at serving customers food and drink at the hotel. If they combined all these things, they could do pretty well, he calculated, and they would be free of the barroom and the smell of beer that made its way into their rooms every night.

My grandmother went along with her husband's idea, and so he pushed his plans even further. A new hardware store had just opened about three blocks up Belmont Avenue on the corner of Norwood Street, one of the new streets laid out by the land company that was selling building lots on the west side of the town. A man named Gaugler had erected a handsome three-story building that provided space for his hardware store on the first floor and a large flat on each of the floors above. My grandfather saw that the corner exactly opposite Gaugler's store was unoccupied, and so he approached the land company, which gave him a price on it. Then he got Gaugler to show him the plans of his recently finished building and, after he had examined them, he decided that the building was just what he wanted—space for a store on the ground floor, rooms for his own family on the second floor, and a flat to rent out for extra income on the third. He would, he decided, hire a builder and have him put the building up for him, reversing the plans so that the two buildings would complement one another and frame the junction of the two streets.

The builder was found and a contract drawn up. I still have a copy of it, and in the specifications I can read, as if with an X ray, where and what kind of timbers are concealed in the walls. My grandfather took no chances; the measurements of every piece of lumber in it are specified—girders six by eight, sills four by six, beams two by ten, and rafters two by six. He spent all his time watching as the structure rose, watching them mortise the beams and tenon the frame, watching to make sure that the poor carpenters put the specified double sills under the partitions, insisting that there be three nails at each end of the studding. I can almost hear his voice: "Three at each end. It's right here in the papers." And if one of the builders called back in frustration with this stubborn Dutchman, "Go tend bar, Brueck-mann. I'm the carpenter," you can be sure that my grandfather was quick to reply, "And I am the owner. I pay the bills." No, they didn't get away with anything. Warped timber had to go, crooked cedar shingles had to be ripped out and done over. When they tried to charge him twice for wood they had used both for cribbing and walls, he caught them red-handed and got his money back. I can still find the deduction in the final bill.

And then there it stood, finished, the house Bill Brueckmann had built, strong and handsome, its interior even finer than the exterior, with cypress woodwork expertly varnished to bring up its grain, large bay windows over both streets, an interior bathroom with hot water, and gaslight throughout the rooms. When the final bills were paid and the keys were in his pocket, my grandfather climbed the exterior staircase in the rear and stood on his veranda looking out at the hills to the west of Haledon and felt exceedingly pleased with himself. The promise might yet, it seemed, come true.

The next day, they brought their furniture up Belmont Avenue on a rented wagon and moved into the second floor rooms. There was a large kitchen just off the back veranda, painted white and awaiting its magnificent Thatcher coal stove. There was an elegant dining room, bay windowed with an ornate mirrored mantle. In front of it was a sitting room whose bay looked out over the avenue. Along one wall they would place the upright player piano they planned to purchase. The children would have their music lessons there, and from time to time the family would have parties and sing around the piano the songs from the old country, filling the new house with the sounds of the past. On the other side of the flat, the bedrooms spread, one for my grandparents, a small one in front for the boy, and one off the kitchen in the back of the house for the girls, for Frieda and Kitty.

Within days my grandfather stocked the store downstairs and opened the doors of what would be known for nearly half a century

Brueckmann in his store (circa 1910).

as "Brueckmann's." Even in the new store, the family had to work long hours seven days a week. My grandfather had to get up at five and travel to Paterson to pick up the newspapers, carrying them back himself on the trolley. As the business grew, he began a newspaper delivery service, hiring local boys, whom he had to supervise every morning to make sure that all the customers got the papers they wanted. When that work was done, he had a few quiet moments later in the morning when he could enjoy a cup of strong German coffee, but the stream of customers wanting tobacco or magazines or candy was constant, and the heavy golden cash register that sat behind the candy counter rang loud the whole day through, sending its message of prosperity through the rooms above. After lunch, Frieda watched the store for a while, and so my grandfather was able to sit for an hour in the morris chair in the dining room upstairs, reading the papers himself. Then he went back downstairs and worked the rest of the afternoon, taking only the light supper that my grandmother brought to him at six when she herself came down to work behind the ice-cream fountain until nine or ten, filling containers of ice cream until her arm and shoulder muscles cried out in pain.

Occasionally my grandmother and Frieda had to work nights in the store alone. My grandfather had meetings of the fire company or of its ladder crew, of which he was a member. And there was politics. He had become more and more active in the Socialist Party and began to have plans for taking a more active part in its campaigns. He had, for one thing, been quick to see that the Old Party (Republican) politicians who had brought about the incorporation of Haledon as a borough had suffered from a single very great weakness: they seemed to be unable to count. Now if there was one thing that my grandfather excelled at it was counting, and he had calculated at once that Haledon had grown so fast in the years before it became a borough that there were now more workers than Old Partyites. What would happen if the Socialists put up a ticket for the newly formed council? What would happen, he wondered, if one of them ran for mayor?

So he made a point of spending some time down in the social club on Clinton Street that came to be known as the Consumers' Club, the accent placed by the mostly German members on the first syllable—the Consumers' Club. There he argued with anybody who would listen, and some of the old members remembered his arguing years later. They told me how it would go.

Some man would say, "What gets my goat is all these greenhorns just off the boat who don't know the first thing about what makes this country go, tellin' you and me how things should be run. Can you beat it?" The man would raise his voice so that my grandfather was sure to hear. "These greenhorns with their socialistic ideas. I say let them go back and kick out the kaiser and put in their socialism over there, if they want it so bad. Why don't you kick out the kaiser, Brueckmann, and leave us Americans alone?"

"I'm a citizen of this country now," my grandfather would say then, looking up from his cards, "I've got nothing to do with the kaiser."

"Maybe you're a citizen, Brueckmann," the Old Partyite would say, "but you don't understand this country, no sir. You don't understand free enterprise. Give every man the freedom to do the best he can, get as much as he can, and as long as he doesn't steal or hurt anybody, leave him alone. That's the way to make a strong country, Brueck- mann, only you can't see it."

Then, as he dealt the cards at his table, my grandfather would say, "What have you got to say about the mill owners who don't work but make a million, when the poor devils who work for them can't even feed their children proper? You call that a strong country?"

"If a man can make a million," the other man would say, "I say more power to him. I'd like to make a million myself. You'd like to make a million, Brueckmann, or what else are you in business for? You can't fool us."

My grandfather would pick up his cards then and say, "The trouble is, people can't see beyond their pocketbooks. Under socialism we would pay everybody the same for the same amount of work. And why not? Work is work whether it's with the hands or the head."

"So that's it then, Brueckmann," the Old Partyite would reply. "You want to pay a doctor who's been to college the same as a ditch- digger, do you? What are you going to pay the president of the coun- try then, fifteen cents an hour?"

The room would fill with laughter then, and my grandfather would feel himself getting hot under the collar.

"Or maybe you'll pay old Teddy a dollar a day," the man would continue, enjoying the laughter around him. "How about that? A dollar a day for being president of the United States of America!"

My grandfather would slam his cards on the table then. "The way things are now," he would retort, "I can see paying a man with an education more for his work because he had to pay for the education himself. Fair enough. But under socialism, education will be free for anybody who can qualify. So what would be the good of making men fight one another for money the way they do now? Now a working man is so busy trying to earn a few more cents than the man next to him that he never sees how much the mill owner is stealing. And that's just what the capitalists want, to keep the workers fighting with one another so that the owners can walk off with the lion's share of the money. It's greed that's at the bottom of it, greed and competition, and that's what socialism wants to put an end to. We want to divide up the profits fair and square among the people who really do the work. What's wrong with that, I ask you?"

"Socialism's against religion."

"Socialism has nothing to say about religion. I say let everybody believe what they want as long as they're honest and treat others as they want to be treated. If you ask me, I don't see what good the churches are, and I think the priests lick the boots of the rich. I knew the priests in the old country. They'd tell the working people that being poor is a good thing, and then they'd eat and drink like the rich. And the poor people believed it. Can you beat that? I say live according to nature, a clean honest life, God or no God. But socialism has nothing to say about a man going to church if he wants to. It has to do with men getting a fair share of what they make, that's all."

"You're a pretty fair talker," someone would call out then. "The Socialists ought to run you for mayor."

My grandfather might laugh then, returning to his card game, but he admitted to himself that it was not a bad idea. And so he went to more and more meetings and argued with more and more people, and my grandmother and Frieda found themselves tending the store more and more often in the evening. It was during one of those late store-tending nights that my grandmother suffered a dizzy spell that sent her to her doctor. After examining her, the doctor told her that she was pregnant again. The news made my grandmother happy at first. Her last pregnancy had been difficult because of her hard life in the hotel. Now, even with tending the store most nights, life was a little more comfortable for her, and so she looked forward to carrying another child, hoping that it would be another boy, for she adored her son and had dreaded having to send him off to school. Things went well for her for the first six months of the pregnancy, in spite of the hard nights she had to endure behind the ice-cream fountain, but in the seventh month the bleeding began. The doctor ordered my grandmother to bed, and her sister Christine came over from Prospect Park, the neighboring town where she and her husband had built a small house, to help with household chores. My grandmother's other sister, Anna, had married my grandfather's cousin Karl and had moved to St. Louis, which meant that Christine was the only family member who could help now. Lying in bed those long days, my grandmother talked with her sister about seeing a specialist, but when she asked her husband about it, he replied that her doctor had told him that specialists were a waste of money. The doctor suggested instead that they try a treatment called "packing," which he said would stop the bleeding. My grandfather had agreed.

My grandmother said years later that she had had serious doubts about the treatment and, as things turned out, her doubts were justified. One night in her seventh month, she experienced severe pains, accompanied by profuse bleeding. They sent for the doctor, who arrived well after midnight, just in time to deliver the baby. My grandmother was in great pain by then, and the doctor had to give her morphine, which made her feel dizzy and faint. "I thought I was going to die," she said as she told the story, "but I told Will and the doctor I wanted to live a while yet. Then I passed out." She remained unconscious for an hour but woke up again just as the baby arrived. Through the sweat and tears that blurred her vision, she saw the doctor take the little creature and hand it to Christine. It was very quiet in the bedroom then, and my grandmother held her breath waiting for the infant's cry. But there was no sound, and she knew at once that it was dead.

"A boy or a girl, Will?" she asked her husband.

"A boy, Katie."

"It's dead, Will.'

"You rest, Katie."

My grandmother slept soundly through the rest of that night. Once or twice, she remembered, she called out for the dead baby, but the morphine and her own exhaustion overpowered her at last, and she slept. In the morning, she awoke and found her sister beside the bed weeping softly. Her sister nodded when my grandmother asked again whether the child was dead, and the two of them wept together for the child and for themselves.

Although she recovered her health within a few weeks, Katie remained depressed. The doctor's warning that she was to have no more children did not upset her; she had Billie and Helen after all. But she often told me that she was haunted by the image of that tiny creature they had taken from her. It had looked very small but perfect in every way. And if there had been nothing wrong with the baby, she often mused, what had killed it? She believed in nature the way her mother had believed in God, and she had difficulty believing that nature could do such a thing. For that reason, she came to believe, I think, that she was in some way to blame, and so in the weeks to come, when my grandfather came back from his political meetings, he often found her sitting in the kitchen before the fire, staring down at her hands and weeping to herself.

4 Stubborn Dutchman

IN 1912 the Socialist party in Haledon nominated my grandfather to be mayor of Haledon, and he accepted the nomination. They nominated two other members of the party for the borough council, Fred Pickering, a quiet unassuming man, and Bill Ritchie, a hot-tempered Scotsman.

I know a good deal about the election that year and about the days that followed it, but not because my grandparents spoke a great deal about it. In fact they did not talk much at all about their years in politics. But after their deaths, I found among my grandfather's papers a small scrapbook that contained newspaper clippings that dealt with those days. That discovery whetted my appetite and so, after reading those yellowing bits of newsprint, I went down to the Paterson Public Library and read my way through about twenty years of the Paterson papers. The reading raised even more questions, however, and so I spent another summer in the '70s pouring over the minutes of the borough council. So you see, I got to know the characters in that political drama and in the sadder drama that followed it pretty well. I still feel as though I can hear their voices filling the Guild Hall where the council meetings took place.

My grandfather and his fellow candidates campaigned hard in 1912. My grandmother brought together some of the Socialist women, and they sewed an election banner that they hung across Belmont Avenue. Bill Ritchie wrote a fiery pamphlet that was distributed to all the voters. I still have a copy of it, proclaiming in bold type:

SOME THINGS THAT SOCIALISM WILL DO: DO AWAY WITH: ALL WAR, ALL POVERTY, ALL BANKS, ALL ADVERTISING, ALL STRIKES, NINETY PERCENT OF CRIMES, MOST LAWYERS, ALL LIFE AND FIRE INSURANCE, ALL PAWN SHOPS AND ALL UNEMPLOYMENT.

It closes with the slogan

IN COOPERATION WEALTH; IN COMPETITION WE CREATE TWO CLASSES; IDLE RICH AND IDLE POOR.

The Socialist victory in Haledon (1912).

After the Socialists distributed a handbill about my grandfather's candidacy, his store was busier than ever. Now he had to spend much of his time arguing. Townspeople he had never seen before came in and bought a newspaper or some tobacco just so they could argue with him. At least the Old Partyites did. The Socialists assumed that they could come in and talk without buying anything. In the end, it all worked. My grandfather won the election 231 votes to 189. He even received more votes in Haledon than the national Socialist ticket—Debs got only 150 votes—and more than the other presidential candidates as well. Roosevelt got 140 votes, Wilson 100, and Taft 50. My grandfather was not surprised by the victory; at the pre-election rally, people had risen to their feet and given him a standing ovation, shouting over and over, "We want Bill. We want Bill." And they were not just Socialists committed to the party's radical agenda; many people simply saw him as a businessman with good sense who would probably run the borough pretty well.

Unfortunately the Socialist victory was not complete. The national ticket lost, of course, and the two candidates for the borough council were defeated by their Republican opponents, Christener and Turner. This defeat was especially troublesome because it meant that my grandfather, although he was mayor, would have to face a council of six Republicans. So it's not unlikely that he had misgivings that election night even as the victory parade formed on Clinton Street and wound its way through the town, past the houses of the Old Partyites, who had forgotten to count, and beneath the small U.S. flag that his little daughter waved from the bay window in the front room above the store.

My grandfather began to meet with members of the council even before the new year and the beginning of his term. He knew that there was going to be trouble, and so he started off in a conciliatory way, agreeing to the reappointment of all borough officials except for the clerk and the chief of police, who happened to be ill. He had judged that if he could make sure that the borough records were accurate and that he was in control of the town's single policeman, he could probably deal with the hostile council at least until the next election. But the Republicans pushed the issue of the police chief, a man named Saner, and got a doctor to say that he soon would be well again. My grandfather gave in when faced with the prospect of having to pay for another doctor's opinion but insisted that he would not pay the man as long as he was not performing his duty, an action that his opponents were quick to point to as an example of Socialist heartless-ness.

That really angered my grandfather, and so he dug his heels in on the question of the clerk. He was determined to turn down their candidate, whoever it was, and to get his Socialist friend Paul Hueck the job. Ready for a fight, he put on his blue suit on New Year's Day, 1913, and walked up to the Guild Hall where the old council would meet with the outgoing mayor, whose name was Pries, and where my grandfather would then be sworn in as mayor and hold his first meet-ing with the new council. He met some of his fellow Socialists on the veranda of the building and talked with them while the old council held its final meeting. Just before noon, someone brought word out that the old clerk, Coon, had resigned and that the council had accepted his resignation. My grandfather was not surprised; he had been informed that the Republicans were planning to elect the outgoing mayor, Pries, as clerk, with the hope that he, with their help, would be able to go on running the borough just as though he were still the mayor.

At noon the new council and mayor were sworn in. The Guild Hall was filled with people, most of them Socialist supporters, who sent forward a delegation with a horseshoe of flowers for the new mayor. They presented the flowers, and then one of the councilmen, a man named Kapp, jumped up and said, "We can't have a meeting, Mr. Mayor. There is no clerk."

"Very well, gentlemen," my grandfather said. "Then I nominate Paul Hueck to be our new clerk. I understand that Reverend Coon has resigned. All those in favor?"

No hands went up.

"All opposed?"

The councilmen all raised their hands.

My grandfather could see from their faces that they thought they had him in a corner. They knew he wanted to deliver his inaugural address while his supporters were present, and they figured that they could prevent him from doing so by insisting that there had to be a clerk to take the minutes. He decided to beat them at their own game. "Very well, gentlemen," he said, "then I will ask Mr. Pries, the ex-mayor, to serve as temporary clerk for this meeting, so that we can proceed with our business."

The councilmen were taken by surprise. They couldn't oppose the temporary appointment of Pries when they wanted him to have the job permanently. So my grandfather was able to deliver his address, and his supporters were able to shout their support while the Old Partyites and the council could do no more than raise their eyebrows and nod in a way that suggested that they knew a few things that the damn fool Socialists didn't know.

During the first three weeks of that January, both my grandfather and the councilmen held their ground on the question of appointing a clerk. Because no one was appointed to the post, the second meeting of the year, which had been scheduled for January 6, had to be postponed until January 20. In the meantime, the Paterson newspapers had begun to cover the story, printing letters from supporters on both sides. The Old Partyites insisted in their letters that they had outvoted the mayor six to one and that they should therefore be permitted to appoint the clerk. My grandfather answered by pointing out that the old council's action in accepting the resignation of Coon was at the root of the problem. He argued that their action subverted the intent of the borough's laws, which provided that the old clerk should remain in office until a new one was appointed. He laid bare the Republican scheme to force him to choose the old mayor, Pries, by using the vacancy to prevent the borough's business from being conducted. What they really wanted, he understood, was a crisis serious enough to force him to resign and so, to make them appear the more stubborn, he announced publicly that while his opponents would settle for Pries and only Pries, he was quite willing to consider other candidates for the job. He was confident that most of the people of Haledon would stand by him if he took this reasonable position and that it would be the Republicans who would suffer in the long run, first in the school board election and then in the general election the following fall.

Before the next meeting of the council, several things happened that further complicated the situation. First, Coon, the old clerk, suddenly turned all of the borough records over to Pries, the ex-mayor, without even telling my grandfather. The Socialists immediately branded the act illegal and threatened to file a formal complaint in the county courthouse. My grandfather was furious. He had always believed that Coon was both lazy and foolish, and he found ridiculous Coon's claim that he could not keep the records in his house a day longer. What made my grandfather even angrier was Pries's claim that my grandfather himself had directed him to keep the records. "I told him to take whatever papers from his own term he might need. That's all," my grandfather said. "I never said anything about the rest of the books."

Well, when Pries learned that the Socialists were planning to make a formal complaint against him, he became frightened, and the Republican councilmen realized that they could no longer rely upon him. So they went to Buckley, the Republican assemblyman from the district, and got him to agree to introduce a bill in the state legislature giving councilmen the right to appoint a clerk in the event of an impasse such as the one in Haledon. My grandfather was indignant when he was told that the state itself might interfere in the town's affairs. "They scratch one another's back, these Republicans," he exclaimed. "There's no two ways about it. We'll have to take over Trenton too, or they will force us to do whatever they want from down there."

On January 20, my grandfather asked my grandmother to watch the store and walked up to the Guild Hall long before the meeting of the council was scheduled to begin. It had been a cold day. The temperature had never risen above twenty degrees, and a strong wind was whipping off the hills to the northwest and scattering blown snow over the already ice-bound streets. He had decided that he had better get to the hall early to make sure that there was enough heat, for Spangenmacher, the Superintendent of Public Works, was sick, and his helper, Gallina, was not very reliable. On top of that, Saner, the police chief, was still ill, and so two marshals had to be sworn in in case of trouble. They had refused to serve at first, pointing out that, with things the way they were in Haledon, they might never be paid, and so my grandfather had to promise to pay them out of his own pocket, twenty-five cents an hour, if the borough didn't meet the payroll.

His precautions proved to be wise. Nearly four hundred people came out for the meeting, most of them complaining and looking for a fight. The seats in the front of the hall had nearly all been taken, most of them by Republicans. Many were old members of the two churches in Haledon, Episcopalian and Methodist. Both men and women gathered around their ministers, whispering in an agitated way and shaking their heads. In the rear of the hall several dozen mill workers had gathered. A few had taken seats, but most of them remained standing near the door, rubbing their hands together, stamping their snow-covered feet and calling to one another in a way that was meant to menace the Republicans in front of them. Ritchie, the Scotsman, who had lost his race for a seat on the council, was the loudest. "There will be no bringing back the wee old mayor tonight," he called to friends across the hall. "We have our own mayor now."

Seeing the angry faces and hearing the catcalls from the audience, my grandfather began the meeting in a quiet and conciliatory way. "Gentlemen," he said, "you have had every other appointive office filled with your own men. Now, I think it is more than right that you should let me appoint a man from my own party as clerk. The mayor is the man who has the most work to do with the clerk, and so I think you should allow me to appoint Mr. Hueck. Never before has an occasion arisen where a mayor had six councilmen bucking him as I have. You are six to one against me, and now I appeal to you as gentlemen to concede me this appointment."

As soon as he finished speaking, Kapp leapt from his seat at the council table. "Not so, not so," he shouted. "This happened once before, and the mayor let the council make the appointment. It's in the minutes. You just read them, Brueckmann, and see for yourself."

As soon as Kapp sat down, Turner, another one of the new councilmen and a man who wanted to be mayor himself, got up and made a long speech stating that the mayor was just the chairman of the council, that the council really ran the borough, and that the council could overrule the mayor whenever it wanted to. Then a man named Belcher, who was seated next to Turner, pointed at my grandfather and said, "It says in the law that you should take the council's advice, but you refuse to take it. You take the advice of your Socialist friends instead. Everybody can see that."

My grandfather realized then that he was in for a long fight, so he leaned across the table and growled, "My party elected me, and I intend to follow its advice whether this council likes it or not."

A number of people in the audience rose to their feet and began to applaud. Abrams, a councilman who was seated across from Turner, leapt up and shouted that the clerk should call the roll.

"There is no clerk," my grandfather snapped back.

"We had a clerk on New Year's Day," Abrams replied. "Mr. Pries was clerk then. Have Mr. Pries call the roll. If the roll isn't called, we have no legal meeting, and we can conduct no business."

"Nothing doing," my grandfather said, hitting the table with his fist. "Gentlemen, I nominate Paul Hueck to be clerk."

"This is not parliamentary," Abrams called out.

Someone in the audience told him to keep quiet and sit down, and Abrams shouted back at the man, warning him to keep his place.

My grandfather struck the table with his gavel and called for order, but Abrams ignored him. Jumping to his feet, he shouted that if there was no clerk there could be no meeting. With that he stormed out of the hall.

When order was restored, Belcher made a speech. "You and your party have made it up," he said, "that Mr. Pries is not going to be clerk. One of your own men told me this morning that you have made your minds up that we might get some things but that we will never get Pries. Well, I tell you something. I'll vote for Pries now and all the time, and Pries is the only man I'll ever vote for."

The hall grew even noisier when Belcher sat down, and my grandfather could see the faces of the Republicans turned in anger at the faces of the Socialists. Every mouth was open in a shout, and fists were waving across the aisles. Struggling to restore order, he hit the table with his gavel again and again until the room grew quiet. Then he nominated another Socialist, John Triquart, but when the vote was taken the five remaining councilmen voted against him. Finally my grandfather nominated John Stewart, yet another Socialist, and the council voted him down just as they had the two earlier nominees.

My grandfather stared at the council and said, "If you won't take one of these men as clerk, we won't have a meeting this year, and I won't resign either." There was a lot of cheering in the rear of the hall then, and a man named Buschmann, one of the Republicans, got to his feet and shouted that there was a clerk after all, because Coon hadn't had the right to resign. The old council hadn't had the right to accept his resignation either, because the law said that the old clerk had to serve until a new clerk was appointed. My grandfather turned to De Yoe, the borough attorney, and asked him whether that was so, and De Yoe replied that anybody had the right to resign whenever he pleased.

It was clear then that they had reached an impasse and that the audience was growing angrier. Even the Republicans, who had sat quietly at first, the church members and their ministers, were now shaking their heads and turning around to return the Socialists' taunts. A number of private arguments had broken out here and there in the hall. My grandfather realized that he might not be able to maintain order much longer, and so he declared a recess and called the councilmen aside. After more off-the-record arguing, they finally agreed that they would have to do something to get money appropriated to keep the school running, and so, to accomplish that, they made Turner temporary clerk, reconvened, and appropriated the $9,733 needed to keep the school open for the next three months. Then they adjourned until February.

After the angry crowd had left, my grandfather strode out of the hall onto the veranda where several of his supporters urged him not to back down. "No, gentlemen," he assured them. "We do not back down, not tonight, not in February. We fight this to the end."

In the days that followed, bitterness grew, and some people who had been good customers stopped going to my grandfather's store. Even the family suffered, for my grandfather had to attend political meetings in the evening even more frequently. This meant that my grandmother was left alone, for the children went to bed early and Frieda had to tend the store. My grandmother would sit by herself in the dining room then, growing increasingly lonely and sad. She thought often of her lost baby and tried, she once told me, to picture that small face that she had seen only once. But the face was gone. She could not recall it.

Even Billy was touched by the ill feeling in Haledon. During the week after the stormy council meeting, Oldham Pond froze over, and he and some of his friends went skating one afternoon instead of returning to school after lunch. When Absolom Grundy, the school principal, learned that the boys were absent, he guessed where they were, walked up to the pond, and caught them. Grundy was a dour man, lofty and a bit pretentious. He spent most of his time in the study of his big house on Zabriskie Street reading, and when he mingled with other people, he visited the Episcopal Minister Watts or wealthier families on the hill, the Mayers and Goodbodys, the Leonards and Haywoods. He was suspicious of foreigners and, although he considered himself above politics, he loathed the Socialists whom he considered godless and anti-American. What was more, some of the Socialists on the board of education had dared to criticize him in the past, and so he had a personal grudge against the party too.

When he found the boys skating on the pond, he brought them back to school, where he took special pleasure in summoning the Socialist mayor to his office and lecturing him and his son. My grandfather endured it. What else could he do? The boy was clearly in the wrong. When Grundy finished his lecture, my grandfather took his son by the arm and steered him out of the school, along Kossuth Street and down the avenue, humming hard all the way, just as he always did when he was holding back his anger. My grandmother was sitting at the window in the front room waiting for them. Her husband had told her what Billy had done, and now she feared that he would lose his temper and whip the boy. But my grandfather didn't whip him. Instead, he sat Billy down in the dining room beside his

mother and lectured him longer and harder than Grundy had, reminding him that he had brought disgrace on his father and on the
rest of the family, shouting that if he wasn't careful he would turn
out to be a good-for-nothing. "Like some of your mother's people,"
he added.

"Don't say such a thing, Will," my grandmother said. She knew
he was thinking about her brother Joe, whose drinking troubled her
husband.

"I say the truth," my grandfather said, glaring at his wife now, "and
he might as well know it. And I won't have you coddling him either.
You see what it leads to."

The boy had been able to endure his father's criticism of him, but
when he saw his father attacking his mother as well, he began to
tremble and, leaping up, ran to his bedroom in tears. My grandmother rushed after him, leaving her husband in the middle of the
dining room, humming to himself. "*Ja*, Katie," he said as she left the
room, "go ahead and spoil him good."

That night my grandmother brought Billy his supper in his room
at the front of the house. When he had finished it, she sat with him
and held his small hand in hers. Then, when the boy went to sleep,
she tucked the blankets in around him and smoothed his fair hair.
She sat watching him as he slept, watched his eyelids flutter, and
heard him sigh. Then, as the last trolley car to Paterson passed the
house, she got up and went to the dining room where she sat crocheting and thinking about what her husband had said to the boy that
afternoon. It had been unfair, she told herself, that he was so hard
on the boy and unfair that he accused her of spoiling him. Didn't he
spoil his Kitty? Every Sunday now he sat her on his lap after breakfast
and gave her a nickel. He would let her carry it down the back stairs
in her hand and then around to the front door of the store where he,
having gone down the front stairs, would let her in and let her buy
five cents' worth of candy. "It was probably the same nickel every
week," my grandmother said as she told me the story years later.
"And he called it 'teaching the value of money.'"

I could see then, as my grandmother told me the sad story, that it
must have been at that time that my grandparents began to drift
apart, that their affection for one another began, under one stress or
another, to cool. She must have thought more and more of the lost

baby in those days and must have begun to wonder whether, if her husband had let her see the specialist, the baby might have survived.

The next meeting of the borough council had to be canceled because there was still no prospect of a resolution of the dispute over the borough clerk. In its place the councilmen convened a meeting of their own to form what they called the "Citizens' League." They invited all of the Haledon Republicans and the few Democrats in the borough to join their league, hoping to line them all up against my grandfather and the Socialists, but the idea backfired when a fight broke out at the very first meeting. The Democrats claimed that the Republicans were wrong, putting the Republicans in a more precarious position than they had been before the league was formed. Now if the councilmen backed down, they would lose the support of their own party; and if they didn't, they would lose the Democrats, whose numbers they needed if they were ever to win an election.

When the council meeting was rescheduled, the councilmen came together a day earlier and decided to spread the rumor that they were going to stand firm. As a result, my grandfather arrived at the Guild Hall on the night of the meeting expecting the worst. The night was not nearly as cold as the night of the previous meeting had been, and although there was still snow on the ground, the air was clear and windless and the temperature was well above the freezing mark. My grandfather walked up Belmont Avenue without hat or gloves, and when he arrived, he found the councilmen not gathered around the stove inside as before but standing on the veranda surrounded by their supporters. "Good evening, gentlemen," he said.

"Good evening, Mr. Mayor," Kapp replied.

"Are we going to have a meeting this evening?" my grandfather asked, scanning the crowd. "It looks like quite a few of the citizens," he chose the word carefully, "are going to attend."

"We would like to have a meeting, Mr. Mayor," Turner said

"I'm glad to hear it," my grandfather said. "I think the citizens would like us to get on with the business of the borough." He narrowed his eyes and fixed them on Turner and the others, watching for their reactions. Three of them stared at the floor, and Abrams pulled nervously at his tie. My grandfather turned away from them then, noting their nervousness and telling himself that it was a good sign.

The room was filled to capacity again, and when my grandfather came in, somebody shouted out, "Stand up to them, Bill!" My grandfather pretended not to hear. He just took his seat, folded his hands before him and waited for the council to join him.

At about eight o'clock, the councilmen came into the hall and sat down around the council table. My grandfather hit the table with his gavel and said, "Ladies and gentlemen, I call this meeting of the council to order and, since we cannot conduct business without a clerk, I once again nominate Paul Hueck for the job." He turned his head slowly, staring into the eyes of each man around the table in turn. "All in favor?"

No hands were raised.

"Opposed?"

All six men raised their hands.

My grandfather paused and shuffled the papers that lay on the table before him. People in the audience were leaning forward in their seats, and there was much angry muttering.

"Very well, gentlemen," my grandfather resumed. "Then I nominate John Triquart. Will those in favor of Mr. Triquart put up their hands please?"

No hands were raised.

"Opposed then, gentlemen?"

The councilmen all raised their hands again, and many of the people in the hall began to shout and whistle. My grandfather struck the table with his gavel and said, "Ladies and gentlemen, this is a meeting of the Council of the Borough of Haledon and it will be an orderly meeting. If anyone speaks without being recognized, out of the hall he goes and no mistake about it. Remember," he added, looking at the councilmen now, "we are a new borough and people are watching to see if we can run our own business in a responsible way." The audience grew quiet then, and my grandfather drew himself up and said, "Well, gentlemen, if you don't find Mr. Hueck or Mr. Triquart acceptable, then I nominate Mr. John E. Stewart. You probably remember that Mr. Stewart applied for the job two years ago when it was given to Reverend Coon. As I recall, everyone agreed then that both candidates were highly qualified. In fact I remember several people at this table saying that Mr. Stewart would also have made a good clerk. I don't think I am mistaken about that. I'm pretty sure the audience remembers." My grandfather looked out at the audience. "All those in favor then?"

The councilmen shifted in their seats. Abrams pulled at his tie again as the audience leaned forward, and my grandfather began to wonder whether in the end he might have to accept Pries after all. Then he saw one hand go up, then another, then two more.

"Opposed?" he asked.

No hands went up.

"Abstentions?"

Two hands went up.

"Then, gentlemen, Mr. Stewart is our new clerk. I thank you for your cooperation."

The crowd cheered and my grandfather struck the table and called for order. Then, as most of the spectators shuffled out of the hall, the Council began what would prove to be a very long meeting. There were marshals to be appointed and bonded, bills to pay, licenses to issue. Almost four hours later, after the long agenda had been dealt with, my grandfather adjourned the meeting and walked down the avenue to his store with some of the other Socialists. As he bid them good night, Paul Hueck said, "You know what they call you now, Bill? They call you 'the stubborn Dutchman.' "

"They could have had it worse, Paul," my grandfather replied, pulling at Hueck's lapel. "I could have made them take you."

"We all have to give in a little now and then, Bill."

"*Ja*, it's the way the world works, Paul. No use talking. But I don't like it. I don't like it, not when I know that I'm right."

5 Strike in the Paterson Mills

....

THE TROUBLE in the Paterson silk mills began in 1912, the year my grandfather was elected mayor of Haledon. Conditions in the city's mills and dye shops were dreadful. Children of fifteen or sixteen worked six days a week for just a few dollars, and men with families to support had to work fifty or sixty hours a week to make ends meet. Some older mills were infested with rats and were so cold in the winter that the workers had to wear overcoats all day as they worked. In the dye shops, men and women often worked for hours standing in icy water.

Doherty owned one large mill in Paterson. He had organized his own baseball team by recruiting his own workers to play for him on Sunday afternoons. Although he underpaid them in the mill, he made a show of giving five dollars to any man on his team who hit a home run. This same Doherty tried to introduce what they called the "four-loom system," which made one man able to do the work of four. The system, if introduced, would jeopardize the jobs of hundreds of workers. Everyone understood that.

The prospect of unemployment obviously angered the workers, who had seen through Doherty's baseball largesse and were ready for a confrontation. But they had a problem: the old-line unions weren't able to organize the workers because most of them were foreigners who spoke little or no English. And so leadership of the workers in the silk industry fell to a man named Katz, who was in charge of the Socialist Labor party in Paterson and who had worked for the IWW in Detroit. In 1912 Katz called a strike against some of the Paterson mills, a strike which lasted for two months, during which time many workers were arrested and thrown in jail—a sign of what would come the following year.

In the end, the mill owners settled the 1912 strike by making new agreements on hours and wages and by promising not to introduce the four-loom system. The workers returned to their looms, but within weeks the owners reneged on their promises, because they learned that there was a split in the IWW and that, in all likelihood, the militants in the union, who had run the bloody strike in Lawrence, Massachusetts, would gain control. They were afraid that if that happened more and more strikes would be organized, and so they abandoned the idea of compromise altogether.

When the workers realized that Doherty and his friends were not going to keep their promises, they went out on strike again. In January 1913, at the very time that my grandfather was struggling with the councilmen in Haledon, eight hundred workers walked out of Doherty's mill and shut it down. Their action gave the radicals in the IWW just the opportunity they had been looking for, and so two leaders of the small Paterson local of the union, Lessig and Koettgen, began to organize the workers again. They took charge of the hastily called strike and distributed handbills at all the mills, calling for a general strike to stop the introduction of the four-loom system. On February 24, they held a mass meeting at the Turn Hall in Paterson and called on all the workers in the silk mills to join the strike.

Because of these events and the long strike that followed, my sources of information about my grandparents' lives grew suddenly much more numerous and much more detailed. Some of the narrative that follows I drew from the records of the Borough of Haledon, but much more is drawn from the newspapers and their coverage of the Paterson strike. What's more, the yellowed strips of newsprint I now had to read were no longer taken from the obscure "Haledon Notes" at the back of the Paterson papers, *The Call* and *The Evening News*, but from the front pages of those dailies, and in fact, as the strike became an event of national importance, the clippings often came from the New York papers as well. Before the strike ended, my grandfather's picture had appeared on the front page of the Socialist daily in New York.

I also have my memories of long talks with my grandmother in the living room of the house on Zabriskie Street, memories that include her own recollection of those difficult strike days in both Paterson and Haledon. My grandfather was less open with me about the strike, but sometimes, on my Sunday morning walks in the woods with him, he shared something of his own experience, dwelling especially on the correctness of what he had done and on the dishonesty and treachery of his opponents. He feared, I think, that I would hear the stories from other sources, and he wanted to make sure that I knew the truth. I talked to other people in Haledon who had lived through those days too. So I am able to paint the picture of what happened fairly accurately. Many of the words I will put in people's mouths were actually reported to me; others are based on what I read and on my knowledge of the people themselves and what they were likely to feel and say.

The workers were not slow to heed the call of the IWW and its leaders in February 1913. Four thousand broad silk workers struck the mills in which they worked. They paraded through Paterson and held another meeting at the Turn Hall. Some leaders of the Lawrence strike, Elizabeth Gurley Flynn and Carlo Tresca, along with the well-known Socialist, Patrick Quinlan, came to Paterson from New York, arriving just in time to see the strike meeting broken up by the Paterson police under the command of one Chief Bimson. Bimson, acting on orders from the mayor of Paterson, Andrew McBride, arrested the IWW leaders and dozens of other strikers along with the new arrivals, Quinlan, Gurley Flynn and Tresca. The trio of outsiders and a few others were released on bail shortly after their arrest, but the arrest of protesting workers continued and hundreds of weavers were thrown in jail during the following days. The owners of the mills and the Paterson police had decided to crush the strike by whatever means were required.

My grandfather told me, that on the day after the beginning of the general strike, he was sitting at his rolltop desk in the rear of the store. Business was slow. He had spent several hours that day putting ashes on the sidewalk outside, where water running down from the roof had frozen. At about three o'clock he looked up and saw Koettgen, one of the strike organizers, coming through the front door. He knew Koettgen because they had both been members of the German *Singerbund* or Singing Society years ago. He also recognized the man beside Koettgen. It was Wilson Killingbeck, the Socialist candidate for governor in the 1912 election. The two men came to the rear of the store and when they reached my grandfather's desk, Koettgen said, "Mayor Brueckmann, I wonder whether Mr. Killingbeck could talk with you? You know Mr. Killingbeck, I believe."

"Yes, I do," my grandfather said, getting up. He shook their hands and brought over two chairs from one of the little tables near the soda fountain. "I would be happy to listen to what you have to say, gentlemen," he said, "as long as I have no customers in the store. As you can see for yourselves, I have no help right now."

"We understand that, Mr. Mayor," Killingbeck said, leaning forward in his chair, "And we'll be as brief as we can."

"I appreciate that," my grandfather said.

"Well, I was arrested down in Paterson yesterday," Killingbeck began, "and now I'm out on bail. I just had to come up to Paterson to talk to the strikers, you see, and when I saw that Bimson's men were going to arrest the speakers at the meeting, I got up and read from the Constitution of the United States. Well, they arrested me all the same. Can you beat that?"

My grandfather shook his head. "How long will McBride let the police go on like that?" he said. "It's not legal."

"He'll let them go on like that as long as he has to and as long as he thinks he can get away with it, Mr. Mayor, and it's the biggest mistake that he and his friends the mill owners could make, because it's making the workers mad, and as a result, more and more of them are joining the strike. They have about five thousand out now. Wouldn't you say so, Fred?"

"At least six thousand today," Koettgen said, "and all that talk of settlement in the papers is hot air. The weavers aren't going back to work, and we have plenty of dyers out of the dye shops now. They want a minimum wage too, you see. And the ribbon workers will be with us soon. You can bet on that."

"Well, gentlemen," my grandfather said, "what brings you to Haledon?"

"Mayor Brueckmann," Killingbeck said, "McBride and his supporters think that they can break the strike, if they can drive away or lock up all the leaders. That's just what they're trying to do now, but their plan is backfiring, because it's driving the workers together." He paused and frowned. "The problem is that if the leaders are locked up and there's no place to meet, the workers will start drifting back to work as soon as things get really tough. You can't keep a strike alive without bringing the strikers together."

"We've got to have a place to meet," Koettgen broke in, "some place where Bimson and McBride can't touch us, some place where a lot of people, thousands of people maybe, can meet."

"Mr. Mayor," Killingbeck said, "we want to bring the meetings up here to Haledon."

"We don't have a big enough hall here," my grandfather said.

"Not a hall," Koettgen replied. "We'll hold the meetings outdoors, don't you see? We could have ten thousand people at an outdoor meeting here in Haledon."

My grandfather stared at them, thinking hard. "I have to look at all sides of this," he said slowly. "It's true I was elected on our ticket, Mr. Killingbeck, but quite some other people voted for me too. I have to do what's right by them."

"That's true, Mr. Mayor," Killingbeck agreed. "You have to protect them and their property. Of course you do. But you don't have to stand by and watch the constitution violated just because some of the people who voted for you might not care about it. You showed this, town just last week that you wouldn't do what you considered wrong. Well, it's wrong for the Republicans in Paterson to trample on people's constitutional rights and it's wrong up here in Haledon too."

"But the strike is a Paterson strike."

"Not any more," Koettgen said. "We have workers out at the Cedar Cliff Mill and at the Columbia Mill right here in Haledon."

"And what about keeping order?" my grandfather asked. I hear there was some brick throwing out in the Lakeview section and that they turned the steam on at one mill to force the non-strikers out. I don't like the smell of it, gentlemen. I've got only one policeman here. That's all."

"I realize that," Koettgen said.

"And I'm worried about Haywood and the IWW," my grandfather continued. "The party kicked Haywood off the executive committee because he was advocating violence. And look at the trouble they had up in Massachusetts. The fact is, Mr. Killingbeck, the party went on record against violence last year and I agree with the party. If we're going to change things in this country, it has to be done in an orderly way, with elections, the way we're doing it here."

Killingbeck got up and came over to my grandfather's chair. "I agree," he said, "and I have the word of the organizers that there won't be any violence. They're telling the strikers right now that if there's trouble with the Paterson police they're to keep their hands in their pockets and say nothing. Don't you see, Mr. Mayor, it's Bimson's men and the private goon squads at the mills who want violence. The strike leaders know this and they're ordering their people not to resist even if they're arrested. You'll have no worries about violence. I promise you that."

"He's right, Mr. Brueckmann," Koettgen said.

"Now what's most important for the party," Killingbeck continued, "what really counts is that bringing the meetings here could show these people that the only party that will look after them and protect their rights is our party. Here's our chance to prove to them that they're going to have to vote Socialist next November if they're ever going to get a voice in the government. It's going to be a big strike, Mr. Mayor, maybe a very long strike too, and it will get a lot of attention. Do you see what I mean? We can show workers all over the country that our party looks after their interests. And that *is* part of our platform."

"And will they win?" my grandfather asked.

"They will win if we can get the workers out of the mills and keep them out long enough," Koettgen replied.

"Now the strike committee will let you and me be the first speakers at the meeting up here," Killingbeck said. "So we can talk about the party, and you can ask the people to be peaceful and orderly yourself."

"What do you say, Mr. Mayor?" Koettgen asked.

"And don't forget," Killingbeck added, "it *is* a question of the constitution, the right to assemble, the right to free speech."

My grandfather was silent for several minutes. He stared out of the back window of the store at the ashes he had sprinkled on the ice outside. Then, turning back to Koettgen and Killingbeck, he said, "Good. Call the meeting in Haledon, and if Bimson and his cossacks try to come up here, I'll call out our marshals and meet him at Burhans Lane."

"Can we meet tomorrow then?"

"Whenever you want."

"And will you speak?"

"Yes."

"Mr. Mayor," Killingbeck said, "we thank you."

My grandfather got up and walked with Killingbeck and Koettgen to the front door. "We thought we would hold the meeting up at the end of Norwood Street," Koettgen said, "in the fields at the bottom of the hill. There's lots of open space there. Do you see any problem with that, Mr. Mayor?"

My grandfather told them that it seemed like a good place to him and suggested that they walk up Norwood Street and look over the spot for themselves. Then, when they left, he called Saner, the policeman who had just returned to duty, and told him to be ready the next day and to have the marshals standing by in case there was trouble. About half an hour later, he saw Killingbeck and Koettgen walk back down Norwood Street to the trolley car stop in front of the store. A few minutes later they boarded the trolley for Paterson.

What, I wonder, was on my grandfather's mind that night after he had closed up the store and climbed the stairs to his bedroom in the family's rooms upstairs? He must have realized that his decision would be unpopular with some of the old families in Haledon, but that wasn't really important after all. He had already made enemies of them during his first weeks as mayor. He might lose customers, of course, and that was a worry, for he had to support his wife and children. But even that anxiety did not make him regret his decision. He must have recalled, as he crawled into bed beside his wife, that he had gone into business in the first place to be free of the mill owners, to be able to say and do as he pleased. And now a time had come when what he said and did might make a difference. He would be foolish to turn his back on the workers for fear of losing a little money.

Nevertheless, he probably didn't sleep well that night. He must have realized that what he was about to do would make many people angry, and not just customers and voters in Haledon. He would be defying the mill owners and the politicians beholden to them. These were powerful men who could do him and his family harm. That possibility must have preyed on his mind that night as he lay awake listening to the old cuckoo clock in the dining room strike the hours.

6 The Haledon Meetings Begin

....

IT RAINED HARD the day after my grandfather's meeting with Killingbeck and Koettgen, and so the strike meeting in Haledon had to be postponed until the following Sunday. There are good newspaper accounts of that meeting, but I learned much of what I know about it from my grandmother who had vivid memories of it, memories that she shared with me. She remembered that the day was cold and windy but, at least in the morning and early afternoon, clear and bright. Thousands of people came to Haledon that day, some in buggies or automobiles, some on foot, most by trolley car. Late in the morning, my grandmother stood at the parlor window, watching trolley after trolley arrive, each filled with strikers and bearing a sign that read "Zabriskie Street Only," for that was as far as the trolley had to run to get its passengers to within easy walking distance of the meeting place.

At about two o'clock that afternoon, my grandfather put on his blue suit and pinned his small golden mayor's badge on its lapel. Then he set out up Norwood Street to make sure that Saner and the marshals had everything under control. A few neighbors called to him as he walked up the street, and a few of the Old Party members stopped him to complain about the meeting, warning him that it was bound to bring on a Socialist defeat in the fall elections. My grandfather listened to them patiently, but as he gazed out over the huge crowd of strikers, it seemed to him that it was more likely that the election would go the other way.

My grandmother left the house an hour later. Stepping out onto the back porch, she shivered as the wind struck her. She stood motionless for a moment, watching how violently it was tossing about the bare branches of the catalpa tree. Below her on the frozen grass, her little daughter was trying to feed bread crumbs to a flock of sparrows, shouting at them indignantly because they would not eat from her hand. Little Billy was trying to catch the catalpa pods as the wind shook them from the tree, but when he saw his mother laughing at his sister, he joined in the fun and began to make fun of her too. My grandmother went down the back stairs. At the bottom, the children ran up to her and pleaded to be taken along to the meeting, but she was afraid of their getting lost in such a big crowd, and so she insisted that they stay with Frieda. She would be back by four o'clock, she explained, for then they would have to reopen the store so that people returning from the meeting would be able to purchase cups of coffee.

My grandmother swung the back gate closed with Billy riding on its bottom rung, still pleading with her. A little reluctantly, for he was her favorite, she turned away and walked up Norwood Street to the place at the edge of the woods where the strike meeting was to be held. When she reached the throng of strikers, she was frightened at first by the sight of so many faces so close together and by the sound of so many voices speaking in different languages, German, Polish, French, Italian, and Yiddish. She made her way among the people with difficulty because they were standing especially close to one another to keep warm. The wind was still blowing fiercely off the mountain, and some of the women had to clutch at their Sunday hats and at the silk ribbons that my grandmother knew at once they had spoiled in the mills and been forced to buy.

Gathered in the open fields and shivering now, the men and women no longer looked as happy as they had when my grandmother had seen them alight from the trolley cars earlier. The bright look of expectation was gone. Here they simply had to confront the incessant wind and the frightening questions raised by the strike. How would they survive? How would they feed their children? How many more meetings would there have to be? The questions lay in their eyes like dying leaves in dark winter pools of water.

My grandmother stopped when she had made her way halfway through the crowd. From that point, she could see the table and chairs that had been set up at the end of Norwood Street beneath the barren trees. The strike leaders were gathered around the table, talking excitedly, and her husband was there with them. My grandmother knew the IWW people, the "Wobblies," as the papers called them. She recognized Quinlan too, the Irishman with the big ears, and Gurley Flynn, young and pretty, looking like a schoolgirl in her plain black skirt, with her fair hair pulled back tight in a bun. And she spotted Tresca too, the Italian with the little beard and the face like an opera singer. In her later tales of the day, she would always stop at this point and whisper slyly, "He was sweet on Gurley Flynn, and maybe she was sweet on him too. And her, married to some man named Jones and with a baby by him too. Can you believe it? She looked so young!"

At the speakers' table, the strike leaders were talking about the size of the crowd. With the wind howling in the trees and nearly ten thousand people gathered in front of them, the speakers would not be able to make themselves heard. So they decided to divide the crowd into three parts. Tresca stood up and asked the Italians to meet him farther down the hill where he would speak to them in their own language, and Killingbeck led the people on the east side of Norwood Street down to Barbour Street where he delivered his speech standing on the front seat of a buggy. Most people stayed where they were, however, and finally my grandfather got up and addressed them.

He welcomed them to Haledon first and then congratulated them on the way they were standing up to the capitalists. He told them that he thought the mayor of Paterson was the one who was an anarchist, since it was he who was taking away their right of free speech. He said that people couldn't really be free in a world run by the Republicans and the Democrats and that the only hope of the workers lay in voting Socialists into office, because only the Socialists would protect their rights and work for them instead of the rich. Finally he reminded them that if Haledon could elect a Socialist mayor, then Paterson could elect one too, and the state could elect a Socialist governor. The crowd applauded when he finished, and then Koettgen and Quinlan and Gurley Flynn got up in turn.

My grandmother was surprised by how quietly the people stood and listened to the speakers. Saner, whom some in the crowd had labeled "our little pink and white policeman" because his fair skin had reddened with the cold, had nothing to do. He stood at the edge of the crowd, swinging his nightstick and shifting from one foot to the other, for the ground around Norwood Street was marshy and cold, and the dampness had soon begun to penetrate everyone's shoes. A few young men actually climbed into the trees, where they sat, swaying back and forth in the wind with their coat collars up, like poor winter birds trying to bury their heads under their wings.

My grandmother left before the last of the speeches were given and hurried back to the store. There she found Frieda struggling to wait on the many people who had also left the meeting early and had stopped in the store to buy hot coffee before boarding the trolleys. Later, when the meeting was over, the two of them had even greater trouble serving the hundreds of strikers who crowded around the soda fountain and the candy cases. Before they finished even Billy had to be called on to help, and by the time the last striker had departed, much of their stock had been sold out—candy, cigars, tobacco, and even ice cream—and there was what seemed a fortune in the cash register. My grandmother knew that her husband would be pleased, but she didn't get to see him after the meeting, and since she was very tired, she did not wait up for him after they closed the store. No doubt he had had to go to a party meeting, she told herself, and so, weary from the cold and the hard work in the store, she went to bed, the images of those thousands of faces still in her head and the wind howling outside her bedroom window.

The strike spread to many more mills in the days that followed the Haledon meeting, until nearly 25,000 workers had left their jobs, and the silk industry in Paterson was completely shut down. The Paterson newspapers reported daily that the strike was about to be broken and that the workers were on the point of returning to work, but my grandfather knew that this was not the case. He kept in touch with the strike committee and read the Socialist daily, *The New York Call*, every day. In fact he ordered extra copies of the paper now so that the workers in Haledon could get the facts about the strike instead of the twisted stories in the local papers. It infuriated him to read about strikers who were supposed to have threatened fellow workers when they tried to return to work. "*Unsinn*," he would mutter, for he knew that the workers in Paterson were still united and that the politicians and the police were just not allowing the truth to be printed. Only a few days earlier, Alexander Scott's Socialist paper, *The Issue*, had been confiscated and burned in his office in Passaic. Scott had dared to call the Paterson police "cossacks" and the politicians "anarchists," and so they burned his paper and threw him into jail.

On the Friday after the first Haledon meeting, my grandfather received a telephone call from Koettgen, who told him that the strike committee wanted to come up to Haledon to see him. My grandfather agreed but asked them to come in the afternoon when there would be fewer customers in the store. Koettgen replied that the afternoon suited them fine and added that they were going to bring along Bill Haywood, who had arrived in Paterson from Ohio the day before. He explained that although Bimson had summoned Haywood to police headquarters after he arrived and had warned him that Paterson was not going to allow outside agitators to stir up trouble, Haywood had not in fact been arrested as some other Wobblies had been on the first day of the strike.

That afternoon my grandfather sent my grandmother downstairs to look after the store, removing the cover from the vent in the dining room floor so that she could call to him if she needed help. The committee arrived just after three in a large automobile that they parked on Norwood Street opposite the back gate. Koettgen was the first to come up the back stairs. Tresca, Quinlan, and Gurley Flynn were right behind him. Then Killingbeck came up with Lessig and Bill Haywood. My grandfather had heard a good deal about Bill Haywood but had never seen him before. He was struck by his powerful build and by the size and roughness of his hands, something he always dwelt on whenever he told me the story of that day. When the committee came into the kitchen, Haywood took off the large hat he had been wearing, and my grandfather could see that he had only one good eye and that the other one was made of glass.

My grandfather shook hands with Haywood and led the committee into the parlor at the front of the house. When they were all seated, Haywood said, "Mayor, I'm going to say straight out what we want. We're here to ask if we can continue to have Sunday meetings up here in Haledon. Everybody has told me what a great success last Sunday's meeting was, and I'm sure you know how grateful we are to you and the good people here for your hospitality. Well, now, we're wondering whether you would allow the workers to come back on a regular basis."

My grandfather remembered that he answered quickly. "Mr. Haywood," he said, "I was pleased to have the strikers here because I believe they have the right to meet and to say what they feel." Then he added, "As long as they behave themselves."

"And they did behave themselves," Killingbeck broke in.

"I can't complain about anything," my grandfather admitted, "but meeting every Sunday is something else again. It's asking the citizens here to have 10,000 or even 20,000 people on their streets every week. And who knows how long it's going to last? It looks now as though it will be a pretty long strike."

"We're ready for a long strike," Quinlan said. "For a year, if it has to be."

"That's quite some Sundays," my grandfather said, and then it was quiet and he could hear his wife ringing up a sale on the cash register down in the store. Little Billy had come from school and was standing at the dining-room door with his sister, peering in at the strangers in the parlor.

"Mayor," Haywood began again, "I know that you're concerned about the strikers' rights and that you want to help these good people from Paterson, but there's more in this than just that, and I think that Mr. Killingbeck here will back me up on this. We thought at first that this would just be another strike in another mill city, like the strike up in Lawrence last year, but this strike could be more than that. We've never had so many people out in so many different mills, and the people seem to be solidly behind us now and determined to see this through. You understand how hours and wages and the four-loom system are issues in other places too. Well, we're going to go to other cities to get other workers on strike over the same issues. We're going to College Point and Astoria where there are mills and to Allentown too. Do you know what I think, Mayor? I think we could have one of the major industries in this country tied up in a few weeks."

My grandfather looked over at Killingbeck who said, "The best thing is, Mayor Brueckmann, that the owners and the Paterson politicians have reacted just as we wanted them to. The police are using violence, the papers are lying every day, and public officials are violating the citizens' rights. You can see what an opportunity we have here. We can convince the people that the capitalists are against them, that the system as it now stands is rotten from the ground up. What's happening in Paterson is the best proof we've ever had. If we can get the people to see that, we can get them to vote the Republicans and Democrats out and vote us in. Then we can really start to change things. That's what we're talking about here, Mayor Brueckmann, something that could change the whole country in the long run."

The room grew quiet again, and all the committee members turned their eyes to my grandfather. He stared at the mahogany table in front of the bay window and at the album of photographs that stood open on the table. He could hear his wife ringing up another sale in the store downstairs. It was surprising how many customers there seemed to be that afternoon, and he thought for just a second of the amount of money there would be in the cash register's drawer.

"Mayor," Haywood began again, "the mill owners and the politicians know that it's not just Paterson that's at stake here, and that's why they've reacted the way they have and why their newspapers are spreading lies every day. They know our hands are on the throat not only of Paterson but also just maybe on the throat of the whole system. They can see the workers uniting someday not far off and maybe taking over the country just the way you took over this town, and they're scared as hell and ready to fight to the death. They can't afford to let the IWW win a big strike in the East and let the word get out that we did it with the help of the Socialist party. Do you see that, Mayor?"

My grandfather thought for a moment. Then he said, "I have to make sure that there will be no violence here. I hear you didn't see eye to eye with our national committee about violence, Mr. Haywood. The party came out against violence last year, and I heard that you didn't agree with that."

"Mayor," Haywood replied, "I don't deny that I had my differences with Debs and Hilquit and the rest of them over that. But Mayor, you ask anybody who was in Lawrence what instructions we gave to the strikers there. 'Keep your hands in your pockets. No violence. No violence at all.' No, Mayor, we didn't cause the violence, the police caused it. The police beat women and children in Lawrence, and it's the same here in Paterson. It's Bimson's violence and the violence of his cossacks, not IWW violence."

Gurley Flynn broke in, "We gave Mr. Killingbeck our promise, and we give it to you, Mr. Brueckmann. If you let us come back to Haledon, the meetings will be peaceful and orderly, just like last Sunday's. Will you let us come?"

My grandfather stared at the floor in silence for several minutes. Then he turned back to Haywood and said, "Yes, come back to Haledon."

"This Sunday?"

"Yes."

"We all thank you, Mayor," Haywood said.

Killingbeck got to his feet and said, "Mayor Brueckmann, we realize that you have to get back to your business, and so we won't keep you any longer." Following his lead, the others rose and made their way through the dining room and the kitchen to the back porch. Haywood shook my grandfather's hand and put on his big black hat. Gurley Flynn and Tresca stepped over to the porch railing and looked out toward the hills at the foot of which the first meeting had been held. "You have a nice view here, Mr. Brueckmann," Gurley Flynn said. "Soon the trees up on the hills will be green and the days will be fine for our meetings. You can't imagine how much it means to those people to come up here to Haledon on Sundays, to be in a nice place, and to feel that the people in authority respect them." She shook my grandfather's hand and then, taking Tresca's arm, followed the others down the stairs. My grandfather watched as they got into their automobile. Quinlan cranked it up, jumped in, and drove away.

My grandfather walked back through the house and down the front stairs to the store. He sent my grandmother upstairs and asked her to send Billy down to help him slip the Sunday papers. A few minutes later, the boy joined him in the store and began to help his father, asking as he slid the sections of the papers into one another about Bill Haywood's glass eye, which had made a great impression on him. My grandfather told him that he didn't know why Haywood had a glass eye but that he had probably had some kind of accident while he was working.

"Can he see through it, Pa?" the boy asked.

"You can't see with a glass eye, *Junge*," my grandfather replied. "But I think he sees pretty fair through the good one."

The boy put his hand over one of his eyes and narrowed the other. "I can see pretty fair with one eye, Pa," he said, laughing, and my grandfather laughed a little too, as his son squinted at him. Then, remembering himself and the importance of teaching his son how to do a job properly, he told the boy to stop his foolishness and finish the papers.

After supper that night, my grandfather called some of the councilmen who he expected would complain about the strikers' return to Haledon. He was surprised at first that they raised few objections, but then he realized that they were worried about how the voters in Haledon would react if the councilmen opposed the strikers. More and more workers in Haledon had joined the strike, and there was growing sympathy for them in the town. The Republicans were worried, he decided, about how the votes would fall in the next general election.

When my grandfather gave the strike committee permission to hold weekly meetings in Haledon, he had hoped that the strike would soon be over. He realized that the longer it continued, the angrier and more difficult to control the workers would become. He feared for the safety of his neighbors and especially for his family, and he worried about how McBride and Bimson would react to his invitation. When he considered how they had treated others who had stood up against them, he couldn't help but conclude that they would try to get him as well, and then what would become of the family and the business?

His hopes for a short strike were dashed. All through March, as the weather grew warmer, the strike continued, and every Sunday a meeting was held in Haledon. The crowds grew even larger until over 30,000 people gathered on Norwood Street each week, and the meetings grew far more animated. Now there was always a band, and the strikers sang the "Internationale" and the "Marseillaise," along with songs from their homelands. Now the speakers delivered their speeches from the second floor veranda of Botto's house, shouting so that the thousands of listeners could hear and stopping from time to time so that people in the crowd could translate for those who could not understand English.

Quinlan was the most popular speaker because he put on such a good show, pacing from one end of the veranda to the other as he spoke, throwing his arms about until the sweat poured down his cheeks in streams. Again and again, he attacked the mill owners—it was the strikers' favorite theme—and came back always to the issue of solidarity. "There are no Germans," he would shout, "no Italians, no Jews. Only workers united under the workers' red flag!"

Quinlan's mention of the red flag produced a fit of rage and patriotism in the Paterson mill owners and politicians. They branded Quinlan a foreigner and an anarchist, and they questioned the loyalty of all the strikers. Mayor McBride responded by declaring Flag Day, a day on which the U.S. flag would be flown all over the city but especially in front of the closed mills. Even that ploy backfired, however, for the strike committee had thousands of small U.S. flags made, and the strikers marched through Paterson on the mayor's Flag Day wearing them in their lapels. And so Flag Day served only to fire tempers further on both sides. More and more strikers were thrown in jail. Tresca was arrested for alledgedly inciting strikers to riot, and in retaliation, Paul Hueck, Haledon's Socialist justice of the peace, swore out a warrant for the arrest of the Paterson detectives who had burned the Socialist paper *The Issue* in Passaic. When my grandfather wrote officially to Mayor McBride about a Haledon connection to the new Paterson sewer line, McBride replied that he would be happy to consider annexing the Borough of Haledon so that the sewer line could be properly extended. My grandfather smiled when he read McBride's response and decided that the sewer connection would have to wait until the strike was behind them.

The solutions to many other problems, however, could not be as easily postponed. My grandfather was as busy as ever with things like trying to get the Delaware, Lackawanna, and Western Railway to run a line into the borough and, of course, with keeping the peace. Boys in the town were always getting into trouble, strike or no strike, and parents turned up regularly at the big desk at the back of the store to ask him to intercede. One morning it was Mrs. Bozzo, whose son Joe had got himself into trouble and was being brought into court on charges. My grandfather didn't think much of the boy, but he knew that his mother was a good woman, and so he interceded with the magistrate, Hovenberg, and got the boy off with a suspended sentence. Decades later Joe Bozzo, a friend of my other grandfather, would become a major figure in Republican politics in New Jersey, his political career having been saved by the Socialist mayor of Haledon.

On the last Sunday in March, Bill Haywood was finally arrested in Paterson. He was speaking at a rally at the Lafayette Oval, and when the police broke up the rally, he shouted, "All right, let's go to Haledon," and led a large crowd of strikers up Temple Hill toward Burhans Lane and the Haledon line. The crowd was just a few blocks from Haledon when the Paterson police moved in on them for the second time, arresting many of the strikers for disorderly conduct, Haywood among them. Killingbeck, who had been standing beside Haywood but who had not been recognized, marched on to Haledon with the remaining strikers. There he delivered a fiery speech in which he complimented the mill owners for recognizing that the strike was in fact a revolution, shouting as he drew to a close, "We want to own what we create. We want to own what we create," until the crowd drowned out his chant with their own shouts and applause.

From that day forward, the press on both sides began to draw invidious comparisons between Paterson and Haledon. The local papers condemned Haledon as a lawless place and a refuge for anarchists, while the Socialist press called it the "civilization" of New Jersey and Paterson its "barbarism." The strikers themselves responded by making Saner, the lone Haledon policeman, its hero, calling out at their meetings: "What's wrong with the Haledon Police Department? *He's* all right!" And so to his great surprise, my grandfather found that the very man he had tried to dismiss when he assumed office had become the symbol of the law and order he himself was now so eager to maintain.

But it was not simply the rhetoric or even the new arrests that increased the bitterness in both camps. People were beginning to suffer. When strikers failed to pay their rent, landlords responded by turning off their water supply. Many families were going without food, and sick children lacked the medicine they needed. In Haledon, Joffe, the Jewish pharmacist whose shop was across from my grandfather's store, grew so angry that he offered free medicine to any striker who brought him a note from my grandfather. Many came, and in spite of the fact that Joffe had three children of his own to feed, no one was turned away. In Paterson, small businesses began to fail because they were without customers, and as a result, still more people lost their jobs. Two new motion picture theaters were forced to close their doors, and so even those few workers who still had some money were deprived of a favorite pastime.

Tempers grew shorter, and panic began to grip the community as the month of April began and, with it, the third month of the strike. As the situation grew worse, greater pressure was placed on the Paterson politicians by the businessmen of the city. Eventually the aldermen arranged a special meeting with Mayor McBride to plead with him to find a solution. They were joined by a Catholic priest named Stein, who came from a church in the Riverside section of the city where many of the mills were located. My grandfather, always deeply anticlerical, entertained a special dislike of Stein and was not surprised when he read that the priest had suggested that the Paterson authorities ask the state legislature to intervene. Stein knew, my grandfather understood, that the legislators were pretty much in the pockets of the mill owners and would do as they were told.

The day after Stein and the aldermen met with the Mayor of Paterson, they sent a delegation to the mill owners, urging them to reopen negotiations with the strikers and the IWW, but the owners refused. They still viewed the IWW and Haywood as outright anarchists who would never rest until they had taken over the mills. Why negotiate with such people? Better to keep the mills closed and continue to manufacture in other places, in the hope that starvation would drive the Paterson workers away from the IWW and back to work.

For some of the owners, however, especially for those who had mills in Paterson only, it was a desperate situation. Stories began to circulate that told of scabs being brought in from other places. When these rumors reached the strikers, whose families were without heat or enough food, their anger exploded. There began to be talk of sabotage, and so, to protect themselves, the owners placed searchlights around their buildings and hired private detectives armed with guns to patrol the mills. The lawyer for the IWW, a man named Marelli, convinced the Bureau of Immigration to investigate the scab charge, but it came to little. He also failed, in spite of his plea to the well-known senator Robert LaFollette, to get the federal government to investigate the entire strike.

The presence of the hired gunmen at the mills caused the first serious outbreak of violence. In mid-April a riot broke out at the Weidmann Mill, and the so-called detectives fired their guns into the air in an attempt to disperse a crowd of strikers. None were hurt, but a stray bullet hit an Italian machinist who was sitting on the porch of his house across the street. When the shooting had begun, Modesto Valentino had risen from his chair to pick up his infant son and was struck by a bullet as he carried the child back into the house. Doctors tried to save his life, but he died the following Sunday. His pregnant wife, when she was told of his death, became hysterical, and her hysteria infected the strikers as well. The murder of a fellow worker was more than they could bear. The Italians among the strikers called for blood. Gurley Flynn proposed that the workers' children be taken out of the city for their own protection, and the Paterson police began to oil their riot guns.

7 Desperation Takes Hold

AN EVIL POWER seemed bent upon the destruction of Paterson. Everything went wrong. The very night after the machinist Valentino died, Mayor McBride called an ill-conceived meeting of the strikers in the Paterson Armory. He invited members of the American Federation of Labor and the United Textile Workers, hoping that Golden, their leader, would be able to persuade the strikers to abandon the IWW and join his union, which would then negotiate a settlement of the strike.

The first mistake the organizers of the meeting made was forcing the strikers to wait an hour outside in the cold before opening the armory doors. Next, there were not enough seats, and that made the already tired and cold strikers even angrier. Since there was no way, in such a large gathering, to keep the IWW leadership from getting inside the armory, they were able to challenge Golden and start trouble with relative ease. As soon as they got inside the armory, Koettgen, accompanied by Haywood, Quinlan, and Gurley Flynn, stormed up to the podium and demanded that they be given time to speak. Golden, who was seated beside a woman named Conboy, who always made a point of referring to Gurley Flynn as Mrs. Jones, told Koettgen that the meeting was an AFL meeting and that nobody from the IWW or the Socialist party would be allowed to speak.

That was all Haywood needed to hear. He jumped up on the platform and began to shout at Golden and, as he did, Koettgen himself walked to the podium, got the crowd's attention and told them that he had just been refused the right to speak. The strikers, already in a foul mood, rose to their feet and began to chant "No, no, no" and refused to stop. In desperation the Conboy woman tore down a U.S. flag that hung behind her and wrapped herself in it. She ran to the podium and tried to get the strikers to quiet down, but the more she hollered at them the louder they shouted, until finally they began to sing the "Internationale" just the way they did at the Sunday meetings in Haledon. Conboy gave up.

When it became apparent that Golden and Conboy had lost control of the meeting, Chief Bimson moved in with his men and began to clear the armory. The police charged, swinging their billy clubs and driving the people before them in a stampede. To the sound of screeching police whistles and screaming women, bodies fell against one another and then to the floor, where they were trodden upon in the hysterical retreat. Astonishingly no one was killed, although many were injured. In the balconies, where terrified strikers could see clearly the abuse of their friends and fellow workers, wild jeering broke out and went on until Bimson brought in still more men and sent them up to the seats above to drive his critics away in the same way in which he had assaulted the strikers on the armory floor.

The IWW decided to make the most of the strikers' wrath. They knew that they had a martyr in the Italian machinist who had been shot trying to protect his child, and so they planned to make a spectacle of his funeral. My grandmother, who felt great grief and sympathy for the man's pregnant widow, insisted on being present, and she carried away vivid images of the day.

The funeral mass was said at the Catholic church on River Street, in the Riverside section of Paterson where my grandmother had worked years earlier. She arrived at the church too late to find a seat inside, and so she had to stand across the street in a crowd of strikers, all of whom, she saw as she arrived, were wearing red carnations. She took her place among them in time to see the hearse arrive, watch as they carried the casket into the church, and weep as the dead man's wife climbed the stairs of the church behind it, one step at a time because of the child she was bearing. My grandmother remained outside on the sidewalk all through the Mass. She could just barely hear the slow hymns being sung in Latin, some of the same hymns she had heard as a child in the old country. When the Mass was finished, she watched as they brought the casket to the door of the church. An Irish priest prayed over it in Latin and sprinkled it with holy water, and then the pallbearers carried it very slowly down the stairs and placed it in the hearse. Finally they led the man's wife down the stairs and helped her into an automobile.

Three bands marched in the funeral procession. One took its place in front of the hearse and began to lead the march in a slow step. A second band marched in the middle of the line, and a third stood waiting in front of the church to follow at the end of the long crowd of mourners. My grandmother had intended to wait for the end of the line, but a striker and his daughter recognized her and called out, "That's Mayor Brueckmann's wife. Make her a place." And so some other people moved aside, and my grandmother joined the procession not too far behind the hearse and began to walk down River Street, glad to be moving because her feet had grown numb from standing for so long in one place.

The procession headed down River Street past the very mill in which my grandmother had once worked, past the nearby stables that reeked of urine and manure. The bands kept playing the funeral march over and over again, and when the wind blew, the marchers could hear two or even three bands playing, very slowly, the same music, echoing one another, and the echoes mingled like confused and bitter memories and stirred their sorrow. The procession turned up Bridge Street and marched between houses with people in their windows. There were children on the sidewalks, and some of them shouted at the people in the procession, but no one called back to them, and their unreturned greetings created an enormous silence that confused the children and pained the mourners. At the end of Bridge Street, they turned down Broadway to Main Street and marched between the shops in the center of the city. Shop owners and their employees stood very still along the curbs, looking tired and a little surprised, as though, my grandmother once said to me, they were seeing something they hadn't expected to see and couldn't explain. They looked, she said, the way the people at Luna Park looked when they couldn't figure out a magic trick they had just seen performed. My grandmother knew some of these people, and she knew others too who were not there because their shops had already been closed.

The line marched slowly up Ellison Street to Cross Street where the strike headquarters was located. It stopped there so that the strike leaders, Haywood, Tresca, Quinlan, and Gurley Flynn, none of whom had gone to the church, could join the marchers. Wearing red carnations on their coats, they stepped behind the widow's automobile, and the march started again, moving slowly toward Market Street and turning down it toward the railroad tracks. They made their way along the trolley car tracks down Market Street, passing city hall where all the lights were on but where no one stood at the windows. McBride had probably forbidden anyone to watch, my grandmother guessed as she caught sight of Bimson's men at the front door. The policemen stood very still, swinging their clubs nervously.

Now city hall was behind them, and they were crossing Main Street again. The procession marched all the way to Spruce Street, where it turned past Roger's Locomotive Works, heading toward the Great Falls. My grandmother could hear the water in the raceway on the left and then, as they drew nearer to the falls, the thundering water, swollen with spring rain and recently melted snow, as it dropped into the gorge beside the city. On the bridge above the falls, the roar was so great that the bands could not be heard, but my grandmother could still see the leading band, climbing the hill into Totowa. She turned to see if the other two bands were still with them and was astonished by the long black line of people that was making its way out of the city now toward the cemetery. It was as if everyone who lived in Paterson was leaving it, as if the houses and the mills, the city hall tower and the tower of the post office, would stand beside the river forever empty

They turned left at Union Avenue and made their way to the city line and the cemetery called Holy Sepulchre. Once there, the crowd flowed around the graves, thousands of people, and my grandmother was certain that she would never be able to see the burial. But once again, someone recognized her and said, "This is Mayor Brueckmann's wife. Somebody take her up front." And so, although she was reluctant to go, they led her up to the gravesite where she watched as they lowered the casket into the ground. She said that she had wished then that she had remained far back in the crowd, because there, in front, she had to watch as the dead man's wife cried out and had to see the face of his little boy as he looked down into the grave, puzzled and trying to understand what was happening.

When the casket had been lowered, Tresca came forward and made a speech in a loud voice so that most of the mourners could hear him. "Remember the principles of the Italian workers," he shouted. "You have to take blood for blood. You must have no peace in your hearts, my friends, until you place red carnations on the grave of your fellow worker as a symbol of the death of capitalism." Tresca stepped back then, and my grandmother watched as they led the wife and little boy away. Then the mourners filed by the grave, dropping their carnations on it as they passed. My grandmother watched for a while. Then, feeling cold and tired, she left the cemetery and walked back to Haledon.

8 The IWW on Trial

··

LATE IN APRIL, as the days grew warmer, my grandfather began to take Billy with him on the trolley to Paterson in the mornings to pick up the newspapers. They always sat in the front of the car, so that Billy could watch the sun come up over the city as they rode down the Hamburg Avenue hill. At dawn the rising sun set all the roofs in Paterson ablaze with its light. The city hall clock tower shone golden in its rays, and the windows of the banks and larger shops were bright with its fire. For a moment, the city seemed one great conflagration, a wonder for the boy, an unsettling omen for his father.

On the last Monday of that month, my grandfather and Billy got off the trolley and walked across Market Street to pick up the New York papers, which arrived on an early train from Jersey City. A crowd of several hundred strikers had gathered at the depot that morning, and some of the union leaders were among them. Koettgen, who was standing at the edge of the crowd, caught sight of my grandfather and came over to greet him. When my grandfather asked him why the strikers had come together so early in the morning, Koettgen explained that Bill Haywood was coming in on the early train and that the sheriff of Passaic County had sworn out a warrant for his arrest. Everyone expected that Bimson and his men would arrest Haywood as he got off the train, and so they had come together to show their support and to let Bimson know that they were not going to back down.

My grandfather nodded, and Koettgen asked him if he could talk with him alone for a moment. My grandfather told his son to wait for him at the steps that led to the depot and stepped aside with Koettgen. When they were out of earshot, Koettgen said, "Bill, I thought I had better tell you how things are now, what with you bringing the boy down here with you in the mornings. The owners are out to destroy us now, you see, because they failed with the AFL and the meeting at the armory, and McBride is behind them because of the pressure he's getting from the businessmen in the city. So they've decided to arrest everybody, put them on trial right away, and throw them in jail. Because of the way things went at the armory, they figure that the workers will hold out as long as they have their leaders with them. That's why they plan to lock us all up. Well, I just wanted to let you know, Bill, that they're mad as hell at you too on account of the meetings. The way they see it, if you hadn't permitted the meetings up in Haledon or if they could be stopped now, the strike would fail. What I want to warn you about is that they might just trump up some charge against you and try to arrest you too. I wouldn't want anything to happen while you have the boy with you. You see what I mean?"

My grandfather thanked Koettgen and rejoined his son. The two of them picked up the papers and carried them to the trolley stop. My grandfather didn't wait for Haywood's arrival; he had to open the store. But later that day, he learned that Haywood never reached Paterson that day. The sheriff's office had placed its own detectives on the train in Jersey City, and as soon as it reached Passaic County, they arrested Haywood and brought him to Paterson in an automobile. He was not the only one arrested. They picked up Tresca and Gurley Flynn too and charged them with inciting to assault and personal injury. They took Quinlan into custody and charged him with unlawful assembly and inciting to the destruction and burning of property. Even an owner of a hall in which the strikers had held meetings was arrested for keeping a disorderly house. Koettgen had been right. The police were determined to get everybody, and in all likelihood, my grandfather concluded, they would try to get him too. He would have to continue making trips to Paterson in the mornings in spite of the danger, but now he would leave Billy at home. Beyond that he could do little. Now that Radcliffe, the county sheriff, was involved, even staying in Haledon gave him no protection. They could come after him there too.

The situation in Paterson grew even worse during the first week in May. Many strikers and even owners of the smaller mills were desperate now, and in their desperation the owners began to call for shop-by-shop settlements. The IWW opposed this, of course, and used one of Gurley Flynn's ideas to try to keep it from being implemented. Gurley Flynn repeated her suggestion that the strikers' children be taken from the city for their safety, and Mayor McBride, sensing that this would give the IWW a greater hold over the strikers, suggested that the city itself take custody of them. In the end, the strikers chose to place their children in the hands of the union, and several hundred youngsters were sent to live with families in New York.

The leaders who had been arrested were, as expected, brought to trial quickly. Quinlan was put on trial early in May. The Passaic County prosecutor, a man by the name of Dunn, tried to prove that Quinlan had spoken at the first strike meeting at Turn Hall in February and that he had urged the strikers to commit violence. Dunn put Paterson policemen on the stand, and they all swore that they had heard him doing this, in spite of the fact that it was established that Quinlan had arrived in Paterson on a train that had not reached the city until the meeting had been adjourned. Not only did strikers testify to that, but a private detective and a reporter corroborated their story. Even the police began to contradict themselves, and as a result, the first trial ended in a hung jury. But Dunn refused to give up. He called a second trial the next week, brought in his witnesses, better rehearsed this time, and got a guilty verdict on the jury's sixth ballot.

Years later I found the transcript of Quinlan's trial yellowing on a shelf at the Passaic County Historical Society. It made good reading. Quinlan, who was fond of referring to the Passaic County Court as the "New Jersey Justice," played with Dunn on the stand.

"Where are you from, Mr. Quinlan?" Dunn asked.

"From the United Kingdom of England and Ireland."

"Is that what they call it?"

"That's what the United States of America calls it."

But Dunn never let up. He was determined to convince the jury that Quinlan and his associates were working for Satan himself: "Do you believe in a Supreme Being, Mr. Quinlan?" "Are you an anarchist, Mr. Quinlan?"

Dunn got his verdict, but it only made the situation in Paterson worse, for the strikers loved Quinlan, and hundreds of them had stood vigil outside the courthouse as the trial was conducted. And Quinlan retaliated. Out on bail, he gave a speech at Union Square in New York in which he threatened that if the IWW didn't win the strike, they would wipe Paterson off the map. "We'll make it a howling wilderness," he cried, "an industrial graveyard, so help me we will!"

To my grandfather's chagrin, violence prowled the city now. At the Lafayette Oval, an angry crowd of strikers gathered after learning about the verdict in the Quinlan trial and began to whisper about blowing up the Passaic County Courthouse. Haywood, who was there, tried to calm them down by focusing their attention on the issue of an eight-hour day, but Lessig, who was the final speaker, gave the crowd what it wanted, shouting that it was time to throw Paterson into darkness. The audience cheered wildly, and Bimson threw a guard around the Edison Company. That Thursday an Erie train had been derailed as it approached Paterson, and a second one had been stopped. Some boys were found in the vicinity, but no one could determine for sure who was responsible. Of course, the IWW was blamed.

The greatest crisis arose when the Price Mill in Paterson made its workers an offer of an eight-hour day and a 10 percent raise in pay. No mention was made of the four-loom system in the offer, but many workers with no food but with children to feed were inclined to go back to work at the mill the following Monday when the whistle blew. Bill Haywood saw the threat clearly. "We have to keep them from going back," he said. "We have to. If they go back to one mill after another, what will happen to them down the road? In a year or so, the owners will bring in the four-loom system with the blessing of the AFL, and a lot of these people will be out of work again. And where will the IWW be? I'll tell you where we'll be. If we're beaten here in Paterson, we'll lose everything we gained in Lawrence, and we'll never get it back. It's just what Gompers and his men want. If we get licked here, it's an invitation to them to organize everywhere, and that'll mean the end of the IWW in these parts, I swear it. And not only that, it'll be a big setback for the Socialist party too, if we lose this fight. By the next election, the people will be back at work again, and the Democrats and Republicans will say to them, 'See what the Socialists did for you, telling you to strike? Where did it get you?' And so they'll have the poor devils voting for Wilson and Billy Hughs and McBride in bigger numbers than ever. No, we've got to stay together, and we've got to keep the strikers out of that mill."

That was the problem—keeping the workers out—but how could it be accomplished? The strike leaders were walking a very thin line now. They wanted the strikers to think that something might happen to them if they broke the picket lines, but they had to be careful not to speak of outright violence, for they knew that there were now stenographers at all the large meetings, taking down every word. With this dilemma facing them, they called a meeting for the following Sunday in the fields of Haledon. As it turned out, it was the largest meeting of the strike. Well-known speakers were gathered from far and wide, and 35,000 people attended. Bill Haywood and the other strike leaders looked out over the throng and realized that it was their last chance to frighten the workers into staying on strike.

My grandfather did not speak at the mammoth meeting that Sunday, but more nervous than ever about the possibility of violence, he walked up Norwood Street to the Botto house and listened to the other speakers as they worked the crowd. Frederick Mohl, the first speaker, began by talking about the U.S. flag. "Its colors are very striking," he shouted, "red, white, and blue, with two or three twinkling stars here and there, but it's not good to eat." The audience laughed heartily and went on to cheer when Mohl told them that the United States was in hock to the pawnbrokers Morgan and Rockefeller. Then Upton Sinclair spoke. He said that he hadn't been able to stand it any more, and so he had left his books to come and congratulate the workers on their solidarity. He mentioned his novel *The Jungle* and said that it had done a lot to improve the quality of meat but not much to improve the workers' lives. "And that's what you're doing for workers everywhere," he shouted, adding that the strikers had the Paterson police at their mercy, if only they knew it, and that he hoped that they would stand fast until they won. A man named Boyd spoke next. He started by attacking the AFL, and then went straight to the question of the Price Mill. "Now I have something to say," he cried. "If there are employees of the Price Mill here, I want them to listen. I want to serve notice on those people that tomorrow morning they have to stay out. Let there be no mistake about it. The Industrial Workers of the World will not permit some to go back to work while others remain out. The Industrial Workers of the World has its hands on the throat of Paterson and intends to keep them there. We are going to keep squeezing that throat until we get eight hours and then some more. We want the Price Mill strongly picketed tomorrow. Remember that!"

My grandfather began to move through the crowd. Before long he came upon two councilmen, Rolando and Christener, and when he stopped beside them, Rolando said, "Looks like trouble, Mayor. I don't like the sound of it.'

"Maybe," my grandfather replied, only half listening to Rolando.

"They'll come up to Haledon now, Bimson and his men. Damned

if they don't," Christener said, stroking his mustache, not taking his eyes off the speakers on the porch.

"There's been no trouble here," my grandfather said. "Ask Saner whether there's been any trouble."

"It won't matter whether there's been trouble or not, Mayor," Christener said. "They're fed up in Paterson now, and McBride has to do something about it. And it's these meetings that have kept the strike alive. You know that. Look at the show they put on."

"They'll bring in the sheriff now," Rolando said. "They'll try to make trouble, and if they can't, that won't matter. They'll just say there was trouble. You heard about the police at Quinlan's trial. They say what they're told to say. I'd look sharp if I were you, Mayor. I'd look sharp from now on."

"Maybe you have something there," my grandfather said and, feeling a chill, he left Rolando and Christener and made his way back to the Botto house, to get it between him and the wind that was blowing off the hills.

Quinlan was getting to his feet to speak, and the crowd shouted so loud and so long that he had trouble beginning. When at last they grew silent, he launched into an attack on the Passaic County courts and their justice. He called the Paterson manufacturers assassins of character and branded their mills slaughterhouses where the workers' blood dyed silk for aristocratic women. He called the sheriff a rotten piece of putty, and the crowd shouted itself hoarse until he sat down.

Tresca got to his feet. Like a lean and nervous tiger, he paced from one end of the Botto's porch to the other as he spoke. The crowd loved his performance, clapped their hands and stamped their feet after every sentence, and when he sat down, roared their approval. Tresca was followed by Gurley Flynn. She reminded the people that all the manufacturers in the country were watching the Paterson strike and supporting the mill owners. "If we win this strike," she shouted, "there will be many more strikes as big or even bigger than this one. Don't go back to work for some half-mad manufacturer. These people are restoring the Spanish Inquisition. Whether we believe in God is no affair of the chief of police of Paterson. But I'm afraid, I'm afraid that when God looks down on Paterson through the mist of the tears of its workers what he sees is the liberty that has been wiped out by the Black Hand villain detectives of this city."

Bill Haywood was the final speaker. By the time he stood up, the crowd was getting tired and restless and was shifting from one foot to the other on the marshy ground. Haywood recognized this and made no attempt to work them into a frenzy again. Instead he told them about a plan he had for showing the world what the Paterson strike meant. He told them he wanted to take the strike to New York, wanted hundreds of strikers to put on a pageant in a big theater like the Hippodrome. He saw at once that they liked the idea, and so he outlined the acts of the pageant in which they themselves would perform—the beginning of the strike, Valentino's funeral, the departure of the children, and the strike meetings. The crowd, weary by now with harangues against capitalism, applauded warmly when Haywood finished. He had given them something to look forward to, something they might enjoy being part of after they got through Monday's crisis and the weeks of picketing yet to come.

When the meeting drew to a close, my grandfather hurried down Norwood Street ahead of the crowd. He knew that there would be many people wanting coffee and ice cream and that his wife and Frieda would need help. He got there just in time, for over a thousand customers crowded into the store that afternoon, and when they were gone there was nearly seven hundred dollars in the drawer of the cash register. He had never made that much money in one afternoon.

9   A Question of How You See It

THE NEXT DAY, as everyone expected, violence broke out at the Price Mill. The strikers placed a strong picket line around the mill to frighten away workers who wanted to return to work, and Bimson's men attacked the line in force, injuring many people with their clubs and arresting scores of others. On the same day, Paterson detectives with pistols under their jackets were discovered at a strike meeting at the Turn Hall and thrown out by the strikers. Predictably, McBride and Bimson seized on the incident as a reason to close all the halls again and to forbid meetings of any kind within the city of Paterson.

As the month of May dragged on without a settlement of the strike, the mill owners and the police grew even more determined to crush the strikers and their leaders by whatever means necessary. They were bent on bringing the entire IWW leadership to trial and jailing them for long terms; and, what was more, they set about preventing strike meetings and systematically broke up the picket lines at the larger mills so that some workers were able to go back to work. The IWW countered by holding daily meetings in Haledon and by pushing forward with plans for the mammoth rally and pageant scheduled for early in June in Madison Square Garden. Even as the IWW carried out these strategies, however, threats of violence grew more frequent both in the speeches of the strike leaders and in the taunts of the strikers who pursued the more and more numerous scabs as they left the mills each day.

When the crisis came, my grandfather found himself in the center of the storm, since he alone was able to provide a safe haven for the strikers. This he continued to do but with greater trepidation each day, for it was becoming apparent that more and more violence would break out, fomented either by the IWW itself or by the agents of the mill owners and the Paterson police. In fact, on the day following the trouble at the Price Mill, my grandfather learned from Kapp, the councilman, that two Paterson detectives had been spotted in

Haledon trying to stir up trouble. My grandfather told Kapp to go find them and bring them to the store.

The two detectives, tall, strapping Irishmen, appeared with Kapp not long afterward and strode to the back of the store where my grandfather was seated at his desk. Their hats were pulled over one side of their heads, and small bulges under their jackets showed where their revolvers hung. They stopped at the desk with Kapp and looked down at my grandfather without removing their hats.

This was the first time that my grandfather had come face to face with the Paterson police. Leaning back in his chair, he said, "I understand, gentlemen, that you are Bimson's men. Is that correct?"

"Paterson Police Department," one of them said. He took out his wallet and, opening it, showed my grandfather his badge.

"This is Haledon, gentlemen," my grandfather said after examining the badge. "Can I ask you what business the Paterson Police Department has in Haledon?"

"We heard," the other man said, "that there was trouble here in Haledon. We heard that citizens who wanted to go to work were being interfered with."

My grandfather got up from his chair and stood in front of the detectives. His eyes grew narrow and he said, "Interfered with? What do mean by 'interfered with,' gentlemen?"

"We mean they were threatened with violence."

"Nobody is threatened with violence in this borough," my grandfather said.

"That's not what we heard," one of the detectives said. "We got a different story."

My grandfather stepped closer to the two men and began to twist the ends of his mustache. "You got the wrong story then, gentlemen," he said. "I'm telling you good and plain, and I'm the mayor here."

The two detectives smiled weakly.

"I am the mayor here, gentlemen," my grandfather continued, staring hard at them, "and *I* keep the peace here. When I want Bimson's help or McBride's help, I'll ask for it, but until then I ask you kindly to keep out of this borough."

The smile faded from the detectives' faces. They stared at my grandfather, and the one who had taken his badge out put it back in his pocket.

"And now," my grandfather said, "as mayor, I ask you to walk nicely down to Burhans Lane, cross back into Paterson, and leave keeping the peace in Haledon to me. Mr. Kapp here will show you the way."

The detectives stood silent for a moment and scanned my grandfather's face. Then one said, "I hope for your sake, Mr. Brueckmann, you keep the peace good. It'll go hard on you if you don't."

"Good day, gentlemen," my grandfather said, turning to his desk again. "I thank you for your advice."

Both men turned and strode to the front door with Kapp. My grandfather waited a few minutes and then stepped out onto the avenue to follow them with his eyes as they walked toward the Paterson line.

When it became clear that my grandfather would not stand for any troublemaking by the Paterson police, the Republicans in Paterson began to put pressure on the newly formed Citizens' League in Haledon to get the strike meetings in the borough suspended. Three days after he threw the Paterson detectives out of town, a delegation from the league, whose members were largely Republicans, called on my grandfather and told him that the residents of the borough were sick and tired of the strike meetings, which they considered a public nuisance. But my grandfather refused to be intimidated by them. He told them the constitution guaranteed the right to assemble and that that right was not going to be taken away from anybody in Haledon while he was mayor. His words angered the group, but they had to admit that he was legally right, and so they left, angrily warning him that they would hold him responsible if violence broke out and property was destroyed.

When neither attempt at intimidation worked, Radcliffe, the sheriff of the county, tried to build a case against my grandfather himself. Later that same week, he was summoned by Radcliffe to appear before the grand jury. Accompanied by an IWW lawyer, he made his appearance and answered the questions about the strike meetings that were put to him. A sheriff's deputy read aloud from notes he said he had taken at one of the Haledon meetings and asked my grandfather if he didn't think that the IWW was preaching anarchy and disrespect for the law. My grandfather replied that, as far as he could tell, there hadn't been any disrespect for the law in Haledon, that all of the meetings had been peaceful and that nobody had ever caused any trouble after leaving them. As the interrogation continued, it became clear that Radcliffe did not have any evidence against my grandfather that would support a formal indictment, and so, at the end of the proceeding, he was simply warned that he would be held responsible if authorities were denounced and anarchy preached in Haledon in the future. Then he was released.

Not all my grandfather's troubles in the following weeks were caused by the politicians and police in Paterson. As the suffering of the strikers grew worse, more and more conflicts among them broke out. Even more workers returned to scab at the mills that had been reopened, and incidents of violence occurred frequently at their gates. This turmoil reached even the Brueckmanns' dinner table.

My grandmother recalled well a warm May evening when, after the family had gathered for dinner, my grandfather had begun humming to himself the way he always did when he was angry. She noticed too that he had scowled at Billy when he took his place at the table. This had frightened her because she knew that the boy had misbehaved the week before, and now she was afraid that her husband had found out about it. On her birthday, she had seen Billy climb Grundy's wall over on Zabriskie Street, sneak through his garden, and steal some lilacs from the bush beside the house. Arms filled, he had run back across the avenue and had given the flowers to her as a birthday present. "You said you liked them, Ma," he said, "so I got you some." My grandmother wept for joy as she put the flowers in water, but for the next few days she continued to worry that perhaps Grundy or his wife Phoebe had seen the boy and talked to his father.

My grandfather put his cup down and said, "So, *Junge*, Saner came to see me today."

My grandmother's heart skipped a beat. She looked at Billy and saw that he was staring at his plate and swallowing hard.

"He tells me some of you boys were down on Clinton Street today."

Billy did not look up.

My grandmother breathed a little easier. Grundy's garden was nowhere near Clinton Street. Something else was on her husband's mind.

"So tell your father, *Junge*," my grandfather continued. "What were you doing on Clinton Street?"

"Just playin', Pa."

"What kind of playing? Saner told me you stirred up a cloud of dust in the road in front of him, so he couldn't see where he was going and fell off his bicycle."

"It wasn't me, Pa."

"He told me you were one of them. Don't tell your father a lie, *Junge.*"

"I didn't do it, Pa."

"What were you doing on Clinton Street at six o'clock in the first place? You should be home with your books by then."

"I went to help Pauly's mother, Pa."

"*Unsinn.* What help does Pauly's mother need from boys your age?"

"She does, Pa, because of the Wobblies."

My grandfather stared at the boy and frowned. "And what do you know about the Wobblies?" he asked.

The boy stared at his half-empty plate, blinking his eyes to keep the tears back but saying nothing.

"I asked you," my grandfather said. "What do you know about the Wobblies? Answer your father, *Junge.*"

The boy swallowed hard twice. Then he said, "Pauly's mother works up at the Columbia Mill, and the Wobblies follow her home at night and spit on her and all that."

"A little spit on the ground wouldn't hurt her."

"Not just spit, Pa. They holler at her, and some of the women pull her clothes and hair. That's why Pauly's big brother meets her at the corner, Pa. And today some men went after him." The boy hesitated. "There were knives, Pa."

No one spoke. My grandmother sipped her coffee. From a late afternoon strike meeting up the street, the sound of voices singing the "Marseillaise" drifted toward them through the trees. My grandmother could hear the voices of the strikers beneath their windows as the singing drew near.

"There are no knives in Haledon, *Junge,*" my grandfather said at last.

The boy looked up, his eyes open very wide. "I saw them, Pa, five of them. Long knives. Some Italians had them."

My grandfather's face grew red. He picked up his soup spoon and struck the table with it. "I won't have my children lying in my house," he said. He began to get up from his chair, and my grandmother jumped up and took hold of his raised arm.

"Will," she said, "don't get yourself worked up like this. What good is it?"

My grandfather stood very still beside the table, looking down at his son. Outside, more and more footsteps could be heard and then, all at once, someone shouted, "Three cheers for Mayor Brueckmann," and many voices called out, "Hooray" and "Hooray" and again "Hooray."

"Go wave to the people," my grandmother said.

My grandfather stood very still, his eyes still fixed on his son.

"Go wave, Will," my grandmother said. "The people want to see you."

My grandfather stepped away from the table and strode through the back door to the porch. He went to the railing and waved at the crowd of upturned faces below him. Some were smiling but most looked tired and frightened. He had seen some of them earlier that afternoon, walking backwards up the avenue in front of a neighbor woman who was a scab. They were spitting at her and tempers were running high, but he had seen no knives.

Even after the crowd left, my grandfather remained on the porch, inhaling the cool air and the fragrance of the lilac blossoms in his neighbor's garden. He looked out at the pale green trees on the hills beyond Haledon, humming to himself as the sun sank behind them. Then he came back into the house and sat in the dining room reading the papers. He said nothing more to his son. The boy had fled to his bedroom.

Early in June, my grandmother and some of the other women in Haledon whose husbands were active in the Socialist party traveled to New York to see the strikers' pageant at Madison Square Garden. My grandmother had not followed the course of the strike very closely, but she had read about the suffering of other women during it, both strikers and strikers' wives. She had read, for example, of a young mother who had been thrown in jail in spite of the fact that she had told the police that her baby had been left alone at home, and she had been touched by the courage of a young Jewish girl named Hannah Silverman, who had actually thanked the judge for sentencing her to six days in jail with her fellow strikers.

My grandmother and her friends did not walk to New York, as many of the strikers and their families did, but took the railroad to Jersey City and then the ferry to Chambers Street, where they boarded a trolley bound for Madison Square. They purchased dollar seats, which had a good view but not as good as that of the boxes, which cost twenty dollars each and were filled with wealthy people from New York. As the pageant began, my grandmother noticed that the people in the boxes spent more time talking to one another, while the people in the dollar seats watched the entire performance with close attention.

The first scene of the pageant depicted the beginning of the strike. As the house lights dimmed, the lights in the arena grew brighter, and my grandmother could make out men and women dressed as mill workers moving down the center aisle. In spite of their laughter and singing, they were clearly on their way to work, for before them rose a high red brick wall, the wall of a Paterson mill with tall glass windows through which the looms could be seen. As the workers entered the mill, my grandmother was struck by the lonely desolation of the imaginary street, which had been so suddenly deprived of the sound of their singing voices. In the place of that sound, she heard the clattering of the looms behind the scenery, and she imagined the workers bending over their work as she had bent many years ago in her mill on River Street.

Then suddenly the looms were silent, and the voices of the workers could be heard again. They burst out of the mill's doors, crying, "Strike, strike," and calling to those still in the mill to join them. The street came alive again, and when all the workers had left the mill, the actors turned to the audience and sang the "Internationale." The audience rose to its feet and joined in the singing.

The second scene of the pageant portrayed the strikers on the picket line outside the mill. They sang songs as they walked along the street, and an Italian worker strummed a mandolin. My grandmother was happy to see the street filled again, but her spirits fell when Bimson's men arrived. At first the police mingled with the strikers without causing trouble, but then suddenly they turned on the workers and began to hit them with their clubs. A shot rang out, and a man fell dead. The audience stood again and shouted in anger at the actors who were playing the police. As my grandmother heard the catcalls all around her, she thought it was no wonder that they had had trouble finding workers to play the parts of the policemen.

Next they reenacted the funeral of Modesto Valentino. A long line of men and women all dressed in black paraded behind a band, which, like the bands at the real funeral, played the funeral march over and over again. The band played better than the bands in Paterson had played, and the line of mourners seemed straighter than it had been that day. So my grandmother was reminded of the funeral but didn't feel somehow the same sadness she had felt then. Eight men carried a casket behind the line of mourners, and behind them a woman, playing the man's widow, wailed even louder than the dead man's wife had wailed. She needed the support of two other women whose faces were draped with black lace veils. As the casket was lowered into the grave, the audience grew still. The leaders of the strike delivered speeches over the grave, and then the mourners filed by stiffly and dropped red carnations on it as they had at Holy Sepulchre Cemetery. Now, however, the carnations remained visible, forming a great mound that was illuminated by a spotlight aimed at the stage from above. As the funeral procession moved off into the darkness with the band still playing the funeral march, my grandmother recalled that the real funeral had not been that way. Instead the mourners had wandered off among the headstones, looking a little lost and ashamed that they were leaving the dead man behind with only the other dead beside him.

The scene in the cemetery left the audience hushed and sad, but the gaiety of the next scene— the departure of the strikers' children from Paterson—lightened the spirit of the audience again. Dozens of children ran into the arena, each wearing a red sash, shouting to one another excitedly about the journey they were about to take. Their eagerness to see New York City and to meet their "strike parents" reminded my grandmother of the eager expectation she had seen on the strikers' faces when they arrived for the first Sunday meeting in Haledon months earlier.

The pageant did not portray a Haledon meeting. Its final scene showed a meeting at Turn Hall in Paterson instead. The actors, all dressed as workers now, came down the center aisle of the arena again, pretending this time to be making their way into the hall. They sat in front of a platform with their backs to most of the real audience, so that the audience itself became a part of the dramatic production.

Bill Haywood mounted the platform and spoke to them about the meaning and importance of the Paterson strike. When he finished, everyone rose, thousands of people, actors and spectators, and sang the "Internationale" again, there in the darkness of Madison Square Garden. My grandmother sang with them, and she trembled as the music sent a chill through her body.

One woman who had accompanied my grandmother and whose husband was an ardent Socialist, whispered that nothing had been said about the party and its role in the strike. My grandmother realized that this was true. There had been no mention of the Haledon meetings, and in the final scene at the Turn Hall, only the leaders of the IWW had appeared, the same old faces, many on their way to jail now—Quinlan, Gurley Flynn, Tresca and, of course, Bill Haywood himself. To the strikers they were heroes, vilified as they had been by the police and the courts, and so the audience applauded them vigorously and shouted themselves hoarse when they appeared on the platform. But nobody mentioned the party.

By the time the pageant ended, however, my grandmother had been swept up in the tide of high spirits and optimism that surged around her. She savored the workers' enthusiasm as she shuffled out of the vast hall, jostled by hundreds of laughing workers, catching glimpses of the pageant's wealthy patrons, whose personal show of solidarity had produced on the workers' lips a fleeting proletarian smile. But outside, while she and her friends waited for the trolley that would take them back to Chambers Street, my grandmother met an Italian woman carrying a sick child. The woman's husband was a jailed striker who was no longer able to provide food for his family. My grandmother sat beside the woman on the train back to Paterson and, grieving for her and for the infant on her lap, she left her friends in Paterson. She insisted on seeing the mother and her child back to their rooms on North Fourth Street in the Temple Hill section of the city.

The house the woman lived in had been divided into seven flats of two rooms each, so that it now accommodated seven families. There was no gaslight. Two candles burned in the kitchen, one before a picture of a Madonna holding an infant Christ, another one on the kitchen table, which, along with four old chairs, was the only furniture my grandmother could see. She sat down across from the woman and watched as the golden light from the candles played across her pale thin face, accentuating the dark hollows around her eyes, deepening the lines about her mouth that made her seem, despite her youth, an aged woman. The pageant had raised no hope in those eyes, no smile on those lips. She was resigned to suffering every conceivable pain, perhaps even her own death. Her only hope lay in the tiny body she clutched to her breast, and even it, too sick to cry, might yet betray her. She spoke in a low voice devoid of emotion about the lack of heat, of water to wash with, of food. The union did nothing for them. They had given her the rail fare and a ticket to the pageant, but nothing to eat. She tried to laugh at that joke, but the laughter died in her throat. *"Dura,"* she said softly, rocking the child that could not cry, rocking it out of habit, not need. *"Dura la vita."* "Life is hard."

My grandmother gave the woman the little money she had with her and left the dark kitchen. As she climbed Temple Hill to Haledon, she could not get rid of the smell of wine and garlic, of sweat and vomit that she had inhaled in that sad room. The confidence she had felt at the end of the pageant in the workers' eventual triumph had drained away, and she could think only of that frail young mother rocking her sick child to sleep beneath the picture of the Madonna.

The pageant was not the great success that my grandmother at first imagined. The next day the papers reported that hungry strikers had fought over the food that had been ordered for the performers and that hundreds of people had been given free tickets to fill the hall. Later, when a final accounting was done, people learned that the great sums of money that were supposed to be used to assist the strikers' families had never materialized and that several large donations had disappeared. Many strikers became bitter now, and stories began to circulate about a party that Bill Haywood and his friends had given the night of the pageant, a party at which guests were served caviar and champagne. No one ever learned whether the stories were true. It didn't matter. True or not, they turned the memory of the pageant into a cancer that killed the workers' spirit and, in the end, doomed their cause.

The Strike Ends

·····································

AS JUNE ENDED and the weather grew hot and humid, it became clear that the strike was going to fail. But the IWW still refused to give in, and both the strikers and the mill owners, embittered and stubborn, became more restless in their desperation. Many strikers turned to violence, and the police responded in kind. For my grandfather, it was the cruel realization of his worst fears. He continued to uphold the right of the workers to assemble and speak freely but found himself increasingly unable to keep the peace. Worse still, he knew that the sheriff, Radcliffe, was watching, waiting for an incident that he could use to throw the "stubborn Dutchman" into jail.

As the will of the strikers grew weaker, McBride and Bimson, with Radcliffe's assistance, pressed their attack against the IWW even harder. All Paterson police officers were made deputy sheriffs of the county, an act that gave them the right to act as law officers in any town within the county's borders. As an excuse for this action, Radcliffe pointed to a riot that had occurred in the neighboring town of Prospect Park, where a bomb had exploded in the house of a scab and police had carried on a pitched battle with several thousand strikers. No one had been killed, but many had been seriously injured.

The strikers and their supporters continued to be arrested and sentenced to imprisonment. Alexander Scott, the editor of the *Issue*, was found guilty of advocating violence and was sentenced to seven years in prison. Gurley Flynn, who was now advocating putting children on the picket lines to ward off brutal attacks by the police, was hastily put on trial. Although the jury was unable to reach a verdict, the trial fed tempers on both sides, not only because of her popularity with the workers but also because, in the middle of the trial, the judge called in Quinlan and suddenly sentenced him to seven years in jail. The judge had promised not to pass sentence on Quinlan at that time, but Quinlan's antics and threats so enraged the Paterson authorities that the judge reneged on his assurances. The papers had been full of reports of the speech Quinlan had just given in Boston, where he called for violence and sabotage, shouting, "God help the Paterson looms if the workers go back defeated." On top of that, as

Gurley Flynn's trial got underway, Quinlan staged a mock trial in the courthouse lobby, ridiculing the judge and what he called the "Jersey justice." It was at that point that the judge lost his patience, called Quinlan in, and sentenced him then and there.

Quinlan's threats in Boston were typical of the IWW's tactics in the face of defeat in Paterson. Although Haywood was always careful not to advocate violence openly, violent incidents occurred more and more frequently. An Italian striker from Haledon was shot and killed while looking for work in Astoria, New York. Some people said that he was shot because of a woman he was visiting there, but nobody knew for certain. It was well known that the continued operation of the mills in Astoria was keeping some of the owners from bankruptcy. Incidents of this kind drove the IWW and the Socialists further apart. Signs of a breach between them were already pretty clear. The Socialists felt that their role in the strike had been unfairly ignored in the pageant at Madison Square Garden, and at the very next Haledon meeting, the IWW leaders deliberately insulted the Socialist candidate for governor. The violence further aggravated the mistrust these incidents had bred, and fear that they would be associated with the union's now inevitable failure was also spreading among Socialist candidates for office and their supporters. Party regulars were afraid that when the IWW left Paterson, the workers would turn their anger and frustration against them and vote their few successful candidates out of office.

My grandfather was less concerned about his own political future than he was about the possibility of violence in Haledon, which, if it came, would almost certainly result in his arrest. The situation in the Haledon mills had turned nasty during the week of the killing in Astoria. The very morning after the murder took place, my grandfather received word that there had been a skirmish between the pickets and scabs at the Cedar Cliff Mill, and so that evening he walked down to the mill to see for himself what was happening.

When he arrived, he spotted Saner, who appeared to be very nervous, his revolver in his hand. My grandfather decided at once that the mere sight of the revolver might provoke trouble, and so he took it away from Saner and put it in his own pocket. Then, before the workers came out of the mill, he called the picketers together and spoke to them, explaining that he expected them to obey the law and not permit any violence. He received assurances from their leaders that they would cause no trouble, and so he left, still in possession of the revolver, and returned to the house for supper. After supper that evening, he learned that Saner had complained to some of the Republican councilmen, who then claimed that the mayor had placed everyone in danger by disarming the only police officer in the borough. My grandfather realized, when he heard the story, that fewer and fewer of his neighbors were prepared to stand with him if charges were made against him by Radcliffe and Bimson.

But he continued to stay in constant touch with the foremen at the large mills in Haledon, calling on them daily to assure himself that no violence had occurred. For another week, the mills remained quiet, and each day the arrival and departure of the workers who had returned to their looms passed without incident. But on the Monday after Quinlan's sentencing, John Grossgebauer called him from the Columbia Mill to report that there had been a fight between pickets and scabs when the mill had opened that morning. My grandfather called Saner to the store at once. They agreed that they would have to deputize more marshals, and so my grandfather called some of the local Socialists and asked them to find eight or ten strong and reliable men who could be counted on to keep the peace if further violence occurred. The men were selected quickly, and at about three that afternoon my grandfather swore them in and sent them out to patrol the mills, some to the mills down the avenue near the Paterson line and others to the Columbia Mill where there had been trouble that morning.

At the end of the working day, my grandfather walked up to the Columbia Mill himself to watch the workers as they left for the day. He walked along the high privet hedge in front of the mill to the gate through which the wagons passed as they delivered the uncut silk and carried away the finished ribbons. He remembered, when he reminisced about the day years later, that he kept his distance from the marshals, standing instead on a small patch of grass along the avenue fifty feet or so from the gate. Then the mill whistle blew and in a few minutes the doors opened and the scabs came out, walking close together and looking straight ahead. The pickets began to shout at them, some in English, others in Italian or German, and many made threatening gestures with their hands. Four new marshals, each holding a nightstick, walked beside the scabs. The pickets kept their distance and no fighting broke out.

A regular meeting of the borough council was scheduled for that very night. Two councilmen, Rolando and Turner, were absent, but those who attended admitted that my grandfather had done the right thing in deputizing more marshals. They were troubled, of course, by the manner in which they had been selected. Most, they pointed out, were Socialists and strike sympathizers, nearly as hostile to the scabs as the strikers were. My grandfather admitted that he had chosen the men from his own party but argued that he needed men he knew he could rely on and control, adding that they had in fact showed no bias in dealing with the workers that afternoon. Still, he promised that he would make the rounds of the mills each day and dismiss any marshal whom he saw not upholding the law.

He kept that promise. Mornings and evenings throughout the next week, my grandmother and Frieda took his place in the store while he visited the picket lines. Inevitably shouting and spitting occurred as the scabs came and went, but he never saw any real violence. What was really angering the mill owners was not the threat of violence but the fact that the mere presence of the picket line was keeping other workers from returning to work and so was preventing the resumption of full production. This was hurting them in their pocketbooks, and my grandfather understood that they would not rest until all the picket lines were removed, as they had already been at some of the Paterson mills.

The following Monday, a warm day in mid-July, my grandfather received a phone call from Radcliffe himself. Radcliffe told him that he had been receiving complaints from the mill owners in Haledon, who claimed that there were not enough marshals at the picket lines to protect their property and that those who were present were not properly armed. My grandfather, who understood at once that the owners were trying to provide an excuse for Radcliffe's intervention, informed the sheriff that he was patrolling the mills himself and that he could report firsthand that there had been no problems. Radcliffe replied that he couldn't understand how my grandfather could be everywhere at the same time and that furthermore he had received what he considered reliable reports of property damage in Haledon and of threats of violence by picketers carrying knives. He said that as sheriff he had the responsibility to keep order in the entire county and that, if necessary, he would send his own men to Haledon to keep the peace.

My grandfather knew what this meant. Radcliffe and Bimson were getting ready to send deputized Paterson policemen to Haledon to stir up trouble and force the withdrawal of the picket lines. Afraid of what might happen if they carried out that plan, he quickly called an emergency meeting of the council at which the councilmen agreed that Saner and the marshals had indeed been keeping the peace, although some reported that they too had learned that whenever my grandfather was not present, a few of the marshals had looked the other way and allowed the pickets to menace the workers as they entered the mills in the morning and left for home in the evening. What worried everyone was the obvious fact that tempers were running short and that, whether or not Radcliffe and Bimson interfered, trouble was almost certain to break out before long. They all agreed that, once the Paterson police arrived, trouble would occur but that it would be Radcliffe's and Bimson's trouble then and not theirs. They argued for several hours about what to do, and it was midnight before a compromise was reached. They decided in the end to meet the following day with the Haledon mill owners in an attempt to work out a settlement for the workers in the borough. The strike committee had recently agreed to shop-by-shop settlements, and so the IWW would be likely to acquiesce if the agreement reached in Haledon was a reasonably good one. At the same time, the council also agreed that if their attempt to settle the strike in Haledon failed, they and my grandfather would call Radcliffe and allow him to take charge.

As my grandfather expected, the meeting with the local mill owners produced no results. The owners now realized that the strike was doomed and probably knew as well that Radcliffe was planning to bring Bimson and his men up to Haledon. Since that was the case, they felt no need to deal with the council and with my grandfather, who, more than anyone else, had been responsible for the length of the strike against their mills and for their financial loss. They listened politely and showed the councilmen the door.

My grandfather called Radcliffe as soon as the meeting was over to tell him that he could send his men to Haledon. Radcliffe replied that he would have them there the next day, and when my grandfather asked him whether the men would call on him first, Radcliffe replied that they might call on him out of courtesy but that they were under no obligation to do so, since they would be acting under the sheriff's orders, not the mayor's. My grandfather told him that he understood that and hung up.

The deputies arrived the next morning. A certain Captain Paterson was in charge, assisted by a sergeant named Murner. Trouble broke out almost at once. The deputies began to harass the pickets, and within an hour, a serious fight began at the Cedar Cliff Mill when one of the pickets tried to hit Paterson with a chair. Paterson had five strikers arrested and taken to the recorder's office. Then he set about making his presence felt in Haledon in other ways, running his patrol car through the streets and even driving scabs back and forth to work in it.

My grandfather remained in the store all day and ignored Paterson when he parked his patrol car at the front door. That afternoon, Bill Ritchie, who had run for a council seat when my grandfather had run for mayor, came into the store and said that he had heard a deputy saying that they wanted to get rid of that "damned Socialist Dutchman" by locking him up. My grandfather thanked him for his warning, and then, when Frieda came downstairs to take over in the store, he said good night to Ritchie and went upstairs for his supper.

He was sitting at the supper table across from my grandmother with the children on either side of him when he heard an automobile stop beside the house on Norwood Street. He assumed that it was one of Paterson's squads advertising their presence again and continued with his supper. But then, when he heard footsteps on the back stairs, he got up quickly and signaled to his wife that she should take the children into the parlor. My grandmother understood at once and led the children away.

Two men appeared at the kitchen door. "Mayor Brueckmann?" one of them asked.

"What can I do for you, gentlemen?"

One man peered through the screen door, clenching and unclenching his fists as he did, biting on a large unlit cigar. "We have a warrant for your arrest," he said. "We're taking you down to Paterson. "Don't ask me what it's about," he added, reaching into the pocket of his jacket and extracting a piece of paper.

My grandfather told the two men that he would have to speak with his wife and asked them to wait on the porch. Then he went into the parlor and told my grandmother in German that he was being arrested and taken to Paterson. He could see that she was on the point of tears, and so he motioned toward the children and begged her to remain calm. Then he put on a jacket and, after instructing my grandmother to call Killingbeck to let him know what had happened, he left the family and walked to the back door where the two men were waiting for him.

My grandmother sat in the parlor with the children until my grandfather and the two men who had come for him had reached the street. Then she ran to the window and watched as her husband was pushed into the automobile at the curb. She cried then; she couldn't help it, and the children, sensing that something was wrong, cried too. When they asked where their father was going, she made no reply. She just watched in silence as the car turned the corner and headed down the avenue. Then she called to Frieda and told her to close the store, for she wanted her sister-in-law beside her. The yellow mid-summer sky over the avenue seemed suddenly wider, and she could not, in her fear of it, endure sitting and waiting alone.

As it turned out, the Paterson detectives had arrested not only my grandfather, but Ritchie too and a third Socialist named Wuentsch. All three were taken before Justice of the Peace Keyes in Paterson and charged with unlawful assemblage. Keyes listened to the charges and to the deputies' testimony and decided that there was insufficient evidence to warrant holding the three men. In the end, he refused to accept the complaint and sent them home.

As my grandfather expected, however, his enemies did not abandon their attempts to take revenge. On July 21, they convinced the grand jury to indict him for malfeasance in office. He had no idea himself that the jury had taken such an action; only when a newspaper reporter appeared at the store and began to question him did he became aware of the indictment and of the fact that a number of witnesses had testified against him.

Two days later, he received a formal notice to appear in court for arraignment, and so, on the following Friday morning, he put on his blue suit and boarded the 9:00 trolley for Paterson. When he reached the courthouse, he found a large crowd of strikers outside it. Questioning some of them, he learned that Quinlan had been brought up from Trenton on a writ of habeas corpus. His lawyers, it seemed, were trying to get him out of jail on bail, and when my grandfather reached the courtroom, the judge, whose name was Klenert, was hearing Quinlan's request. So my grandfather slipped into one of the

back rows and listened as Quinlan's lawyers presented their arguments. The room in which he found himself, the largest in the courthouse, had a high ceiling and tall windows through which, in spite of
the dust, the morning sunlight fell on the marble floor and the mahogany benches.

The discussion of Quinlan's plea went on for nearly an hour. When
it concluded, Judge Klenert set Quinlan's bail at five thousand dollars
and, after the bond was produced, Quinlan was set free. A few minutes later my grandfather could hear the crowd outside the courthouse shout as they greeted their hero. Then, after Quinlan's lawyers
had left the courtroom, the assistant prosecutor, whose name was
Force, called my grandfather forward. "Mayor Brueckmann," he
asked, "are you represented by counsel?"

"I am not," my grandfather replied. "I don't think I need a lawyer.
I have done nothing wrong."

Force turned to the judge, and as he did, one of the IWW lawyers
rose and said that he would provide my grandfather with legal counsel if he needed it. The judge thanked him and then asked Force to
read the indictment. Force picked up the papers that lay on the table
before him and began to read. The indictment charged my grandfather with willfully neglecting his duties as the chief executive of the
Borough of Haledon in connection with the maintenance of law and
order during the silk strike. It also charged that he had appointed
deputies and town marshals who were members of the IWW and
who were not qualified to act as officers of the law. Finally, it charged
him with joining the picket lines himself.

When Force finished reading the indictment, the judge leaned forward and asked, "Mayor Brueckmann, how do you plead to these
charges?"

"Not guilty," my grandfather replied.

The judge then asked Force at what figure he wanted the bail set.
Force suggested $25,000, but the IWW lawyer got to his feet and
argued that $25,000 was far too high in view of the fact that my
grandfather was a property owner and an elected official. They argued over this for some time, and Klenert finally set the bail at
$2,000. "Mayor Brueckmann," he said, "can you post a bond?"

"I cannot," my grandfather replied.

"You realize," the judge said, "that you will have to go to jail if you
do not post bail and that you will have to stay there until you're tried."

"If upholding the constitutional rights of citizens is a crime, Your Honor," my grandfather replied, "then I am ready to go to jail."

It was obvious that neither Judge Klenert nor Force wanted to send my grandfather to jail. There were hundreds of strikers outside the courthouse, and Quinlan was still with them. Nevertheless, it was clear that my grandfather had no intention of giving in, and so Klenert called Force to the bench where they conversed for some time in a whisper. Several times Force shook his head and indicated by his gestures that there was nothing he could do. Motioning him away, Klenert turned back to my grandfather. "Mayor Brueckmann," he said, "you own your own home, I understand. You have a piece of property and a business in Haledon."

"That is correct, Your Honor," my grandfather replied.

"Well then," Klenert said, "you can put up your house as bail."

"I will not do that," my grandfather replied. "If you think I have done something wrong, then put me in jail."

The judge was clearly perplexed. He called the IWW lawyer who had offered to help my grandfather to the bench. After they had whispered together for several minutes, the lawyer came over to my grandfather. "Mayor Brueckmann," he said, "The judge would like you to put up bail. He feels that it is dangerous to have to put you in jail today."

"That is his problem," my grandfather replied.

The lawyer stared at my grandfather for a moment, and then returned to the bench. Klenert listened to what he said, and then called a fifteen-minute recess.

Most people in the courtroom left their seats and withdrew to the corridor. My grandfather got up from the bench on which he had been sitting and walked over to one of the room's tall windows. Outside he could see the crowd of strikers at the courthouse steps, and in front of them, he could see Quinlan, standing on the top step and waving his arms about violently as he always did when he was addressing a crowd. My grandfather stood very still at the window, watching Quinlan's performance and thinking about his wife and the children and his half-sister Frieda. What, he wondered, did he owe to them, what to the people standing out there on the steps, what to himself? Suddenly the crowd outside clapped their hands in applause and began to shout. He could hear their faint cries through the windows as they lifted their faces up toward Quinlan. How many times, my grandfather wondered then, had he looked into those faces, how many Sundays had he heard their cries? What had they suffered at the hands of the same men who now wanted him to suffer as well? Sometimes a time comes, he told me many years later, a time that makes you see as if in a magnifying glass the way everything is, not the way it looks every day but the way it really is, and then you know, he added, what you must do.

Judge Klenert returned to the courtroom and called for order. People returned to their seats and Klenert asked, "Mayor Brueckmann, have you reconsidered your decision about bail?"

"No, Your Honor," my grandfather replied, "I have not reconsidered. I refuse to put up bail."

People around my grandfather whispered in agitation to one another, and Klenert, angered by them and impatient with my grandfather, pounded on the bench with his gavel and called for order. For several minutes, the courtroom was silent and the faint cries of the strikers outside drifted in through the windows. Then my grandfather heard the door of the courtroom swing open and the sound of footsteps coming down the aisle beside him. Turning, he caught sight of De Yoe, the borough attorney of Haledon, as he made his way down the aisle to the judge's bench.

Klenert leaned forward when De Yoe reached the bench, and De Yoe whispered something to him. Klenert leaned back in his chair, obviously reflecting on what De Yoe had said. People in the room coughed nervously, and their coughs echoed against the high ceiling, resounding ominously like a child's cry in church. Klenert leaned forward again and asked De Yoe a question, and De Yoe responded by nodding his head in the affirmative. Then Klenert turned to my grandfather again. "Mayor Brueckmann," he said, "Mr. De Yoe here has offered his own house to satisfy your bail, and I have accepted it. That concludes these proceedings," he added. "You are free to go home. I am placing your trial on the court calendar for September 18. You will have to come back then." With that, the judge rose and left the room without giving my grandfather a chance to reply.

My grandfather got up and left the courtroom. Out in the corridor, he faced a group of newspaper reporters who asked him to comment on what had happened. He hesitated for a moment and then said, "Gentlemen, I am not worried about this indictment. It is just another attempt by the Old Party to discredit the Socialists, and it won't work. The deputies we appointed in Haledon preserved order and were of more service to the community, I tell you, than the whole Paterson police force was in this city. There was no violence in Haledon, no violence, I tell you, gentlemen, until the sheriff sent his deputies in. Why then did they bring *me* here? Tell me that. Why wasn't the mayor of Prospect Park indicted for neglect of duty? In Prospect Park, men were shot and clubbed, but in Haledon we didn't have a single fight or arrest. No, the only reason that I am indicted today is that I represent the working class. I was elected on the Socialist ticket, and the mayor of Prospect Park is an Old Party man. I say to you again, if it's a crime to protect the right of free speech and free assembly, then I go to jail."

"Isn't it true, Mayor Brueckmann, " one of the reporters asked, "that you refused to protect the mill owners' property?"

My grandfather smiled and replied, "The mill owners wanted twenty men with nightsticks, not to protect their property but to break the strikers' heads open and force them back to work. And now, gentlemen, you will have to excuse me. I have my own business to run."

My grandfather's indictment received a great deal of coverage in the days that followed, not so much because of the strike, which was all but over by then, but because of the upcoming general election in November. The Republicans and the Democrats were afraid of losing Paterson to the Socialists and were eager to do all they could to discredit my grandfather and his Socialist administration in Haledon. When Wilson Killingbeck came to see him in the store the night after his appearance before Judge Klenert, he pointed out to my grandfather that his trial had been set just six weeks before the election.

"You watch," my grandfather said. "They will never go to trial. They're afraid of what might come out in the open if they do."

"Maybe so, Bill," Killingbeck replied. "Still we have to get our side of the story out. I have a reporter from the *New York Call* coming to interview you tomorrow. They're going to do a front-page article on your case."

"I'll be happy to talk to them."

Killingbeck picked up his hat and started toward the front door of the store. "The strike is just about over, Bill," he said, "and the IWW has been beaten. I don't think they will ever have power in Paterson again. The people don't trust them."

My grandfather opened the door for Killingbeck and stepped out onto the avenue with him. "It's a pretty big setback for the Wobblies and for Haywood," he said.

"But you know, Bill," Killingbeck said, "they really thought that they had the beginning of something here. They really thought they might get something important started, and when I think of those thousands of people up here, the speeches and the singing, I can see what made them believe it."

"It's over now," my grandfather said, "and things will be hard in Paterson for quite some time if you ask me." Further up the avenue, he could see the Haledon car making its way toward them.

"We've got to turn Paterson into another Haledon now," Killingbeck said as he stepped out to the trolley tracks. "We've got to get out the vote.'

"Maybe," my grandfather said, "Maybe." A customer had entered the store and so, waving to Killingbeck, he hurried inside. He sold the customer a pouch of tobacco as Killingbeck climbed aboard the trolley, and then, ringing up the sale on the register, he locked the store and went upstairs to the family.

Family Matters,
Party Matters
································

THE PATERSON STRIKE ended as the summer of 1913 drew to a
close. By September the silk mills were once again in full production.
Some had given the workers small raises in pay; others had reduced
working hours slightly, but many weavers and dyers were still working
fifty-five hours a week for disgracefully low wages. No one made any
further attempt to stop the introduction of the four-loom system, and
this meant that more workers would soon be dismissed, swelling the
ranks of the unemployed, both those who had been blacklisted for
their union activity and those who had worked at mills closed permanently when some of the manufacturers decided to leave Paterson
altogether.

In September my grandfather appeared in court again, only to be
told that his case had been postponed indefinitely. It was the last he
heard of the charges against him. He had been right; the Paterson
politicians had more to fear from a further investigation of the strike
than he did, and they were afraid of what other issues might be raised
if they put him on trial. Months later, the Commission on Industrial
Relations, which held hearings on the unsuccessful strike in Paterson,
published a report on its findings. My grandfather read it with care.
It concluded that during the strike the Paterson police organization,
coupled with the police magistrate's court, had become a tool of op-
pression that acted in the capacity of a despot. It also reported that
the police authority of the state had been turned over to the mill
owners. Private detectives had been brought into Paterson, clothed
with the authority of the police and the sheriff, and employed as the
private army of the mill owners. Finally it declared that all the violence committed had been on the part of the police officials and the
inferior courts, which had trespassed upon every natural right and
constitutional guarantee of the citizens of the city.

Although the report of the commission vindicated my grandfather
and his fellow Socialists, it proved not to be an important factor in

his election to a second term as mayor in 1914. He was reelected not so much because he was a Socialist but because people generally felt that he was honest and worked hard at being mayor. Most of all, they knew that he spent the taxpayers' money as grudgingly as he spent his own. The Republicans attempted, in their campaign against him, to argue that he had increased the borough's expenditures, but my grandfather was quick to respond that the Republican council members were responsible, and the people believed him. Beyond that, they had seen him, in the calmer days after the strike, walking the streets, supervising the laying of sidewalks and sewers, even checking reports that stray dogs had wandered from time to time into the gardens of irate householders. People told a story of the foreman of a gang laying new sidewalks who tried to have my grandfather arrested when he found him helping himself to a cup of cement. My grandfather was, in fact, checking the cement to make sure that it met the borough's specifications. The foreman had never seen a mayor doing that before. Nor had the people, but they liked it, and so they reelected him and added one more Socialist to the council, to which they had already added two Socialists in the 1913 election.

As a result, my grandfather had fewer difficulties with the council during his second term. Now he was able to meet Fordyce, the new Mayor of Paterson, and discuss the trunk sewer connection, knowing that his own council would support him. He also began to accomplish many other projects he had planned when he took office in 1913. Hundreds of shade trees were planted along the streets of the borough, and his plan for bringing a natural spring on the hill above Haledon to the center of town was now being seriously discussed by the councilmen.

For the family, life was quieter after the strike but not without problems. As my grandparents grew closer to their fortieth birthdays, they found themselves arguing more frequently, especially about how they should raise the children. My grandfather pushed his son more and more to study, to work hard, and especially to save money, while my grandmother, who doted upon the boy, spoiled him, gave him money and presents secretly, and even told him that too much reading might make him sick. My grandfather saw what was happening and, in his resentment, began to treat the boy even more sternly. Billy was no longer given any present at Christmas but a five-dollar gold piece, which he was permitted to hold on Christmas Day but which was then put back in his father's safe. Money was to be saved, not spent.

My grandmother, on the other hand, spent long hours in her kitchen with her son, as she did many years later with me, telling stories about the old country and making jokes. One New Year's Eve, the boy ran to his father when he came up from the store. "Ma says she saw a man today who had as many noses as there are days in the year," he shouted. "Is that true, Pa? Is there a man like that?"

"Better ask your mother, *Junge*," my grandfather replied impatiently. "That's what your mother is good at—making jokes."

Billy stared at his father for a moment and then ran back into the kitchen where he buried his head in his mother's apron. His father had made fun of them both, and he felt, as always, a sweet sadness that drew him closer to his mother. "Pa doesn't like jokes," he said, his lips moving against his mother's stomach as he whispered to her.

"We're different," my grandmother replied.

"Tell me about the man with the noses, Ma."

My grandmother explained the joke to him loud enough for her husband to hear, and my grandfather, who had settled into his chair with the papers, muttered *"Unsinn"* to himself when he heard his son's laughter.

With the little girl, Helen, or Kitty, as my grandfather insisted on calling her, he was just the opposite. My grandfather gave in to her every wish. He continued to indulge her by giving her a nickel for candy every Sunday morning and spending what seemed a fortune to my grandmother on a new piano, so that the little girl could take lessons with Mr. Kruse, their tenant in the rooms upstairs.

My grandmother loved her daughter too, but she resented a little the attention her husband gave the child and found herself frequently making comparisons with the way he treated his son. She seemed to lose her temper with the little girl more than with her son and seemed to find more in her to blame, especially when her husband was present. Years later my mother, for Kitty was my mother, of course, told me the story of a hot summer day when she was seven years old. My grandmother sent her down the avenue to Henseger's store for butter. She had run such errands before and so had no difficulty purchasing the butter, but on her way home, she caught sight of the freshly spread tar and oil that the county spread on the road in the summer to keep the dust down. It was black and shiny and glistened wonderfully in the sun. Fascinated, she bent down and touched it and, when it stuck to her fingers, she put the butter down and wiped one hand with the other. But the oily tar was so sticky that she drew threads of it from the road with her hand. Next she began to rub it on her dress and then, when she began to perspire, on her face and hair. Finally, becoming frightened, she picked up the butter she had placed on the curb and ran home.

My grandmother had been suffering all day with indigestion, a complaint the July heat always aggravated. When she heard her daughter screaming as she came up the back stairs, she ran to the porch and found the little girl standing before her, her body and her clothes covered with tar, her hair clotted with it, the butter in her right hand melting and streaked with oily black. She took the ruined butter from her and threw it on the kitchen floor. Then she dragged the child into the bathroom, striking her as she went and shouting, "Look at yourself. Just look at yourself, what you've done."

The child did not understand what she had done but, gathering from her mother's reaction that it was something dreadfully serious, became hysterical herself. My grandmother tore her clothes off, still shouting at her each time she found another smear of tar and oil. Then, when the little girl was naked, my grandmother ran to the kitchen for a bottle of kerosene and, dousing a dish towel with it, returned to the bathroom and scrubbed her daughter from head to foot. The harder she scrubbed, the more difficult it became to get the tar out of the child's hair, and the angrier my grandmother grew. Finally, trembling herself, she threw the towel down and ran away, unintentionally locking her daughter in the dark bathroom. The child became even more hysterical herself then, screaming and beating on the door until her father, who heard the noise from downstairs in the store, dashed upstairs and freed her.

My grandmother was sitting in the chair beside the kitchen window, sobbing to herself, a knotted handkerchief in her right hand. "What is this, Katie?" my grandfather asked, holding the little girl in his arms. "What is this?"

My grandmother did not reply. She waved him away, and my grandfather had to call to Frieda to have her finish washing his daughter. After he had gone back downstairs, my grandmother ran to the bedroom where she threw herself on the bed and lay there for a long time, sobbing softly into the pillow.

Several days later, my grandmother saw her doctor, who told her that the many pressures of her life, and especially her husband's difficulties during the recent strike, had taken a serious toll on her health and her state of mind. She would have to rest, he explained, for if she did not, she would run the risk of suffering a serious nervous collapse. When my grandfather heard the doctor's diagnosis, he decided to send his wife and daughter to the country in the summer. They needed to escape from the hot summer days in Haledon, he told himself. His wife needed a cooler place where she could sleep the whole night through. And so he found a farm near Unionville in Sussex County, which was run by a family named Morris, and he sent his wife and daughter there for a rest.

My grandmother and mother stayed at the Morrises' farm for a month that summer, the first of many months that they would spend there in years to come. My grandmother found herself free of work for the first time in almost thirty years and spent her time walking in the fields with her daughter, occasionally helping Mrs. Morris with the chores—milking cows, feeding chickens, and hanging laundry to dry in the sun. She loved the farm but missed her son, for in spite of her pleading, her husband had kept Billy in Haledon. And so she had to clutch Kitty's hand as she strolled beneath the apple trees, but Billy, with his round blue eyes and his yellow hair and his laughter at her jokes, occupied her mind much of the time. Would he cry, she wondered, alone in Haledon with his father who was bent, more than ever now, on teaching the boy to work hard and who thought more and more of making something of him?

In spite of the election of additional Socialists to the council, the Republicans and especially Turner, who still wanted to be mayor himself, continued to harass my grandfather and to cause him as much trouble as they could. And so, when war broke out in Europe, they turned it to their advantage. Even at the beginning of the hostilities, people harbored much anti-German feeling, and this, along with the U.S. Socialists' condemnation of the war as a capitalist venture, made my grandfather especially vulnerable to charges of being unpatriotic. In fact, my grandfather agreed with the party about the war in Europe and hoped that the United States would stay out of it. His only regret was that some socialists in Germany had declared their support for the kaiser.

The Republicans in Haledon were both anti-German and anti-

Socialist. They wanted to see the kaiser beaten and felt that the U.S. Socialist Party's condemnation of the war was an act of disloyalty. As McBride did during the strike, they began to play upon fear of foreigners, using the U.S. flag as a symbol of loyalty to what they called "the American Way" and of rejection of whatever was foreign. On the Fourth of July, the year after the war in Europe began, Turner had the Citizens' League organize a flag-raising ceremony on the lawn in front of the Goodbodys' house just beyond the end of the trolley line. Staunch Republicans, the Goodbodys were one of the wealthiest families in Haledon. After the event was planned, Turner invited my grandfather and the rest of the councilmen to attend, an invitation that put my grandfather in a difficult position. He knew that they had organized the Citizens' League at the beginning of his first term to remove him from office, and he understood that it was a political organization pure and simple. He knew that Turner was hoping that he would refuse to attend the flag raising so that Turner could point to my grandfather's absence as proof that he was unpatriotic.

My grandfather decided to turn down the invitation, and as he expected, Turner immediately called the newspapers and issued statements about his lack of patriotism. There was even talk of organizing a public meeting to protest his refusal to attend. My grandfather was furious, and when a reporter from a Paterson paper appeared in the store, he gave the man a piece of his mind, pointing out that the Citizens' League was simply a front for the Republican Party and that it had been fighting his administration for years. "If we're going to have a Fourth of July celebration," he said, "let it be a proper one, run by the borough and paid for with public funds, not by some organization like this one. That's all I have to say."

The flag-raising incident passed and was forgotten, but the political skirmishing continued, as feelings about the war grew stronger. Later that summer, the Republicans planned a rally across the avenue from my grandfather's store and invited several guest speakers to attend. They announced that the purpose of the rally was to attack socialism, and then they spread the word that the Socialists in Haledon were planning to break up the meeting and harm the speakers. When he heard this rumor, Kapp, who had served as a councilman during my grandfather's first term, came to the store and suggested to my grandfather that he ought to introduce the speakers himself, to make sure that there would be no trouble.

My grandfather wasn't sure of Kapp's motives, but because he was eager to avoid trouble, he agreed to make the introductions. On the day of the rally, he put on his blue suit and, leaving Frieda in charge of the store, crossed the avenue to the corner of Zabriskie Street where they had erected a speakers' platform and draped it with flags. As he made his way through the crowd that had gathered in front of the platform, he noted that it contained an almost equal number of Socialists and Old Party men and women. At the front of the crowd, he came upon Kapp, who informed him that the two guest speakers, a congressman and a prominent anti-Socialist named Urban, were already on the platform and that it was time to begin. My grandfather climbed onto the platform himself and, with a nod to the others seated here, raised his hand and called for silence.

The crowd grew quiet, and my grandfather began. "Ladies and gentlemen of Haledon," he said, "I hear there has been a story going around that we have no free speech in Haledon, and so I came over here this afternoon to make sure that everybody understands that it's not true. If I remember correctly, ladies and gentlemen, Haledon was about the only place around these parts a few years ago where there was any free speech."

The Socialists in the crowd began to applaud, and Urban and the congressman smiled painfully and stared at the sky. "Now ladies and gentlemen," my grandfather continued, "we have with us this afternoon two gentlemen who want to talk to us, and Mr. Urban here says he wants to show us what's wrong with socialism. If you ask me, Mr. Urban is a hot-air merchant, but he has the right to talk here in Haledon just like anyone else, and I intend to protect that right. So I say, nice and plain, to my friends and supporters, no trouble this afternoon. If you don't like what Mr. Urban says, then you just walk away, and if Mr. Urban insults anybody, just report it to the marshal over there, and don't try to take things into your own hands. I thank you."

My grandfather's display of tolerance threw Urban off balance, for he had intended to begin by portraying the Socialists as a pack of narrow-minded and ill-informed foreigners who were hotheaded and crude. Unable to pursue that line, he tried instead to provoke the crowd in another way. "You know, good people of Haledon," he began, "whenever I talk to a group of citizens like this, I always look around at the faces before I begin. And I did that today and couldn't help noticing a drunken woman standing with some of the Socialists in the crowd. And I asked myself when I saw that poor woman, *Is this what Socialism wants for all of us—drunken women?* So help me, if I saw my mother drunk like that I'd disown her, yes, I would."

There was a lot of muttering among the Socialists in the crowd, and one man called out, "You've disowned her already; you call yourself Urban instead of Urbansky, which was her name."

Urban shot a wrathful glance at the man and then turned back to the Republicans at the front of the crowd. "What can we expect from these Socialists?" he asked the Republicans, forcing a smile. "They don't believe in God. They don't believe in morality. They don't believe in marriage. Did you hear that, ladies? Marriage is old fashioned, don't you know? Now, what do think about that? So what do they believe in? I'll tell you what. They believe in economic determinism. You know what that means? That means nobody's responsible for what he does. A man steals; it's the economic system that's to blame. A man lies; it's the system's fault. A man murders; the same thing all over. So just let him go free. How would you like to live in that kind of society?"

The Socialists at the rear of the crowd could contain themselves no longer. They asked Urban to name a single Socialist in Haledon who was not married, and when he admitted that he couldn't, they began to pick apart his talk of economic determinism and morality with a sophistication that took him by surprise. Then they took the offensive by attacking the capitalist system and calling the industrialists and bankers a pack of despots.

"Despots?" Urban cried at that point. "Despots? I'll show you the biggest despot of them all—this Socialist mayor of yours. Yes, sir. He told the good people here that I wasn't a fit person to associate with. I heard about that. Now that's a despot for you, a man who tells you who you can associate with. I don't know any capitalists who do that. No sir, you've got the biggest despot of them all right here."

With that the Socialists began to shout and holler so loud that Urban could no longer make himself heard, and in spite of the Republican head shaking and tongue clicking up front, he was finally forced to give up. Then he and the congressman, who had uttered not a word, climbed off the platform and, nodding to their supporters in a knowing way, made their way amid boos and taunts to a waiting automobile.

Urban's appearance in Haledon had been a circus, it was true, but more serious attacks on the Socialists were made as well. More and more anti-Socialist editorials appeared in the newspapers, and some of the Catholic clergymen began to preach against the party in an attempt to win the Italians and Irish and Poles away from the Socialist ranks. My grandfather read about a priest named Toohey who was making the rounds of the Holy Name Societies, delivering attacks on Marx and his ideas. He told his audiences that Marx had called for the abolition of religion and that he had lived out of wedlock with several women, one of whom had committed suicide. He reminded them that Debs had called Christ "the tramp of Galilee" and that Berger, another prominent Socialist, had once said that working men had no time to pray. Toohey made no bones about his support of the rich. He told his audiences that the Socialists' plan to take over the mills and the railroads amounted to nothing more than stealing. "What can we expect," he would cry out, "from men who are in favor of divorce?" It was a line saved for the end of his speeches whenever there were women in the audience.

As the war in Europe dragged on and stronger anti-German and anti-socialist feeling aggravated old animosities, my grandfather began to be concerned not only about his political career but also about the family and the business as well. Men like Urban and Toohey grew more vehement, and the newspapers began to report cases of sabotage by German sympathizers. Inevitably my grandfather lost customers, and my grandmother found that there were a few women who no longer greeted her in the stores along the avenue.

Worse still, the children began to suffer. Billy was thirteen years old in 1916 and due to graduate from the grammar school that June. In April, Grundy, the principal, called my grandfather and told him that the boy was weak in arithmetic and might not receive his diploma if his work did not improve. Grundy's dislike of my grandfather had grown over the years, and now he sounded especially pleased to have found another way to cause the Socialist Dutchman pain. My grandfather, on the other hand, made up his mind that his son would graduate with his class. He worked with him every night during April and May and saw that the boy studied hard and made progress. Confident that his son would pass the final examination, my grandfather had my grandmother take Billy to Paterson to buy him a suit for graduation.

But Grundy said that Billy had failed the examination, and when the list of graduates was posted, his name was not among them. The boy came home that afternoon and locked himself in his room. He was afraid to face his father, who had worked so hard with him and who had wanted, the boy understood, to beat Grundy at his own game. Billy felt that he had failed his father and was thoroughly discouraged. To my grandmother's surprise, her husband was gentle with the boy this time. He told her that Billy had done his best and confided in her the suspicion that Grundy had marked the test as strictly as he could to keep the boy from graduating with his friends and to shame the family.

Billy himself had to take special lessons that summer. He went to the house on Zabriskie Street each morning to be tutored by Grundy himself, until, late in August, he passed the examination and was given his diploma. My grandmother remembered watching him from her kitchen window as he ran down Grundy's front steps and across the avenue with the diploma in his hand. My grandfather was waiting for him in front of the store. He shook the boy's hand and gave him a ten-dollar gold piece, admonishing him, as always, to save it but not insisting that it be put in the safe upstairs with the five-dollar gold pieces he had received on Christmases past. The boy grew so quickly that he never wore his graduation suit, and my grandmother never saw it hanging in the closet without thinking of Grundy and enjoying a brief moment of hatred for the man.

To make up for the graduation ceremony her son had missed, my grandmother threw a party for Billy the weekend after he received his diploma from Grundy. She invited the whole family, her sister Christine and her husband, John Lischer, and her brothers August and Joe, both of whom were married as well and had children. My grandmother prepared some of Billy's favorite German dishes and persuaded her husband to buy a dozen jugs of elderberry wine and some schnapps for her brother Joe, who had a prodigious capacity for alcohol and who indulged freely at celebrations of all kinds. Many toasts were made at the party, and the jugs of wine were being emptied quickly. My grandmother watched her brother Joe closely, noting that he didn't drink much at first. But then, after a few hours, she heard him talking loudly to her husband and August, and she told herself that it was a bad sign.

So my grandmother moved her guests into the front room where the piano stood. Before the singing began, they called upon August to read one of his German poems, and he obliged by reading from a long one called "Auf Wiedersehen," one stanza of which went

> *Ich hatte einsteins einen Sohn.*
> *Der kühnste Jäger weit und breit,*
> *Zu seiner Mutter Schmerz und Leid,*
> *Sprach er auch jeder Warnung Hohn.*

> I once had a son,
> The bravest hunter far and wide,
> To his mother a pain and a sorrow,
> He met every warning with scorn.

When August finished his poem, they called upon Christine Lischer to recite one of her English poems. She was the better known of the Ruhren poets. Her poems, thick with nature images and heavy with sentiment, often appeared in the poetry columns of the Paterson papers, which she shared with another Paterson poet, the infamous Mr. Ginsburg. As senior English teacher at Central High School, he drove terror into the hearts of my mother's generation and produced not only hundreds of literate graduates but also a leading U.S. poet. Christine was hopelessly shy, however, and, giggling in embarrassment, refused to recite at the party. She enjoyed seeing her poetry in print but reciting it was beyond her powers. And so the guests drifted apart, the women gathering around the piano for the singing of the old German songs, the men retiring to the dining room for cigars and talk of politics

As the political discussion grew more heated, centering now on the question of whether workers should send their children to high school, Joe Ruhren lost interest. He wandered away from the dining-room table and came into the kitchen where the women were washing dishes. My grandmother watched as he finished another glass of schnapps. She could see that his left eye was twitching, an especially bad sign, and she couldn't help wondering what he was up to, as he wandered among the dirty pots and pans. Then, as his sister Christine turned from the table to the sink, he reached into his pocket and placed something on the table. As she turned back to the table and the dirty dishes, Christine saw what was there, screamed, and dropped her dish cloth. My grandmother came across the room at once and found on top of one of the dirty dishes one of the papier-mâché artifacts that Joe often made to amuse his sisters, this time not a beautifully painted bird or an insect with a grinning face but a small pile of glistening dog dirt, realistically rendered with painstaking care. Christine, who enjoyed hysterics and the illusion of hysterics, continued to scream, punctuating her cries with tentative bursts of laughter. My grandmother, who understood perfectly how this kind of comic scene was to be played in the family, reached down and picked up her brother's artwork, knowing she would elicit even further screams and laughter from her sister. These followed in due course, and by the time Christine had begun to sob with hysterics and dab her eyes with the edge of her apron, my grandfather had come into the kitchen to find out what was going on. He was already annoyed with his brother-in-law because he had interrupted his discussion with August several times, and now, looking down at Joe's handiwork, he frowned and shook his head to express his disapproval. When he looked straight at Joe, however, he was surprised to find that he was neither enjoying the women's laughter nor chastened by his brother-in-law's censure. Instead he just smiled and nodded at my grandfather in a way that made him realize that Joe was mocking him and his talk of politics in a way that he did not want to understand.

My grandfather turned away from Joe and pretended to ignore his mockery, and Joe himself wandered back into the dining room and poured himself yet another glass of schnapps. Then, with the women still in the kitchen and his brother and brother-in-law still talking politics, Joe called little Billy into the front room and poured him a glass of schnapps too. The boy had already been permitted several glasses of elderberry wine, and so it was not surprising that a half hour later my grandmother found him trembling and vomiting in the bathroom. She put him to bed, pale and forlorn, and got him to tell her what had happened. She did not, however, tell her husband about it. She had always indulged the little weaknesses of the men in her family, and besides, there was already ill will between her husband and her brother. The party had been a success, and my grandmother saw no reason to upset everyone. Billy would recover by morning, in time to begin his new job in the store, as his father had decided when the boy told him that he didn't want to go to high school in Paterson. As she drifted off to sleep that night, my grandmother thought about how lovely it would be to have her son downstairs in the store all day. She knew that her husband still dreamed of his attending high school, but she herself was secretly pleased that he had decided against it. Hadn't August said just that afternoon that too much education gave children foolish ideas about what life was all about?

12 The War

······················

IN 1917, as the United States moved to the brink of war and then over it, neighbors put greater pressure on my grandfather to declare his loyalty, just as the Socialists pressed him to support publicly the party's condemnation of the war. In Haledon, some Socialists, Ritchie among them, had left the party, and although my grandfather had been reelected to a third term in 1916, he understood that his party affiliation had been a liability in the election and that it was unlikely that a Socialist, especially a German Socialist, would be elected mayor of Haledon again. But as one of only two Socialist mayors in New Jersey, he continued to be courted by the leaders of the party, especially by Ludwig Lohr, who was working closely with Leon Trotsky in New York in those days and editing the Socialist daily *Volkzeitung.*

My grandmother told me several times the story of their meeting Trotsky and of his reading a poem at a public lecture and dedicating it to her. I never quite knew what to make of the tale, and then one day, as I went through my grandfather's papers, I came across a handwritten note from Lohr, inviting my grandfather to address a meeting in Brooklyn and pleading with him not to disappoint his friends. The note struck me as important, first because it tended to confirm my grandmother's story—Lohr and Trotsky were close associates then, and Trotsky was probably at that meeting—and second because it revealed Lohr's misgivings about where my grandfather stood politically.

I'm reasonably certain that my grandfather accepted that invitation and allowed himself to be introduced as the "Red Mayor," as the party leaders were fond of calling him. I can only wonder whether Trotsky, in what were to be his last days in New York, not only read his poem for my grandmother but spoke as well of the vision he had of the Socialist world to come. I wonder too whether my grandfather saw in Trotsky's eyes a part of his thought that his words did not give away, a part that was waiting for another day in another place and that prompted insignificant gestures like flattering a small-town mayor and dedicating a poem to his wife.

This pressure from the Socialist camp was, however, distant and sporadic; the pressure in Haledon, once the United States entered the war, was close and constant. One afternoon a group of Boy Scouts came into the store to ask for a contribution for a new U.S. flag, and my grandfather heard them whisper, "He won't give; he's a German." As soon as war was formally declared, he began to receive official communications from the adjutant general of the state in Trenton, demanding that he outline what steps were being taken in the borough to assure preparedness and calling for the formation of a home-defense force, a census of boys eligible to serve in the Army and, most ominous of all, the constitution of a secret service committee. My grandfather was in favor of ignoring the letters, but several of the councilmen took these matters very seriously and displayed their seriousness in public as a badge of their patriotism. Even the fire company, of which my grandfather was an exempt member, sent a letter to the Congress of the United States, promising "full, free, and individual support of any action the President and the Congress might take in the present contest." The following week, a tavern on Barbour Street burned to the ground, and my grandfather took advantage of the occasion to remark that the fire company would do better to pay attention to putting out fires and leave the war to the federal government.

The Republicans, and especially my grandfather's old foe Turner, experienced an especially dramatic reawakening of patriotism. Turner threw himself into organizing Liberty-Bond drives and put his daughter to work organizing collections for the Food Administration and the War Camp Recreation Fund. Even his opponents' posturing, however, concerned my grandfather little. It was the talk of disloyalty and sabotage that was spreading across the country that frightened him. In December, just before Christmas, he received a letter from an organization calling itself the American Defense Society, which asked him and the council to sign a petition calling upon congress to punish any citizen who was found to be disloyal. He found these things deeply troubling and was particularly disturbed when he learned that people were spreading rumors in Haledon that he and some of the members of the council were not loyal citizens. The Paterson newspapers picked up the issue at once and began to run editorials about the position of the Socialist Party and about Hilquit's famous war resolution. The *Press Guardian's* coverage caused

such a stir in the borough that at the last council meeting of the
year, Adams, a Republican councilman, put forward a resolution that
affirmed the loyalty of the mayor and the council. Adams got to his
feet at the meeting and read the resolution aloud:

> Whereas the citizens of the Borough of Haledon desire an open state-
> ment as to the sentiments of the Borough officials on the present
> Council Board as regards the present war between these United States
> and Germany, and feeling as we do that the patriotic citizens are justly
> entitled to an answer to their question, be it resolved that the following
> signed members are in full sympathy and accord with the government
> of the United States in the prosecution of this war and do fully sub-
> scribe to the statements of President Wilson in condemnation of the
> unlawful, brutal and murderous acts of the German government in
> causing and carrying on this war, and to any further action that the
> federal government may see fit to take in bringing this war to a success-
> ful end. And be it further resolved that the Borough Council is willing
> and will do all in its power to assist the national government to bring
> about the decisive defeat of Germany and her allies, and that we do
> recognize the governments of Great Britain, France, Italy, Russia, Bel-
> gium, Romania, Serbia and Japan as allies of this country in a war of
> democracy against autocracy.
>
> And be it further resolved that this Council has done and intends to
> do all in its power to assist the government in the raising of any funds
> that may be necessary to further the cause of the present war, and that
> we are in full sympathy with the national government in the raising of
> any further Liberty Loans that may be deemed necessary.
>
> And be it further resolved that this Council is not in sympathy with
> the International Workers of the World nor with any other organization
> that in any shape or form endeavors to interfere with the carrying out
> of the plans of the national government in its efforts to bring this war
> to a successful end.
>
> And be it further resolved that a copy of these resolutions be spread
> full upon the minutes and a copy sent to the Paterson newspapers
> circulating in this borough.

When Adams had finished reading the resolution, my grandfather
asked whether there were any questions. No one spoke. It was obvious that the Old Party men thought they had put him in a tight spot
and that many an old debt would now have to be paid. They remained
silent, waiting to see what he would do, and the Socialist councilmen
waited too, anxious to hear his response before they responded them-

selves. My grandfather hesitated. He probably thought then of the Socialist leaders, of Lohr and Trotsky who had begged him to stand fast with them, and he had to admit that he shared some of their views on the war. Perhaps he thought of that day in the courthouse not long ago, when he had stood firm against intimidation. And now? He must have thought also of the customers whose faces he no longer saw in the store, of the suspicious glances on the streets of the town, and of his son running down Grundy's steps with the diploma in his hand that he had not been permitted to receive with his friends. The IWW was weak now, the Party weakened, the country in the clutches of war fever. He looked up at the councilmen and said, "Well, gentlemen, since you feel this resolution is necessary, I will sign it with you, but I want to let you know that I consider it an insult to me and the members of my party."

No one else spoke. The entire council signed the resolution, which was then placed in the minutes and sent to the newspapers. Then the meeting was adjourned. Walking down Belmont Avenue after the meeting, my grandfather reflected on what had happened. He knew, of course, that his decision to sign the resolution was also a decision not to stand with Lohr and the radicals in the Party who still imagined that they would build a socialist state in the United States. Did he believe that? His six years as mayor had taught him that most of their hopes were, at least for now, empty. In Haledon he had seen the United States in a way that Lohr, living in Brooklyn, had not seen it. He had experienced the power of the capitalists during the strike and the super-patriotism of his neighbors during the war. A revolution might happen in Russia, where the people had so little, but here things were not that bad. Some immigrants had hard lives, it was true, but, as Haywood and the IWW had discovered, there were not enough of them to change the whole system. There might not even be enough of them to win another election.

Seeing these things, my grandfather made his peace, still regretting and even hating the war but keeping his thoughts to himself. Now he gave his time to the business and to the borough, getting a building code passed, planning for the extension of the reservoir, agreeing reluctantly to the sale of bonds to finance its construction. He struggled in vain to keep the cost of running the borough down in the face of the inflation caused by the war. Each month he agonized as the costs rose—a marshal's pay up to thirty cents an hour,

gasoline for the fire truck twenty-five cents a gallon, thirty-two dollars for four tons of coal to heat the firehouse. These costs were
disgraceful and yet another indication of the evils that war could
work.

A few Haledon Socialists continued to support the national party
and the position of people like Hilquit and Lohr. Paul Hueck, who
had been one of the organizers of the party in Haledon, was too
stubborn to accommodate himself to the hysterical patriotism of the
war years and stated openly that if he were to say publicly what he
felt about the war, he would be thrown into jail. As the reports of
sabotage spread and the papers published the names of dead and
wounded U.S. soldiers, statements like Hueck's increased the fury of
his neighbors, who grew more and more determined to crush him
and the other Socialists in their midst. And so, when Hueck protested
the school board's decision to invite the Reverend Watts of St. Mary's
Episcopal Church to address the graduation ceremony on the
grounds that the minister prayed for the war effort, my grandfather
was not surprised that the Republicans petitioned the state commissioner of education to have Hueck removed from the board.

And still the hysteria grew. Now people were intimidated into buying Liberty Bonds they could not afford. There were endless collections of money and food and clothes. Newspapers printed the names
of young men who did not volunteer for the Army, and in Paterson a
serious attempt was made to forbid the teaching of German in the
high school. But my grandfather had made his own peace. He spoke
at the Fourth-of-July flag raising that the borough itself now ran. The
Reverend Watts of St. Mary's was also on the platform and spoke at
some length about his own imminent departure for France, not, my
grandfather noted to himself, to serve in the trenches but to work for
the YMCA in Paris. When my grandfather rose to speak, he avoided
any larger political issues and emphasized instead the sacrifices of the
local boys who had fought in Europe, some of whom had returned
wounded, some of whom had been killed. No one at the ceremony
could find fault with his words, not even the Old Party men, not even
the Socialist holdouts who still opposed the war publicly. Only the
Reverend Watts seemed a little ill at ease. His service in Paris seemed
to lose a little of its luster in the shadow of my grandfather's words
about the wounded and the dead.

Not long after the flag-raising ceremony, my grandfather decided not to run for reelection in the fall. Given the situation, it would be nearly impossible for a Socialist to beat a Republican. My grandfather had been mayor for six years. Perhaps, he told himself, Turner's hour had come.

13   Good Times

BOTH THE WAR and my grandfather's third term as mayor came to an end as 1918 drew to a close, and these two events marked the beginning of a quieter and less public time in the life of the family. This time brought some sorrow and loneliness, but more than anything else, it brought the good times that everyone seemed so eager to enjoy after the war ended.

Billy was now a handsome young man, still a joy to his mother but now a friend sought after by most young people in the borough as well. He had never taken piano lessons as his sister had but had learned to play the piano on his own, just as, my grandmother recalled, her brother Joe had taught himself to play the zither. "It was just in him," my grandmother would say. "You can't teach something like that." And so Billy was the first to be invited whenever a party was thrown. He and the druggist's son, Abe Joffe, would share the piano playing and lead the singing.

Sometimes there were parties at the Brueckmann house too. The young people would crowd into the front room and gather around the upright piano as Billy played and sang. He loved the songs of Irving Berlin, my grandmother told me. Years later, my grandmother would lead my mother to the old piano and make her play one:

> Come on and hear,
> Come on and hear,
> Alexander's Ragtime Band.
> Come on and hear,
> Come on and hear,
> It's the best band in the land.

I can still hear the sound of that old piano, just as my grandmother could later recall her son's voice and the tears that had welled up when she saw how much his friends loved and admired him. He could always make them do whatever he wished and often made them sing along:

> Come on along,
> Come on along,

Let me take you by the hand,
Up to the man,
Up to the man,
Who's the leader of the band.

Years later, my grandmother's eyes still filled with tears when she remembered the way he would throw his head back as he sang, letting it rest on some girl's shoulder and looking up at her in a way that made his mother jealous but happy too.

From what I can tell, my grandfather did not appear at the parties. He would have been downstairs, watching the store. He must have heard the music, must have told himself that the boy was growing up and that it was only natural for him to have friends. But I think the music must have annoyed him. It was not like the music he sang in the old country or, in later years, at the Singing Society in Paterson.

It's just the bestest band what am,
My honey lamb.

To him lyrics like those must have been almost meaningless—cheap and somehow tasteless. He must have been puzzled by what they saw in it.

They can play a bugle call
Like you never heard before,
So naturall,
Makes you want to go to war.

He no doubt recalled that only a few months earlier they had played a bugle call for the boys who had been killed in the war. He had still been mayor then. Now this. The war had just ended, but all they could think about was having good times.

Up to the leader man,
Ragged leader man.

How many times, I wonder, had he muttered "*Unsinn*" to himself as he heard the strange music and bent over the books making up the newspaper bills for the delivery boys to take out with the papers the next morning?

Soon Billy began to walk home with one or another of the local girls after the parties ended. My grandmother told me about one night when, seated at the kitchen window, she saw him standing

across the avenue at the corner of Zabriskie Street with Emma
Brauch. She watched them talking together for some time and then
saw Billy put his arms around Emma and kiss her long and hard. It
took my grandmother's breath away and, when Billy came up the
stairs and into the kitchen, she couldn't help baiting him a little.

"Where was the party tonight?" "

"Birch's, Ma. We had a swell time."

"Quite some girls there?"

"Some girls, Ma."

"You walked Emma Brauch home."

"Just to the corner, Ma."

"I know. I saw you."

Billy's face turned red then. "I kissed Emma good night, Ma."

"So I saw. You better be careful with the girls. You're young yet."

"I just kissed her once."

"The girls these days, they'll take advantage of you if you don't
look sharp." My grandmother turned away, knowing that she had said
more than she had intended.

"I love you best, Ma."

"Get away now," my grandmother said, "and go to bed. You know
you have to help your father with the papers in the morning."

"OK, Ma."

"And you had some beer."

"Just a little."

"I can smell it all the same. Don't let your father find out."

"I won't, Ma."

Almost everybody had good times then. People loved giving parties. Even my grandfather had to attend some of them. A lavish reception was thrown in his honor after he had finished his third term
as mayor, and the Young People's Socialist League, although its mem-
bership had dwindled in recent years, raised enough money to present him with a silver loving cup inscribed to "Comrade William
Brueckmann." The cup, which stood for decades on the mantelpiece
in the front room, now lies in a trunk in my attic, seldom displayed
as a curiosity these days, the title "Comrade" having grown less outrageous politically.

My grandmother and grandfather threw a party for their daughter,
my mother, when she graduated from the school on Kossuth Street.
My grandfather was especially anxious that everyone should know

that his Kitty had graduated as an honor student and was going to attend Central High School in Paterson. They invited many people to the party, and when the house was filled with guests, my grandfather walked to the window several times and looked across at Grundy's house. He hoped that the principal could hear their celebration.

His half-sister Frieda, who had lived with the family for so many years, had grown to be an attractive young woman and was nearly as popular as young Billy. On the nights that she worked at the soda fountain in the store, young men were always present, drinking their ice-cream sodas very slowly—sometimes Lou Meyer, whom she married eventually, and sometimes Andrew Heller who was a reporter for a Paterson paper. Twice a week, my grandfather allowed her to go out with a young man, dancing in the fine weather or skating and bobsledding on Gaede's Hill when snow fell and the pond was frozen over. Once, she later told me, he even permitted her to go to Atlantic City; she was, after all, over twenty.

Money fueled the good times that followed the war, and the abundance of money also meant that people bought more and more. Inflation grew. When my grandmother visited Paterson to shop, the prices appalled her. She often went to Quackenbush's vast department store on the corner of Main and Ellison Streets. There were sales on Fridays, but even the sale prices seemed high to her. She was no less startled by the new styles, by the daring cut of the new clothes for women—the vests with their crocheted yokes and low necklines, the blouses and georgettes with the same revealing lines. She told me that she would have been embarrassed to be seen in the street wearing them.

The machines that appeared then were even more astonishing. One afternoon my grandmother heard people shouting on the avenue and, thinking it was a fire, ran to the window. She saw people standing in the middle of the street looking up into the sky, and when she looked up, she saw a machine, hanging in the clouds, winged like a bird, with a tail of yellow paper or cloth, moaning as if in pain as it pushed its way through the sky. My grandfather told her later that day that soon people would be riding in airplanes just as they did in trains, and my grandmother exclaimed, as she would until her dying day, that she would never do it, that she would be too afraid of falling. Then, when Billy told her that someone had already invented a way of jumping to the ground from an airplane, she was seized by a moment of terror just thinking of it, her body falling through the empty air with nothing for her hands to touch, with no way to stop her unimaginable fall.

At about that time, my grandfather bought an automobile, a Ford Model T. He was selling so many newspapers now that he and Billy had difficulty carrying them up from Paterson on the trolley car. Besides, if one of the paper boys failed to appear in the morning, he had no way to get his papers delivered. The car, which my grandparents always called a "machine," would solve all these problems, and so my grandfather had a salesman bring one up to Haledon one afternoon. My grandfather paid for it in cash right at the curb, and the salesman had him climb in and taught him how to start and drive it. My grandfather liked the idea of owning his own automobile and built a small garage for the machine behind the house.

One Sunday not long after he had purchased the Ford, my grandfather decided to take the family for a ride in it. My grandmother's sister Christine, the poetess, and her husband John walked over from Prospect Park for Sunday dinner, and after they had eaten, my grandfather went down to the garage where Billy was busy polishing the brass headlamps of the new Ford. My grandfather started the engine with a crank and maneuvered the machine out of the garage and onto Norwood Street. Then he turned it around and pointed it toward Belmont Avenue. At the back gate, he stopped for my grandmother and her sister and brother-in-law. Frieda stood on the porch with Kitty who, my grandmother had decided, was too young to ride in a machine. Indeed, when my grandmother heard the noise the Ford made and saw the way it shook, she was not at all sure that she wanted to ride in the thing herself. She hesitated at the curb for a moment and then, seeing her sister boldly perched on the rear seat and afraid of appearing foolish to the others, she climbed in beside Christine and pulled her hat down firmly on her head.

My grandfather drove the Ford to the corner and stopped to see if anything was coming down the avenue. When he had determined that the road was clear, he turned the corner and steered the machine along the trolley tracks, picking up speed as he went. Christine clutched her husband's arm and, predictably, began to laugh uncontrollably, giving the impression that she might surrender to hysteria at any moment and hurl herself into the street. My grandmother was terrified by the speed at which they were traveling and was convinced that the wind in her face would prevent her from breathing. She tried to shout to my grandfather that he should drive more slowly, but the noise the machine made was so deafening and he himself was so intent on mastering the trembling, clattering vehicle that he never heard her. Billy, on the other hand, kept urging his father to make the Ford go even faster, until my grandmother felt it her duty to lean forward and hit him on the shoulder to keep him from getting them all killed.

My grandfather stopped the machine again at Burhans Lane, the Paterson line, to make sure that no wagons were coming. Perhaps some fear of pushing the rash enterprise into another municipality also gave him pause. In any case, he came to a halt just across from the new movie house that a man named Schlink had just built. The man had built the house in Haledon because the Paterson authorities, in an unintended parody of the strike-meeting prohibitions years earlier, had forbidden him to open on Sundays. My grandfather had had no such scruples about movies on Sunday and so, in the final days of his term, had invited Schlink to build in Haledon. He still had the free pass the man had given him, although he had never used it. People were lined up outside Schlink's movie house as my grandfather brought the Ford to a halt. Many waved and shouted, "Hello, Mayor Brueckmann," and the children on the line marveled at the shiny new automobile and noise it made.

When my grandfather reached the next important intersection at North Seventh Street, he decided not to stop but reached out instead and squeezed the horn. To his surprise, no sound emerged from it, and so, as he was hurtling toward the intersection, he squeezed it again. Again no sound, and a third frantic attempt produced no result. The machine rolled across North Seventh Street without incident, but my grandfather, badly shaken, steered it at once to the curb and brought it to a halt. Then he and Billy leapt out and examined the horn, prodding the bulb and sticking their fingers into the trumpet, their brows furrowed, their eyes narrowed in alarm. But despite their best efforts, the horn refused to produce a sound, and so my grandfather announced that they would proceed no further that day. They would have to make their way, once the machine was turned around, back the nine or ten blocks to Norwood Street with great caution.

He and Billy climbed back into the front seat and my grandfather, struggling manfully with the gears and the brakes and tugging at the mammoth steering wheel, turned the Ford around and drove back up the avenue at a walker's pace. Several boys went by them on bicycles and, when they reached the movie house again, all the people in line laughed and waved. This time, my grandmother smiled and waved back, for she was much happier now that they were moving at a reasonable speed, and she was relieved to be going home. In a few minutes, they turned the corner of Norwood Street. Everyone climbed out of the machine, and my grandfather put it carefully back into the garage. My grandmother and her sister climbed up the back stairs and, once safely back in the kitchen, laughed until they wept, as they told Frieda the story of the family's first ride in an automobile. My grandfather ignored the women. He took John Lischer into the dining room where they smoked cigars and discussed the internal combustion engine.

The drive past Schlink's movie house prompted my grandmother to ask her husband whether they might go to see a moving picture themselves, and so, several weeks later, he invited her to go with him, not to Schlink's but to the far more elegant Garden Theater on Market Street in Paterson. There they watched a movie starring Lillian Gish, in which a poor girl whose father is a drunkard is befriended by a lonely Chinese man. The man takes her in and treats her with respect and affection, things she had never known at home. The story enchanted my grandmother. She cried with the rest of the audience when the father, in a drunken fit, struck the girl, and she wept even more bitterly at the end when the kind Chinese man killed himself. She was pleased to learn that a short movie starring Buster Keaton would follow the main feature, and indeed, Keaton's antics restored her good spirits and made her forget the sad young woman in the Lillian Gish movie.

When they left the Garden, my grandmother felt her mind swimming. Feeling just a little dizzy in the bright world outside, she tugged at her husband's sleeve and said, "Can we stop for some ice cream, Will?"

My grandfather, who had just lit a fresh cigar, clenched it between his teeth. He took off the new straw hat he was wearing and wiped the sweatband nervously. He put the hat back on with a sweeping gesture but didn't get it on straight and so had to take it off again, looking a little self-conscious now, and then put it back on more carefully.

My grandmother knew, she told me years later as she recalled her first movie, that my grandfather was worried about spending more money. The tickets to the movie had been fifty cents each.

My grandfather began to search in his pocket as they stood there in front of the movie theater, looking for his wallet, first in his right-hand jacket pocket, then in the left-hand pocket, then in the right-hand one again. He tried his back pockets, first one and then the other. Then he tried his jacket again where, in the breast pocket, he finally found the wallet, which he opened and examined. He then replaced the wallet and removed his hat again. Scratching his head, he said, "Ice cream is pretty dear at Wieda's, Katie. We can have some ice cream back at the store."

My grandmother nodded and kept her head bent as they walked to the trolley stop. She understood that spending money for the moving picture had been hard enough for her husband. Spending money on ice cream, something that he himself sold, would have been an outrageous extravagance. "The Scrooge of Haledon," his cousin Karl had once called him. My grandmother laughed softly to herself whenever she told the story, but clearly she had enjoyed the movie immensely and was grateful to her husband for it. Of course, she had to admit that it would have been nice to have the ice cream sundae too, and in later years, whenever I went shopping with her in Paterson, we always went to Wieda's. I had a banana split. She insisted.

14 Loss
....

IN A NUMBER OF WAYS, sadness came to the Brueckmann family, even in those good times. Suddenly one day my grandfather received word that his brother Paul was dead. Paul had moved from Paterson to Baltimore with his family to take a job there during the war and now, while working in the same factory, had stepped on a rusty nail and contracted lockjaw. He had been taken to Johns Hopkins for treatment, but the infection had spread too quickly, and he died several days later. His brother's death was a source of special grief for my grandfather, for the two of them had come to America together, and the earliest memories of life in Paterson were memories he shared with Paul. Now he was gone, just as some of the boys who had gone to France were gone, their faces fading from his memory despite the fact that many had worked for him as delivery boys. He realized then, he told me years later, that life could end suddenly without warning on the most ordinary of days, and the sad understanding of that truth staggered him, when he learned of his brother's death, more powerfully than the fist of the drunken man in the barroom had on that night years earlier when his daughter had been born.

They brought Paul back to Paterson for cremation, which was the fashion among the Socialists. My grandmother took a grim delight in telling about it—the sight of the casket dropping into the furnace, the muffled roar of the flames, and the sound of an organ somewhere out of sight playing "Nearer, My God, to Thee." There were no Socialist hymns appropriate for funerals, and so religious music was played to keep the less comforting sounds of the cremation from the mourners' ears and to provide some small consolation. For my grandfather, there was no consolation; there was only a gnawing sense of resentment at the intrusion of religion and the pain of irrevocable loss.

Loss came in other ways too. A year later, Frieda married one of her suitors, Lou Meyer, and moved away from the family. They arranged a modest wedding for her with a reception at the house after the ceremony, and my grandfather, as the festivities drew to a close, took Frieda out onto the back porch and gave her a thousand dollars as a wedding gift. She had been with them for many years, first at the hotel and then at the store, and she had worked hard to make him a successful businessman. It pained him to part with that much money, but he felt that it was a debt that had to be repaid.

Frieda's departure meant that my grandmother was alone in the house for most of the day. Kitty now attended high school in Paterson and often did not come home until late in the afternoon. My grandmother sometimes felt lonely those days in her empty house, but she reminded herself how fortunate she was to have her husband and son working close to her, downstairs in the store, where she could see them whenever she wished or call through the vent in the dining room floor if she needed them. But then, without warning, Billy announced that he wanted to enlist in the Navy for three years and go to sea. His heart was set on it, and although my grandfather tried at first to ignore his requests for permission, the boy wouldn't let the subject drop. And so my grandfather had to decide; Billy was only seventeen.

My grandfather thought hard about it for several days. After all, he told himself, the war was over, and so there would be little danger of the boy being injured or killed. And the training in the Navy might be a good thing, might make a man of him, give him some backbone and ambition to make something of himself. He had always felt that his wife had coddled the boy and even now wanted to keep him tied to her apron strings. She gave in to him too often, as my grandfather saw it, took the boy's side, even liked that music he played and sang all the time. Perhaps it would be good for the boy to get away from her, from his friends, especially from the girls who seemed to be chasing after him all the time.

Where would the Navy send him? What kind of friends would he make on a ship? Then again, he might have fewer temptations there. No drinking. No women. He was a good-looking boy, no two ways about it, and he liked the girls. Something of the Ruhrens in him, my grandfather had decided, some of their blood that makes the men like women and drink and good times and music.

> Play a bugle call
> Like you never heard before,
> So naturall
> Makes you want to go to war.

And he wasn't the only boy in Haledon who wanted to go into the Navy. With the times we've got now, my grandfather thought, the town isn't big enough for them; they want to see the world. More experience. More fun. And suppose he went ashore someplace with a bunch of no-good friends. With that Ruhren blood. Plenty of people there at the waterfront, just waiting for sailors—women—and him always wanting a good time with music and dancing and drinking. He had smelled beer on the boy's breath several times lately. And only seventeen.

Well, there were temptations everywhere, even in Haledon, maybe even more in Haledon. Haledon. It would be a good thing for the family in the borough. "Young Brueckmann's gone into the Navy," people would say, "Mayor Brueckmann's son." Good for the family's name, good for business too. My grandfather decided in the end to let the boy enlist.

When my grandmother learned of her husband's decision, she wept and pleaded with him to change his mind, but her tears could not move him. He went with his son to Paterson the very next week, signed the necessary papers, and bought the boy a new suit and a pair of shoes. A week later Billy left. On the day of his departure, the family gathered on the sidewalk in front of the store to wait for the trolley car. My grandmother always recalled the day as one of the darkest in her life. My grandfather held his son's small valise as the boy kissed first his sister and then, when the car appeared, making its way down the avenue, his mother. My grandmother pressed her son tightly against her, resting the side of her head against his head and watching through the soft blond hairs on his neck as the trolley car rolled toward them, growing larger and larger, until she could hear it rumbling over the switch just beyond the store. Then she pressed her lips to his face, tasting her own tears as she did and hearing her husband calling to the boy from the curb.

"I'll miss you, Ma," Billy said, removing one of the big hairpins from her hair. "And I'll keep this for luck," he added. "Goodbye, Ma." He broke away from her as the trolley came to a halt. The screech of its wheels on the tracks found its way to the inner pain my grandmother was suffering and made it even worse. As she turned to watch her son shake hands with his father and then leap onto the car, she felt, she once said, the way she felt when she imagined drowning or being trapped in a grave. But she waved bravely along with her husband and daughter, and Billy, standing at the rear of the car, waved too, as the trolley grew smaller and smaller and finally disappeared from view as it went around the bend in the avenue beyond the Cedar Cliff Mill and their old hotel.

The days were even harder for my grandmother then, and at night she often slept fitfully and dreamed frightening dreams. In the afternoons, she would walk about the empty house, imagining her son's voice: "Hello, Ma. You mustn't feel blue." And she would stand before the photograph of him that stood on the piano and hear him playing the German songs for her or singing

> Come on along,
> Come on along,
> Let me take you by the hand,
> Up to the man,
> Up to the man,
> Who's the leader of the band.

And sometimes she would go into his bedroom and, opening up the dresser drawers, take out his shirts and hold them to her face, trying to catch in them the scent of his body. When it came, something would clutch at her stomach and move up through her chest so that she would lose her breath and grow first very hot and then suddenly cold.

Her nights were the worst. She told me of the dream she often dreamt. In it she was trying to reach California where Billy had been sent. She found herself always in the same vast railway station, like the station in Cologne in the old country, searching for a train, which she could never find. She would become frantic in her search and the sun, streaming through the glass vault of the terminal, would strike the rails and blind her. Then she would wake up, only to find that it was morning and that the sunlight was streaming through the bedroom window and falling on the pillow where she lay.

Sometimes, she recalled, the dreams would come earlier in the night, and she would awake in fright, her heart beating so violently that she would get out of bed and walk around the kitchen table to compose herself. On those nights, however, even the familiar objects in the kitchen seemed strange and terrifying to her, and so, when the pounding in her chest would not be stilled, she would open the back door and, if the weather was warm enough, go out onto the porch.

One night, when her dream had been especially frightening, she
went out onto the porch and stood there, staring at the trees on the
mountain to the west and at the stars above them. She had just received a letter from her son, informing her that he was now on a
destroyer in the Pacific. Might he be keeping watch now? she wondered. He had written about the watches he had to keep alone and
about how, in his loneliness, he would study the sky and the thousands of stars above his head. My grandmother chose a bright star
and imagined that he too was looking up at it. She stared hard at it
and tried to hear his voice and catch his thoughts, but they would
not come. She could hear only the rumble of a freight train on the
Lackawanna line in West Paterson. The train made a noise like the
wind blowing over the sea, and that made her think of Billy again.
That's what he would be hearing now, she told herself—the sea rolling under the ship, driven by the wind, slapping against the bow just
as the waves had struck the ship that had carried her to the United
States years ago. Was he safe? Now? This very moment? How strange
it seemed that a child whom she had carried inside her could be so
far away, so utterly beyond her protection. He might be injured or
even killed without her knowing it. And if such things could happen,
she asked herself, what was all the work and the struggling for? She
thought of the tiny creature they had taken from her once. Silent and
still it had been, nature's mistake.

Her brother Joe had come to see her earlier that week, my grandmother remembered whenever she told the story of that terrifying
night, and she had given him a shot of schnapps because she could
see that he was sad. When she told Joe how worried she was about
Billy, he sipped his schnapps slowly and told her that it was foolish to
worry. It didn't matter what happened, he explained. Life was a joke
after all.

"What a thing to say," my grandmother had protested.

Joe took another sip of schnapps and with one eye twitching in a
spasm of protest against heaven, added, "Life is a joke, Katie. *Ja*, life
is a joke and children are the biggest joke. It's no use worrying."

My grandmother stared out into the darkness, remembering her
brother's words. Was it a joke, she wondered? Could nature be a
joke? Could it be a joke, making children, loving them? The thought
frightened her, and she wanted to go back into the house but found
that something was holding her there on the porch. Was it the sound

of the train or was it something up on the hill moving among the trees? She strained to see it in the darkness and imagined that she could see something very black moving in the woods on the hillside, like an animal but bigger. She kept trying to make out its shape, but whatever it was, it didn't have a shape that remained the same; it changed and moved and sometimes came closer to her and sometimes went away. Its presence held her fast there on the porch, with the rumbling of the train or the memory of the rumbling of the train in her ears and her heart pounding in her chest. Then at last she told herself that she would die there by herself if she didn't move and go back into the house; and so, turning with great effort, she walked slowly through the back door, hearing her brother's final words as she went, "Dying is a joke too, Katie. Dying is the last big joke."

15   A Visit to Morrissee Avenue

THE SPRINGS of my grandfather's loneliness ran even deeper than his wife's. The emptiness of his days was due in part to the absence of those who had been closest to him, but he also felt that he had lost his ties to the past and to the old country. The loss had taken place gradually during the war as the hatred of Germany grew and had been completed after the war by the humiliation of his native land and by the sad picture of the country his people there drew in their letters. As U.S. editorials took pleasure in the "plucking of the German goose" and branded Germany as a "savage and criminal nation," my grandfather read his relatives' letters about the harsh treatment they were suffering at the hands of the occupational forces and of the economic distress that had spread across the land in the wake of the signing of the treaty at Versailles. So he lost the happy vision of his boyhood home and discovered in its place a vague foreboding about the future of that sad land oppressed by poverty and shame.

He lost his political hopes as well. In Haledon the Socialists had been beaten by the Republicans in the last election, and his old opponent, Turner, had at last become mayor. On the national political scene, the party was in even greater disarray. The radicals had broken away to form two new parties, the Communist Party and the Communist Labor Party. Unlike the old leaders like Debs and Hillquit, the radicals now rejected the idea of working within the U.S. political system and instead began to advocate a revolution like the one that had just taken place in Russia. They took their orders from the International and, like Haywood in the old days, called more and more for the violence they thought inevitable.

My grandfather received a letter from his cousin Karl in St. Louis, announcing that he had joined the Communists and urging my grandfather to do the same. But my grandfather stayed out of the quarrel. He remained convinced that the radicals were mistaken about a revolution in the United States. There was too much prosperity now. The Republicans were in control and the rich seemed willing to give the working people enough to keep them satisfied. Working with Gompers and the AFL, they could control the country for a long time. America had just won the war, and profits were high. You can't, he told himself, make a revolution out of good times.

Nor was there much hope for the old-line Socialists. They had lost strength during the war, and the split with the radicals left them too weak to elect candidates even in most local elections. As far as my grandfather could see, the socialist dream for the United States was all but dead. He had said that to Killingbeck even before the war, as the strike in Paterson drew to a close. "We're not going to get any kind of revolution in this country. The people don't want a revolution. The people won't even want our party, if the Republicans give them enough to fill their bellies and some hope for a better life." Convinced now that he had been right, my grandfather stayed clear of politics and tried to fill the new void in his life with his concerns about his family and his business.

After his son left home for the Navy, however, he seemed to drift further and further away from his wife. She thought only of the boy and seemed to blame him for his absence, seemed to blame him, he often thought, for not being Billy, for his strong will and his carefulness about money, for all the ways in which he was the very opposite of the boy. His wife kept more and more to herself now, he noticed, staying up late after he went to bed and leaving him alone with Kitty at dinner by feigning indigestion or bad nerves. Days passed when they spoke to one another almost not at all.

As a result my grandfather spent more and more time in the store, strengthening the business and taking advantage of the prosperity around him to increase his own wealth. He found, as the months passed, that he was becoming if not rich, then very comfortable indeed. Late at night, he would sit at the big rolltop desk at the back of the store, going over the growing receipts and checking the delivery boys' collection books. He ran seven paper routes now, covering the entire borough and parts of Prospect Park and North Haledon. There was scarcely a family anywhere in Haledon that did not receive its daily newspaper from him. He could almost recite their names from memory as they appeared in those books, books that I can still read today, a kind of epic catalogue of the old clans of Haledon.

Something else happened in those days. Another woman came into his life. I learned this from my mother only months before her own death. When she discovered that I was writing this book, she called me into the small bedroom she occupied in my sister's house and told me the tale. "There was a woman he was sweet on," she said, employing my grandmother's delicate phrase. "He used to go over and see her on Morrissee Avenue. He didn't know we knew." What made her tell me, I wondered? She adored him of course, adored him all her life. Was it the indignation of a child angered because the love that was hers had gone elsewhere? The first, best love spoiled? She loved him, I think, until his death, but she felt a resentment that never quite faded, and she wanted the story recorded.

The intruder, whoever she was, probably came to the store one of those nights when he was poring over the books, running his finger along the columns of names—Ormezzano, Pourtfleet, Post, Parkin, Quazzo, Rolando. Rolando had served on the council when my grandfather was mayor and had stood with him during the strike, but now he owed $5.50. People took advantage sometimes. Raffino, Regis, Rosso, Riva, Rolentino. His eyes moved across to the next column. Turner, and beside the name, $12.00. My grandfather smiled. Now that he's mayor he thinks he doesn't have to pay his bills. "If people only knew what was in these books," he often said to me in later years, "the debts, the way their friends behaved. . . ." Terboren, Vola, Van Hassel, Van De Voort, Westerfield. Did a pretty fair job as superintendent of the Department of Public Works but we paid him too much all the same. Welch, White, Wilcome, Zennacher—$2.48.

Then, quite suddenly, she was there beside the desk, a woman whom he knew as a customer but who had never come in that late before. Did she call him "Mayor" then, as some people still did at times? Perhaps, in making conversation, she mentioned how steady a man he was, how well he had taken care of his family, how he had run the borough so well for so long. She probably had a problem of some kind, perhaps a legal problem. People were always coming to him with their problems. She probably asked if he would come over to her house on Morrissee Avenue one day and look at some papers. When he agreed, she no doubt leaned over the desk in a provocative way and touched his arm as she thanked him.

My grandfather would have gone back to the books quickly, dismissing the image of her tanned shoulders and neck. Ceccerelli,

Christi, Christmann, Cerrutti, Clifford. Now the second column—
Franz, Farmer. Farmer owed over thirty dollars. How was he supposed to make a living? he asked himself. Farrassier, Feldlein, Frey.
All those people, and most of them felt about him pretty much as
that woman did. What was it that hot-air merchant Urban had said
about him the day he came to speak in Haledon? "The candy kid: he
sells candy to the children just the way he used to sell booze to their
fathers." Wrong. They respected him. Even if they didn't pay their
bills all the time, the people respected him, mayor or no mayor.

He closed the books, got up, and walked to the front of the store
to lock up. Out on the avenue, one of the jitneys the Hambloch boys
had begun to run back and forth to Paterson passed the store. The
street was deserted at that hour, and the empty stillness made him
feel suddenly alone. His wife and daughter were at the farm. He
climbed the stairs and went to bed alone. Perhaps he thought of the
woman's flattering words about him as he drifted off to sleep.

He must in time have gone to her house on Morrissee Avenue,
gone to sit in one of those dark Haledon front rooms with lace anti-
macassars on the furniture, cute dioramas of alpine scenes hanging
on the walls, the elegant photo album erect on the table, its mother-
of-pearl cover daubed with roses. And she must have produced whatever paper it was she wanted him to look at. When he had answered
her questions, they must have talked about local news. A carnival had
come to town about that time, and a gypsy who traveled with it had
shot a marshal in a fight. When they took the gypsy up the avenue to
the jail, his hysterical wife ran after him, half clothed, protesting his
arrest. Perhaps she talked of that, resting her arm on the back of
the sofa. Did my grandfather catch sight of the small silver beads of
perspiration on the soft hair that covered that arm, so slim but firm,
turned golden by the sun?

So many lonely nights at the rolltop desk at the back of the store.
Romano, Schroeder, Sanfelici, Schlink, Siegel, Sweetman, Tortoise-
shell, Wallerius, Wimmershoff, Zabriskie. Upstairs, back from the
country, Kitty was playing the piano. She was playing a new piece
that he had bought for her, "The Dance of the Paper Dolls." It was
a difficult piece, and she was having trouble with it. He could hear
her having to stop and start again from the beginning. She was a
stubborn child and refused to give in. A strong will, my grandfather
reflected, like me. My blood, that's for sure. He thought about how

she played at being a teacher some nights. She'd make a good teacher, he told himself, everything in order, no nonsense. She'd keep the students in line all right, and no mistake about it. One more book. Ebersbach, Frignoca, Faletto, Giardino, Gallina—$6.72. Hadn't paid in two months. Yes. He had had trouble with Gallina. He worked for the DPW and had gone on strike for more money during the strike in Paterson. He thought going on strike was the fashion then. My grandfather closed the book. Upstairs Kitty had stopped playing and had gone to bed.

Why not a walk over to Morrissee Avenue? Get the books off his mind. She probably had begun to offer him a schnapps by then. "Just a glass to take your mind off things, Bill." "Bill" now in her own house. Perhaps she brought over the stately album with the mother-of-pearl cover with roses on it and began leafing through it, displaying her family. He could see the beads of perspiration on her wrist now and feel her thigh against his. He caught the smell of her hair as she bent over to turn another page. The schnapps made him feel hot and a little light-headed. The faces in the album seemed suddenly to be grinning at him, mocking him. Him, a man of fifty, a successful businessman, ex-mayor of the borough, sitting with a woman whom, he now had to admit it, he desired. And surely she knew. He could tell from the way she spoke, from the way she touched his arm. She knew what he wanted and was enjoying his wanting it. He hated her then, hated the easy control she had over him, her triumph. How could she fail to recognize his own fear and foolishness? Surely she would laugh when he left, confident that he would be back, that the inevitable conclusion would come sooner or later. He rose suddenly and made an excuse to go. Did he say, perhaps, that he had promised to listen to his daughter play a new piece on the piano? In any case, he left hurriedly and made his way back to Norwood Street.

Letters came from Billy more frequently now. The boy was back in San Diego, and he wrote again and again saying that he needed money. My grandfather was suspicious. Good times, he thought to himself, that's what it's for—good times. He pictured his son in a speakeasy somewhere, playing the piano, not the kind of songs his daughter played to please him but Billy's kind of music, ragtime. He'd be popular there, just back from the sea, strong and brown from the sun. My grandfather could picture him with his head thrown back, singing

If you want to hear the Suwannee River
Played in ragtime,
Come on and hear,
Come on and hear
Alexander's Ragtime Band.

And there were sure to be women. He pictured them too, dressed the way they dressed now in short skirts. "Flappers," they called them. They'd be looking for a boy like him, handsome, strong, lots of fun, like Katie's people.

Thoughts of his son hung over him all day in the store and wouldn't go away. It made him irritable. He nearly lost his temper one morning. Hobart came into the store, complaining to him, as if he were still mayor, about a jitney driver who had taken his passengers for a tour of Hobart's three-hundred-acre park up on the hill across from where Katie's people used to live. Hobart said he was thinking of getting out of Haledon the way the Goodbodys had. He made my grandfather furious. A rich man—son of the man who had been McKinley's vice-president and who might have been president if he'd lived—with his three hundred acres and forty-room house, his tennis court and polo field. The worst of the capitalists, and he won't even let a few neighbors look at his castle on the hill! My grandfather held his tongue, but the lingering anger Hobart had provoked persisted through the day and dogged him that evening as he did the accounts. Boyle, Bradley, Barbero, Butz, Bunzli. These were the worst summer days, late August. The yellow sky hung low over Haledon's valley and was filled with incessant, inescapable noise. Over on Zabriskie Street, Otto Martin was rebuilding the little house next to Grundy's house, and the hammering went on from daybreak to sunset. My grandfather went to the back door of the store to escape it. In the garden, a few dozen starlings were chattering raucously. One more book perhaps. Koiman, Knapsack, Lopez, Meyer, Mensa, Martin, Manger. He put the book down. He was tired. He needed to take a walk.

He locked up the store and walked up Norwood Street. There seemed to be thousands of birds in the trees calling to him, and Cohen, the junk man, rolled by on his wagon, slouched behind his dirty white horse. "Sleeping Jesus," the boys called him, sometimes throwing stones. How many years had he been dragging junk out of cellars and barns? The cow bells strung over the wagon grew fainter as Cohen drove down the street. Had there ever been a time, my grandfather asked himself, when he had not heard them going by, over and over again. Their sound and the sound of the birds made him feel desperate, and he wanted to cry out. *I'm here,* he said to himself. His hand was on the gate.

This was the fated night. Perhaps he had two glasses of schnapps, perhaps three. Its perfume mingled with the scent she was wearing. Did she say something about life being short, about having to have some fun now and then? The sun fell through the front-room window upon those firm arms, touched golden by its rays, the slim legs pressing his knee. And he knew that he would not have to decide anything. She had removed from him the burden of decision. No awkward questions, just the touch of her arms and the warmth of her breath on his neck. He would not be required to play the fool. He must have felt joy at first, filling his veins and his lungs, but he must also have felt, when he gathered himself to himself again, a desperation greater than any he had felt before. He must have felt as if he were falling into a black river, swept along among nameless objects and terrifying waves. Nothing would have a name there. There was no order in that swirl of formless things, none of which had a place. He must have felt himself a drowning man, surrounded by presences he could not describe but that, he must have felt, being William Brueckmann after all, were bent on his destruction. "You only live once, Bill," she probably said, sensing his distress. "You deserve a good time now and then."

Who was she? I don't know. I remember once, at a party for my cousin, Billy's son, who had just come home from the Army, a large blond woman sat upon my grandfather's lap and kissed him on both cheeks, laughing wildly. My grandfather reddened with embarrassment. The children were aghast, the adults uncomprehending, all but a few perhaps. Was she the one, and what was her name? I don't know. My mother took that, along with the fingering of "The Dance of the Paper Dolls," with her to her grave. Some elder members of the old clans of Haledon may know it. Not many though. They are a dying breed.

16   Bad Times

....

IN THE AUTUMN OF 1923, after three years in the Navy, Billy came home. My grandmother threw a party the night he returned, and most of the family and many of his friends came to welcome him. After dinner they gathered in the front parlor around the piano. My grandfather insisted that his daughter play some new songs she had learned, but most of the time Billy played, first the German songs that made his mother and aunt cry and then his own favorites. "Play 'Alexander's Ragtime Band,' Bill," one of the local girls cried.

"Beer first," he shouted back.

My grandmother knew that Billy had already drunk several bottles of beer, and so she looked at her husband out of the corner of her eye when Billy called for more. He seemed not to have heard or was perhaps pretending not to have heard, and so Katie went to the kitchen for another bottle. When she brought it to her son, he tossed his head back and drank half of it without stopping. Then he began to play and sing

> Come on and hear,
> Come on and hear
> Alexander's Ragtime Band.
> Come on and hear,
> Come on and hear,
> It's the best band in the land.
> They can play a bugle call
> Like you never heard before,
> So naturall
> Makes you want to go to war.
> It's just the bestest band what am,
> My honey lamb.

He leaned his head against one of the girls he had written to while he was away and she ran her fingers through his hair.

> Come on and hear,
> Come on and hear,
> Let me take you by the hand

Up to the man,
Up to the man
Who's the leader of the band,
And if you want to hear the Suwannee River
Played in ragtime,
Come on and hear,
Come on and hear
Alexander's Ragtime Band.

My grandfather stepped out of the parlor and walked through the kitchen to the back porch. It was a clear October night, and he stood at the porch railing for some time, filling his lungs with the cool air and enjoying the sweet smell of the newly cut grass that drifted up to him from the garden below. He hummed to himself the way he often did and thought about how much his brother-in-law Joe had drunk that night. And the boy. His first night home, of course. But he had nearly fallen off the piano stool once. A feeling of foreboding settled over him and he decided to take a walk.

After my grandfather left the party, the singing and drinking continued, and Billy drank so much beer, my mother recalled, that she and my grandmother had to help him to bed. My grandmother was relieved that her husband had left. The boy deserved a good time his first night back, after all, and as long as his father didn't know how much beer he had drunk why should she make anything of it?

But the good times continued. One night about a month after Billy's homecoming, my grandmother woke up to the sound of shouting beside the house on Norwood Street. She got out of bed, threw on a robe, and walked to the kitchen window. Through the leaves of the catalpa tree outside she could see figures moving about in the street. She thought at first that they were children because of the strange way they were running, but then she heard their voices and realized that they were young men. Shifting her position to see better through the leaves, she strained to make out their faces. They were still moving in that same strange way, lurching in one direction, then turning suddenly, bobbing like puppets on a string. She saw one dash across the street suddenly and throw his arms around a tree, and she knew then it was a bunch of drunks she was watching. They probably had been having a good time in a saloon that served bootleg liquor, and now they couldn't find their way home. She was about to return to bed when a drunk right under the window looked up, and she saw that it was her son. She was startled, for she had imagined that he had gone to bed hours earlier. She watched as he stumbled against the curb, and then she opened the window a little to listen.

Another drunk called, "Hey, sailor boy, goin' home to Mama?"

They laughed.

Another called, "Hey, Brueckmann," mispronouncing the name, making it sound like "Brockmann." "Hey, Brockmann, go get some candy for the girls, Brockmann. How about an ice-cream cone, Brockmann?"

Billy was trying to get through the back gate now as the others kept stumbling around in the street and calling out to him, "Brockmann, Brockmann, get us some candy please, Brockmann."

After fumbling with the latch for several minutes, Billy came through the back gate and began to climb the stairs. My grandmother moved from the window to the back door. She opened it and listened to her son's unsteady steps on the stairs. "Go to hell," he shouted to the drunks in the street as he reached the turn in the stairs. Then pulling himself up, he climbed the last five steps. At the top, he leaned against the side of the house and ran his hand along the side of the door until he found the handle. Then he pulled the door open and saw his mother. "Ma?" he said, a puzzled look on his face. "I'm sick, Ma. Let me come in."

My grandmother pushed the screen door open and helped her son step inside. She guided him past Kitty's room, which was just off the kitchen, and into the dining room where he fell against the telephone table. My grandmother was terrified. Had her husband heard? Would he get out of bed? She led her son, more quickly now, into the front hallway, where he stopped suddenly and said, "I'm really sick, Ma," and then, leaning against the railing of the front staircase, he vomited on the floor.

My grandmother led him into his room, took off the soiled clothes, and put him into bed. As she pulled the blankets up, he took her hand. "Oh, Ma," he said slowly and then again, "Oh, Ma," and then, turning his face away, he fell asleep.

Before she went to bed, my grandmother scrubbed the hallway. Then, after emptying the bucket and washing her hands, she went out onto the back porch where she stood for some time, staring out at the moon and the silver leaves of the trees as they swayed gently in the breeze that was blowing down from the hills to the west. She filled her lungs with the cool moist air, but no matter how much she inhaled, she could still smell the sweet whiskey and the sour vomit, and she had to swallow hard to keep herself from being sick.

Before long my grandfather learned how his son was spending his nights. Laurence Garbaccio, who ran a taxicab in Haledon and had taken a job as helper in the store after Frieda had left, told me about some of the worst mornings. My grandfather usually got up at about six-thirty, relying as he did upon his son to rise even earlier and to let the paper boys in downstairs so that they could fold their papers. One morning when he got out of bed, he heard the boys shouting outside. Going to the window, he saw that they were not loading the papers onto their bicycles, as he had expected, but were just roughnecking as they often did when they were waiting for the store to open. My grandfather turned from the window and walked to his son's bedroom to wake him up, but the bedroom was empty. The bed had not been slept in.

My grandfather dressed, went downstairs, and opened the store himself. Then when the boys had loaded their papers and left, he called up to his wife and asked her to bring him a cup of strong coffee and a Swiss roll. My grandmother brought these to him, and he sat down at his desk, waiting for Billy to appear. Customers came and went, a few salesmen appeared, and Laurence, the helper, arrived at about nine-thirty. My grandfather was still at the desk at ten when Billy came through the front door. He had a broad smile on his face, but he obviously hadn't shaved, and his clothes were dirty.

My grandfather got up slowly and walked toward his son. "Pretty late for work," he said. "I didn't see you here at five-thirty."

"I know, Pa," the boy said.

"You know? What do you know? I had to get up and take charge of the boys. Your mother's worried until she's near crazy. Do you know that?"

"I'm sorry, Pa."

"What good is being sorry? I'm paying you good money—to work, not to spend your nights singing and drinking and your days hung over, looking like a rummy."

"I said I was sorry, Pa."

"You're turning into a no-good. No use talking. I can see it. You shame your family, your mother and your sister. The whole borough knows how you behave. And us, a respected family, a prominent family. Wasn't I mayor six years?" My grandfather stopped and stared into his son's haggard face. "And what's in it for you, *Junge*? What do you get from it? That's what I'd like to know."

Billy leaned against the long table they used for slipping papers. "Pa," he said, "I had more fun last night than you've had in your whole life."

My grandfather stared at the boy but said nothing. Then he turned to Laurence. "What am I going to do with a son like that?" he asked. "What can I do?"

"He's only young, Bill," Laurence replied. "He's just come home. Don't be too hard on him."

Humming to himself, my grandfather left Billy and Laurence and went upstairs to let his wife know the boy had come in. He reported the conversation they had had downstairs, but my grandmother made no comment, and her silence made him even angrier. Now she has nothing to say, he reflected as he drank a second cup of coffee, but a lot of it is her doing and no mistake about it. He has her blood to begin with and then she coddled him all those years and now the boy's turning into a rummy like the rest of them. My grandfather worked only a short time in the store that afternoon. At about four he walked over to Morrissee Avenue.

In 1924 my grandfather ran for mayor again. Many of his neighbors had lost their patience with the free-spending ways of the Republicans, and they saw my grandfather's success in business as a sign that he was a shrewd manager who watched money carefully. For his own part, as the family's life together grew more painful, he found himself searching for excuses to get away from the house. And so, when the Citizens' League, which had been formed ten years earlier to get him out of office, asked him to run again, he gladly accepted, enjoying the irony of their request. But it was as a Progressive that he ran this time, for socialism in Haledon was all but dead.

On New Year's Day 1925, having won the election, he delivered his seventh annual address as mayor, taking care, because of his reputation for stubbornness, to strike a note of openness and cooperation. He asked the council to cast aside political differences, and then, stressing the fact that he did not want to sound dictatorial, he gave them a list of things the borough needed—new water pipes, new curbs, more shade trees. They needed as well to unify the jitney and trolley schedules and bring the number of building permits under control. At the end of the speech, he touched upon the things that he knew were troubling the residents of the borough more than any-thing else—increased noise and lawlessness in the town, young peo-ple driving too fast, loud speakeasies and saloons. He noticed, as he spoke of these things, that the councilmen stared awkwardly at the table. He guessed what they were thinking and winced. "I would beg you, gentlemen of the borough council, again," he continued, "to abolish all party lines and to work together for the betterment and welfare of the borough, and for my part—*What were they thinking?*, he must have wondered as he spoke. *Why did they all stare at the table that way? 'His son's one of the worst rummies in town.' Was that it?*—and for my part—*Or is there something else they know?*—and for my part, you have my sincere assurances at this time that I will do my utmost to accomplish these aims—*You never know.*—to accomplish these aims, so that at the end of our terms, we may look back over our work with perfect satisfaction and in the knowledge that we have done our duties—*Was there a trace of a smile on several faces?*—we have done our duties as good and faithful citizens of the Borough of Haledon."

Billy's good times affected my grandmother in a different way. For her there were no council meetings in the evenings; she had to re-main at home. Sometimes Billy stayed with her, tinkering with his crystal set, but generally he disappeared as soon as he had finished dinner, leaving his mother to a lonely night of worrying about when he would come home. As the weeks passed, she became increasingly nervous. She lost weight, grew short-tempered, slept only fitfully, and lost her appetite. By the spring of the following year, she seemed so ill that my grandfather decided to let her take Kitty on a trip to the old country. The business was doing well, and he could easily afford the fares on one of the new liners that he saw advertised in all the New York papers. It would be good for her to get away from Haledon and from the boy, he told himself. How many nights, after all, had her low moaning awakened him, thinking it the wind at first, until he heard her footsteps on the porch and the uncontrollable sobs that shook her thin body? Perhaps visiting new places and seeing old friends would bring back her strength and a little of her former joy. And he would be alone.

And so, that summer my grandmother and mother sailed for Europe on the SS *Resolute* with a close friend of my grandmother, a woman named Mrs. Risser. The ocean voyage itself did little to restore my grandmother's spirits, for it stirred in her other sea memories that had troubled her nights and cast a shadow of remembered sorrow across her days. And she remembered her voyage to the United States as well, the rolling cabin in steerage with its foul and inescapable odors of fish and garlic and bodies too long unwashed. Her brothers' mischief, the way they tormented the poor Jewish family beside them, came back to her now, and the laughter in the cabin-class salon of the *Resolute* recalled their malicious laughter then and made her melancholy even in the midst of mirth. And always she recalled her sorrow and longing for her son during those years when he was on the destroyer. Standing on the deck alone in the morning, she listened to the waves as they struck the ship's hull, and she remembered how she had stood on the porch in those days, thinking of her son listening to the same slapping of the waves against his ship as she had heard on her first voyage, the same sound she was hearing now.

But when they reached Europe, it was quite different. In Paris they were always having to dart into ladies' rooms to extract traveler's checks from the money belts my grandfather had insisted that they wear. How my grandmother laughed at their antics and how, she told me years later, she rejoiced to see her family in Krefeld again, to visit the old rooms on Gladbacher Strasse that held her childhood in them and evoked its sweetness—the smells of her mother's kitchen, the sound of the small loom beside the stove. The tribulation that life in Haledon had made hers receded as she sailed along the Rhine, gazing at fabled castles and listening to the tale of the Lorelei and the maidens from the sea who beckoned to sailors and then destroyed their ships on the rocks. By the time she reached Switzerland and Christine's husband's people, the world had reshaped itself, and its lovely aspect had restored her. She laughed as she rode the cable car to the peak of the Matterhorn and exclaimed at the alpine beauty on every side. Her appetite returned, and her body grew sound again. The world of her journey seemed a benevolent world, and my grandmother thrived in it.

On the return journey, darker thoughts of Haledon came to her from time to time, but she denied them a lodging in her mind. She drove them out by throwing herself completely into the fiction of shipboard life, the nightly programs of theatrical merrymaking and the daily melodrama of victory or defeat at shuffleboard and cards. She believed, as she listened to the extravagant Tyrolean band that entertained them every night, that the insouciance and gaiety of her tourist's life would continue even in Haledon after their return.

When they did return, her hopes were, it seemed, fulfilled. Within a few months Billy married Emma Brauch, one of his first girlfriends. He had always been popular with the girls because of his good looks, and the family's obvious prosperity made him a good catch in spite of his reputation for being wild, something which Emma told herself she would put a stop to. After they were married, the couple moved into rooms that Emma's family owned on North Seventh Street in Paterson, and the Brueckmann household itself enjoyed a tranquility it had not known since Billy's return from the Navy.

Encouraged by his son's marriage, my grandfather bought another business, a store much like his own on Park Avenue in Paterson, and put the boy in charge of it. My grandmother regretted not having Billy near her in the store downstairs, but now her nights were quiet, and her spirits remained high. The gaiety of her days in Europe had passed, but her life was tranquil and so her health, so precarious a year ago, remained sound.

Then, as December winds began to shake the trees beside the house and rack their dry branches, other clouds cast a shadow over the family's newfound hope. My grandfather was seated at his desk one night, going over the books and thinking about his decision to run for mayor one more time. He ran his finger down the list in front of him—Christener, Dick, Ellis, Esselmann, Edson, Ford, Fehren-bach, Flubacher. He paused. Flubacher had come into the store that very morning, complaining that he couldn't work on the battery jars for the fire alarm system because the Republicans had all but taken over the firehouse and were using it to play cards in. Can you beat that? my grandfather fumed silently. They use the firehouse, when Hobart, who is one of their big shots, has a house with forty rooms in it up on the hill. And do you think he'll let the poor suckers from down here set foot in his park? No sir. Posted, all three hundred acres of it. And yet, he comes down here to play poker in the firehouse. Hecht, Hambloch, Haycook. He was having trouble keeping the figures in his head. They're no better than they were years ago, the Republicans. Take that banner they hung up last year on Belmont Avenue: "Elect a Native American for Mayor." Just like it was during the war. But I put them in their places. We hung up one of our own: "The Only Native Americans Are Indians." He had to smile to himself, thinking of how he had got the best of Hobart and his friend Joe Bozzo. Chiselers, the lot of them. Bozzo was never much good, even as a boy. Some say he even cheated his father out of his house.

The phone on his desk rang and my grandfather picked it up. It was an editor at the *Paterson Morning Call*. The man said that he was calling to let my grandfather know that the newspaper bill for the store in Paterson hadn't been paid for several weeks. He said that he knew that my grandfather was an honest businessman and that he would want to look into it. My grandfather thanked him and hung up. As he put the account books away, a new fear began to take root in his mind. There had been no trouble with his son for several months now, and he had begun to hope that marriage and responsibility for the new store had straightened the boy out. Now this. What did it mean? He closed the store and went out for a walk.

The next day was Sunday. My grandfather was busy in his own store all morning, but in the afternoon, at about two-thirty, he closed up and drove over to Park Avenue with Laurence Garbaccio. When they arrived, he found two customers in the store, both of them complaining because Billy had not opened up until two o'clock. My grandfather could see that there were two piles of unsold newspapers on the counter, and he guessed that most of the regular customers had walked several blocks to a nearby store on Broadway to buy their Sunday papers. The boy would be left with the unsold papers and no money in the register.

One man walked out of the store with his paper tucked under his arm. "You're no businessman, Brueckmann," he shouted at Billy as he left. The other customer bought a pack of cigarettes and walked out without saying anything, but my grandfather could see that he too was angry and might never come back. What was more, Billy forgot to charge him the tax.

"You have to charge the tax, *Junge*," my grandfather said.

"It's only a few pennies, Pa."

"That's your profit, those few pennies. That's the way it is in a

store. That's the way it is when you sell something somebody else
makes. You make a little each time you sell. If you don't make anything, you can't stay in business. That's all there is to it."

"Don't get so excited, Pa."

When my grandfather told his son that he wanted to look over the
accounts, Billy reached under the counter and removed the ledger
that my grandfather had given him when he opened the business. My
grandfather carried it to one of the tables at the rear of the store and
sat down. Opening the ledger, he began to scan its pages, and in just
a few minutes he saw that the accounts were hopelessly confused.
Unpaid bills stretched back several months and on many days, Billy
had entered no income. "How is it there is no money down here?"
he demanded.

"I guess I forgot to put it down, Pa."

"And where is the money?"

"I don't know, Pa.'

"Have you got the money in the bank? Do you make deposits
regular?"

"There's no money in the bank, Pa. Emma needs the money for
the house and for eats."

My grandfather saw quickly what the situation was. Four hundred
dollars in unpaid bills and no money to cover them. "Did you pay the
rent on the store this month?" he asked.

"I forget, Pa."

"It's no way to run a business, *Junge*," my grandfather shouted,
losing his temper now. "You know what I have to do now?" he cried,
shaking the ledger at Billy. "I have to pay these bills from my own
pocket. Four hundred, maybe five hundred dollars with the rent,
from my pocket."

"I'm sorry, Pa."

My grandfather made for the door with the ledger under his arm.
"And we close this place up. That's for certain," he shouted back at
his son. "You come back to Haledon and work for me, *Junge*, so I
can keep an eye on you." With that he followed Laurence out of the
store and got back into the car. "What's wrong with the boy?" my
grandfather asked as Laurence drove down Broadway. "Can you tell
me that? No idea of what business is about. No responsibility. All
that money . . . where did it go? A lot on drink, you can be sure of
that, that rotgut they make up at Van Breutigan's farm. What can I

do with him? What was it Ritchie said to me? 'Mayor, you should have taken a strap to him years ago.' Laurence did not reply. He turned the car down West Broadway and headed for the Hamburg hill.

But my grandfather kept talking. "I never hit him," he said, "Never. What good would it have done? It's in the blood. None of Katie's brothers have made much of themselves. In the blood. So what good is a strap? You can't change what nature makes. And she was always too easy on him, forgave him no matter what he did. He always came crying to her, and she would tell him that it was all right, and so he'd go and do the same thing again. And the times we have now, that doesn't help either. Look at the saloons we've got—the Castle at the end of the car line, the Mountainside Inn. Nothing but bootleg liquor and gambling and women. Good times, Laurence. That's what they all want—good times."

They stopped on Norwood Street beside the store. Laurence said nothing that afternoon, but he remembered the conversation and the scene in the store and told me about them years later. "You know," he admitted then, "Maybe Ritchie was right. Maybe he should have talked less and taken a strap to him. It was the talk that really hurt the boy. You could see that."

17   Just Not in Him

·······································

MY GRANDMOTHER was secretly pleased to have her son back in the store in Haledon. Just as in years gone by, he would come up to the kitchen in the morning for a cup of coffee. She always knew when he asked for it very strong that he had been out with friends the night before, but she never made an issue of it. Sometimes he came upstairs in the afternoon to play for her and to see his sister when she came home from high school. My grandmother would stand in the front parlor and watch his hands moving over the keys, hoping that he would throw his head back the way he did when he was really enjoying the music:

> O my honey,
> O my honey
> Come along now
> And let's meander.
> Are you comin'?
> Are you comin'
> To the leaderman,
> Ragged leaderman?

And if he lingered too long, she might have to stop the music, reminding him that his father was listening and would be angry if he stayed away from work too long. "Your father doesn't like the new songs," she would say. "But he knows that it makes me happy to hear you play."

Did Billy say anything then about whether his father cared about others being happy, about *her* being happy? Did he ever say anything else? Did Kitty, who in time would feel it necessary to tell me about my grandfather's infidelity, feel obliged to share the gossip of her friends with her mother? Here, reader, you can only join me in speculation, for I have no answer to that question. Two things only I know—that from the time I was a child, when their marriage had not yet reached its fortieth year, they slept always apart and treated one another with an odd and formal cordiality, and that not long after Billy's return to the store in Haledon, my grandmother suffered a serious nervous collapse.

And so perhaps it did slip out. Perhaps, in a moment of anger, Billy said something like, "He doesn't care about whether any of us are happy, Ma. He only cares about money and himself. There are things I could . . ." He would have caught himself, of course. He loved her after all. But then, if Kitty had been there, might my grandmother not have turned to her, after Billy went back to work, and might she not have asked what her son was talking about? And might Kitty, my mother, have felt then, as she felt later, that she had to say what her friends had said about her father? My grandmother, the least suspicious woman in the world, might have grown suspicious then, might have watched and seen her husband walking up to Morrissee Avenue and turning the corner toward Barbour Street, not just once but many nights.

They found her standing on the porch one night in the rain, watching the dark clouds roll over the hills to the west and listening to the large drops of rain splattering on the branches of the trees and the street below. She was feverish and dizzy and seemed transfixed, mesmerized by that black presence that she had seen come drifting out of the woods, growing larger and larger, formless and terrifying. My mother found her there and called her father and they led her back into the house.

In the morning she was no better. She got out of bed but made no breakfast for the family. Instead she sat alone in the front room, her head in her hands and when my grandfather tried to approach her, she snapped, "Get away, Will." That was all. "Get away, Will." She talked almost incoherently of her dead baby then and of her son, and when they asked her what was wrong, she replied, "I used to love nature. I used to love nature. No more." They called the doctor then, and when he came, he told them that she had suffered a nervous breakdown and would have to be hospitalized.

My grandfather was frightened and dismayed by my grandmother's illness. My mother told me that. She told me that he would sit for hours in his leather chair in the dining room brooding, sometimes humming softly to himself the way he did when he was troubled by something. What was he thinking then? Perhaps he remembered a day long ago, lying in a field beside her, wondering whether she loved him and then, to his astonishment, hearing her say that she did. He had not given it much thought in recent years. She was just there, beside him in bed, at the stove in the kitchen, crocheting in the dining room at night. And now, when he tried to approach her, she muttered, "Get away, Will," and refused to look at him.

He must have wondered about the reason. The boy? The aggravation he caused her? But for my grandfather it kept coming back to the same thing. Wasn't it her fault? He had tried to make a man of him and she had always found fault with that, didn't want the boy pushed too hard. Let him spend his whole life playing and singing with the rest, with the Ruhrens. Life was a joke for them. So why not get drunk and forget about it? Or did she know something, something he thought had remained secret? What could he do after all. It was only natural. A man had natural needs. Natural. But Katie wouldn't understand that, wouldn't try to understand that. "You put too much in your head, Will," that's what she would say, what she always said. "You think too much, Will. What's going to happen will happen. You get yourself all worked up. What does it matter? What does it matter?" That's what they all say, the Ruhrens. What does it matter? With them it's all the same, no matter what you do; the trees against the sky, the bells on the wagons on the street, the birds singing, year after year, on and on, and nothing to be done about it. So maybe Katie thinks that it's all a joke too and doesn't care about whether the boy makes anything of himself. But she's crying now and pretty sick and that matters and that's not a joke.

As the dry leaves fell from the catalpa tree beside the house and scraped their way across the street in the wind, he made a firm decision to send his wife and daughter to the farm in Sussex for the whole summer. Katie always felt best after a rest in the country. And so they went for that entire summer and my grandmother returned in late August much improved, her spirits lifted by her vacation and by the news of the birth of her first grandchild, a boy, whom they named William after his father and grandfather. The baby's arrival cheered everyone in the family and not long after he came their spirits were lifted still higher by the news that Kitty, who would graduate from the Paterson Normal School that year, had been promised a job at the Haledon School by my grandfather's old enemy, Grundy.

My grandfather began his fifth term as mayor that same year. When he took the oath of office in January, he was presented with a second silver loving cup. "From His Friends and Admirers" the inscription read this time. The cup still lies in my attic beside the one presented earlier by the Young People's Socialist League. The second cup was, I think, more important to my grandfather, because it had come from many more people, who, as the years passed, had to admit that he had served the Borough longer and probably better than anyone before him. Few political feuds arose now. His fourth term had been marred only by a squabble with the Fire Company, whose members continued to use the Fire house as a private social club. My grandfather had had to threaten to disband the company, but even that political storm had passed. Before long he found an opportunity to even the score with the Fire Company by encouraging another group at the far end of the Borough to organize a second company. He promised to help them and even sent his son over to the organizers, Farmer and Ulrich, who convinced him to join them.

This too seemed a stroke of luck for the family, for, like the birth of Billy's son, Billy's joining the second fire company seemed to give him new strength. He came into the kitchen one afternoon and sat with his mother, talking with her about the new baby and the work on the new Fire House. He had helped with all the work on the new building, digging the basement and hoisting the roof beams into place. My grandmother listened attentively and rejoiced in the healthy glow on his tanned face.

Later that afternoon, after Billy had left, her brother Joe Ruhren came to visit my grandmother. She told him at once about how well her son was doing. "And whenever there's a fire," she said, "he gets Will's machine out of the garage and runs to it. He even drives the second-hand fire truck they got from Paterson. He's a good boy if you give him a chance, Joe.'

"Will expects too much of him, Katie," Joe said, "but the boy doesn't have it in him. He doesn't have it in him, but Will won't admit it. He keeps trying to make him do what he can't do."

"I wish he'd leave him alone, Joe."

Joe nodded and smiled. Kitty came into the kitchen to get some milk from the ice box. She sat in the chair next to the kitchen window. She liked hearing her Uncle Joe talk. Joe winked at her with his twitching eye. "Not everybody's a genius, Katie," he reflected. "I am but most others aren't."

My grandmother and my mother laughed.

Joe took a swallow of the coffee my grandmother had given him and ran his fingers through his short curly hair. He put the cup down very carefully because he knew that his sister was watching him closely to see whether he had had too much to drink before he came to see her.

"I'd rather have him digging ditches," my grandmother said, "as long as he was happy, instead of working in the business with Will, having to live up to what Will expects of him. Sometimes I almost wish he had stayed in the Navy. He looked so good when he came home. Do you remember? But then, you never know whether we might get another war again. I'd worry myself sick if he were out there on one of those ships then."

Joe smiled over his coffee cup. "We won't get any more wars, Katie," he said.

"How do you know that, Joe?" my grandmother asked.

"I know, Katie," he replied. "I invented something. We won't get any more wars now."

"You invented something, Joe?"

"Everybody's inventing things now, Katie. Airplanes, radios, Victrolas. So I figured that, since I was pretty clever, I could invent something too. So I did."

"Get away, Joe. You didn't."

"*Ja*, Katie. I pretty near invented something, and when it's finished, we won't get any more wars."

"What is it, Joe" my grandmother asked, not sure now whether it was a joke. She had, after all, been very impressed with the way he had taught himself to play the zither. And there were his plaster-of-paris models.

"It's right here," Joe said, reaching into his overcoat and removing what appeared to be two pieces of lead pipe joined together at right angles. At one end there was a rubber bulb like the bulb at the end of the Ford's horn, only larger and then, just beyond the bulb there was a hole in the top of the pipe.

"What is it, Joe?" my grandmother asked.

"It's a gun, Katie," he replied.

"A gun?"

"That's right, Katie. You can touch it but be careful. I wouldn't want you to hurt yourself."

"Joe," my grandmother laughed, "they invented guns years ago. This is just two pieces of pipe put together."

"They never invented a gun like this one, Katie," Joe said. He reached across the table and tapped on the end of one of the pipes. "This gun can shoot around corners, Katie."

"Around corners, Joe?"

Joe nodded. "This is what the inventors call a 'prototypist'," he said, "but when I get it working nice and proper, we won't get any more wars."

My grandmother gazed at him in astonishment. "How's that, Joe?"

Joe leaned forward and whispered. "Once they've got a gun that can shoot around corners, you see, Katie, nobody will be able to come out from behind what they're behind, and as long as the armies are all crouched behind walls, we can't get any wars." Joe tapped his forehead. "I figured it out, Katie, by myself."

My grandmother thought about it for a moment. Then she said. "Suppose both sides rush out at once, Joe?"

Joe shook his head. "Impossible, Katie. If both sides have got my gun, it'll be mutual, don't you see? They'd be killed on both sides, all of them. They won't risk it."

My grandmother touched the gun and pushed it gingerly back across the table to her brother. "Does it work, Joe," she asked, "with bullets, I mean?"

Joe shook his head. "Not yet, Katie, not with bullets yet. But I'm working on it."

"What does it shoot then, Joe?" my grandmother leaned forward, whispering in a conspiratorial manner.

Joe reached into his other pocket. "Right now, Katie," he said, "I use table-tennis balls." He put a ball on the table in front of her. "Like I said, this is just a 'prototypist.'"

My grandmother picked up the ball. "Joe," she said, frowning, "you can't kill anybody with a table-tennis ball. They don't hurt much."

"I know," Joe said, loading a ball into the gun through the hole in the top of the pipe with the bulb on it. "I know that, Katie, but it's the principle of it that's important, and the principle of it works. You put the ball in here, you see, and then," Joe turned and pointed the gun across the table, "you squeeze once and the ball goes down the pipe to the corner, and then you squeeze again and it goes down the other pipe like this."

Just as Joe had predicted, the ball emerged from the second length of pipe and shot across the kitchen into the dish closet. My grand-mother gave a small cry. Joe smiled with pride.

"Can you do it with bullets, Joe?"

"I'm working on it, Katie," Joe replied. "But it's the corner that's hard. I'm working with springs and oil now. I'll get it right yet, Katie, you'll see."

My grandmother leaned further forward. "Could I try it once, Joe?" she asked.

Joe loaded another ball into the pipe and slid the gun across the table. "You shouldn't break anything, Katie," he warned. "Be careful."

My grandmother closed her eyes and shot a ball into the old iron Thatcher stove. The ball bounced off the stove and flew through the door into the dining room. My grandmother was delighted with her success and demanded more ammunition, which her brother pro-duced from his overcoat pockets. Soon the kitchen and the dining room were dotted with expended balls. My mother joined in of course. She had always been keen on table tennis.

Before long my grandfather came up from the store. He picked up several balls from the dining room floor as he passed through it. Then he came into the kitchen. Joe put the gun away at once and looked up at my grandfather, who was looking distressed. He always suffered from indigestion after seeing his brother-in-law.

"Quite some table-tennis balls in the house, Will," Joe said, picking up several balls himself.

"*Unsinn*," my grandfather muttered.

"You could use them in the store, Will," Joe continued as he col-lected the balls. "A nice little decoration around the display window maybe."

"Something for children," my grandfather said, dismissing him.

Joe shook his head. "Not just for the children, Will," he said. He came across the kitchen and put his face close to my grandfather's face. "Advertising, Will. Paint something on the table tennis balls."

"Advertising?" my grandfather stared at him in disbelief

"*Ja*, Will. They've got all kinds of advertising now: streamers be-hind airplanes, skywriters. Have you seen that, Will? *Wunderschön*! They've got searchlights in the sky now and balloons with letters on them. You could hire one for the business or when you run for mayor next time and you could put your name right here on the table tennis balls too. It's the modern way, Will. You have to advertise, Will, or people forget who you are." Joe Ruhren shuffled to the back door."

"I thank you for the advice, Joe," my grandfather said, relieved to see him at the door.

Joe tapped his curly head. "What I've got here, I give to my friends," he said. "Katie knows. *Wiedersehen*, Will."

Although my grandfather decided not to run for mayor a sixth time, he hoped to stay involved in local politics, and so when some the members of the Citizens' League asked him to run for Tax Collector in 1930, he gave the idea serious consideration. Given some of his other plans, taking the job of tax collector might make sense. He had decided that the store was too small and that he needed to build a second store on the empty lot next to it. He would put the soda fountain in the new store and put his son in charge of it. He himself would manage the stationery and newspaper business and create a small office at the rear of the store where, if he won the election, he could carry out his responsibilities as Tax Collector. With this in mind he went to see Rheiner and Melhorn, who were running the Citizens' League in those days, told them that he would run, and accepted their offer of support. That done, he began drawing up plans for the new store and getting bids from builders.

Then, even as the masons were laying the foundation of the new building, matters took a turn for the worse. Emma called one night, quite beside herself, to tell them that Billy was in the hospital. The problem was not just drink; he had also taken drugs.

18   I Had a Son

....

NOT MUCH MORE than a week before my grandfather died, he told me about his son's drug problem. I was about to leave for service in the Army, and he was obviously troubled by my going away. He was staying with my mother in the house on Zabriskie Street. I remember that he called me into the little sun porch at the front of the house the day before I was due to leave. He was seated in the rocking chair, looking very pale and weak after the operation he had had.

"So, *Junge*," he said. "Tomorrow?"

"Yes, tomorrow."

"Look sharp, *Junge*." He hesitated. "I had a son," he said. "I had a son, but they took him from me. *Ja*, they took him from me. He got in with the wrong people and . . . and they gave him dope. Do you know what that is, *Junge*?"

I said that I did.

"It killed him in the end." He was rubbing one hand with the other, clearly troubled, not by his own illness but by some fear of endless tragedy, the reenactment of yesterday's tragedy, the final dashing of hope. "Look sharp," he said again. "Don't let them make a monkey of you . . . like my boy. They took him from me."

I promised that I would look sharp. I sat with him for a while in silence and then left. I never saw him again.

The drug problem was worse than Emma and my grandparents knew. The morning after Emma's call, my grandfather went to see the doctor who was caring for his son. My mother went with him. "He has been taking the drugs for some time now," the doctor said. "He can stop if he has the will. It takes a lot of strength, and there is always the temptation. The alcohol complicates things." My grandfather asked how it had happened, how the boy had started. "Who can tell?" the doctor replied. "Perhaps while he was in the Navy. He was in the Far East, I believe. And then, these are strange times, you know. People have lots of money to spend and what with prohibition and the places people have to go to get a drink, to have a good time—"

"He likes good times," my grandfather said. "Drinking, singing, playing the piano . . ."

"Sometimes the musicians . . ."

"Did he get it from them?"

"Hard to know," the doctor shrugged. "He has lots of friends. Perhaps he knows one who knows someone in a hospital or a drugstore. Perhaps it's just a dealer on the street. Did he go to New York much?"

"Sometimes."

"He'll be all right this time. He's healthy otherwise."

"He looked so good for the last few months," my grandfather said. "Worked all last summer on the new Fire House, sunburned, broad shouldered, good strong muscles in his arms. I thought it was going to be better, thought he might make something of himself. I had a house for him, wanted to put him in charge of the new store. I wanted to give it all to him."

"I'm sorry," the doctor said. "Perhaps, if you watch him closely, it will still work out."

I think that somehow they could not bring themselves to believe that it would still work out, not my grandfather, not my grandmother. Those were bad times, my mother always said when she spoke of the end of her brother's life. Most of all she remembered the hours of silence, her father and brother never speaking to one another in the store, her father and mother sitting in the dining room at night in silence. But the inner voices must have been eloquent enough.

Billy first: "You sucked my blood, Pa. You gave me this life and then you made it a Hell for me. You were never satisfied with anything I did, never had a good word for me, never praised me, never thanked me. You decided everything ahead of time, had to have it all your own way. I had to try to make myself what you wanted me to be and, if I got it wrong, you hollered and hollered until it near drove me crazy. You sucked my blood, Pa."

My grandmother: "You have nobody to blame but yourself, Will. Who made him this way? You expected too much of him, tried to make something out of him that wasn't in him. So how can you blame him? Everything was for you, Will. Look at me. I slaved for years in that hotel, cooking for forty dinner boarders every day, taking care of the children. Even here, there were days when I stood for hours packing boxes of ice cream until I couldn't stand the pain in my arms.

And what did I get from it? Once to the movies maybe. No, it all went into your pocket, into the safe in the bedroom. Not a penny to me for all the cooking and washing and sick children. All for you, so you could play mayor and be respected. Who respects me? And what do I have from it? A son who will kill himself with drink and dope and a husband who . . . I'd be better off working in the mills. I was happy then."

My grandfather: "I wanted to make something of the boy, like I made something of this family. We were working in the mills years ago with no money in the bank. We had nothing over there on Doremus Street. Nothing. Does she remember that? But when the bad times came and the strike, we weren't in the mills any more, and there was always food on the table. And now we have more money than most people here, more even than those poor suckers who put their money in Wall Street. Fools. I can buy them from my coat pocket now. That's what we have. I did that, and I wanted it for him too and for his boy, but he was weak from the beginning. Bad blood, the Ruhrens, singing and drinking and good times."

Nothing went well that year. My grandfather lost in his bid to become Tax Collector, defeated by another local businessman named Frignoca. He thought at first that it had been the Depression that had beaten him, that the people had had enough of Progressive candidates, but then he learned that the Republicans had guaranteed his opponent's victory. They had registered all the patients at the new county hospital on the hill above Haledon and had brought them down in automobiles to vote against him. After the election he went to see the new Republican Mayor, Bernascone, who ran the grocery store in Gaugler's building just across Norwood Street. My grandfather complained about the people from the sanatorium, but Bernascone just leaned on his meat cleaver and smiled. "People have a right to vote," he said, "even if they have consumption. And why shouldn't they vote where they are if they're too sick to get home?" My grandfather smiled and left Bernascone's store. Let the Republicans run Haledon for a while, he decided. He had other things to tend to.

He had the boy, who was out of the hospital now and back at work in the store. Billy spoke very little, but my grandfather kept after him, trying to find some way to get him to take control of his life. One day he took him over to the house on Zabriskie Street that he had taken from Otto Martin, when he defaulted on the mortgage my grandfather had given him. The remodeling was nearly finished now, all except for the bathroom and the third floor. It was a large bright house, with chestnut trim in the rooms. My grandfather walked Billy through it, suggesting that he and Emma take it and bring the baby to Haledon. Billy said they might do that, but my grandfather could see that the house meant little to him. He lived in another world now, uncommunicative, often so sick and dizzy when he came to work in the mornings that my grandfather would have to send him upstairs to bed.

Within a few months, they had to put him in a sanatorium in West Paterson. My mother recalled the night she drove her mother and father there in the new Model A Ford my grandfather had bought her. Once inside the sanatorium, they followed a nurse down a narrow corridor. She explained to them as they went that they would be able to see Billy but not speak to him. Then when they reached his room, she simply pointed to a small window in the door. My grandfather stepped up to the window and looked into the room. He stood very still for a minute or two and then stepped away and took his wife's arm, as if to lead her away. But my grandmother pulled her arm free and, approaching the window, looked in. My mother came to her side and looked in as well. What they saw was a small room with padded walls. The padding looked like bed sheets with rags stuffed behind them. In a cage in the ceiling a single light bulb burned, bathing the room in a harsh white light. Billy was kneeling in the far corner, his face turned from the door. He wore a white hospital gown and white mittens. He was swaying back and forth on his knees, his hands flat on the floor. Perspiration glistened on the back of his neck, and some drops of it fell to the floor as he struck his head again and again against the padded wall.

My grandmother stepped back from the door and took my grandfather's arm. They walked together down the corridor and out to the Ford, saying nothing. My mother followed them and, getting into the car, started it and drove back toward Paterson It was dark and the road was empty. As they passed under the Lackawanna railway trestle, they could hear the sound of a train passing overhead and the metallic echo of the Ford's little engine bouncing off the pillars of the trestle. "Why does he do it?" my grandmother said suddenly.

"There's no use talking, Katie," my grandfather said.

"He could have had it so nice. The new house, the store—"

"No use talking," my grandfather said again.

They crossed the Spruce Street Bridge, circled around the Passaic Falls, and made their way back to Haledon. My mother put the car in the garage and, coming upstairs, sat by herself in the front parlor. My grandfather went into the bedroom where he remained alone. Before long, my grandmother, who was seated in the dining room crocheting, heard him pacing back and forth humming to himself. The faster he paced, the louder his humming grew. It grew so loud that my grandmother finally had to call out, "Will, be quiet," but the humming and pacing continued until she had to summon my mother and with her push open the bedroom door.

My grandfather had opened the black safe that stood in the corner of the bedroom and had spread its contents on the bed. He had stacked the gold pieces by denominations, eagles and half eagles, and now he was walking back in forth in front of them, humming, as if in a trance. When the door swung open, he turned suddenly and stared at his wife and daughter.

"What's wrong, Will?" my grandmother asked.

My grandfather crossed the room and began to strike the dresser with his fist. "*Genug*, Katie," "Enough," he cried, and then over and over again, "*Genug, genug, genug.*"

"Will," my grandmother said, "You'll make yourself crazy. Stop it." But my grandfather went on pacing, and my grandmother, in fear, ran out to the back porch. She stood out there for a long time, watching the familiar black shape moving in the woods. It grew larger and larger as it moved closer to her. It seemed to cover almost the whole hillside now, but she was not afraid. She felt nothing. It might have come right onto the porch and touched her, and still she would have defied it. Now I have seen the worst, she said to herself. There is nothing more to be afraid of.

In the following months, Billy spent more time at the sanatorium than at home, and it became increasingly clear that there was no hope of his recovery. Without his help, my grandfather was forced to close the new store, and not long after he did, the boy died. He was twenty-eight years old.

They held the wake at the Gloors' house, in the rooms of Emma's people, where Emma and her little boy had stayed as Billy's condition grew worse. On the day of the funeral, my grandfather went with his wife and daughter to see his son for the last time. My grandmother stayed at the parlor door with Mrs. Gloor, and my mother led her father across the room to the casket. My grandmother watched her husband from the door, seeing a confused look spread across his face as he stared down at the body, and she grew afraid when his face began to move, almost as if he were going to laugh, but it wasn't laughter coming, she knew, but something else. My grandfather moved a little, swaying in front of the casket, and my mother, afraid that he was going to fall on top of it, took his arm and led him to a chair. "Sit down, Pa," she said, "until it's time to go."

When the other visitors had departed, Emma and her son joined my grandparents for the closing of the casket. Then they left the house, got into the waiting automobiles and followed the hearse to the crematorium in Union City. There, seated in the first row, my grandfather kept his eyes fixed on the floor, but my grandmother watched as they rolled the casket in and placed it behind the glass door. They played "Nearer My God To Thee" then, the way they had at the funeral of my grandfather's brother years earlier. My grandmother paid it no heed. She heard another song:

> They can play a bugle call
> Like you never heard before,
> So naturall
> Makes you want to go to war.
> It's just the bestest band what am
> My honey lamb.

The hymn grew louder as the casket began to descend, but once again the roar of the furnace below rose above the music and above the sound of her son's voice in my grandmother's head. It was a low, roaring noise that made her grasp her husband's arm and then put her face against it. My grandfather took her hand and held it tightly, whispering her name over and over. Then it was finished and they left.

My grandmother waited outside the crematorium with her daughter while my grandfather went for his son's ashes. A half hour passed and then he came out to them, carrying a small urn wrapped in cellophane. He got into the Ford, sitting down in the front seat beside my mother, who started the car and then drove back through Passaic and Clifton to Paterson. They said nothing to one another. My grandfather sat with the urn on his knee and watched the faces on the streets go by. They looked back at him and had, he reflected, no idea that he had just cremated his son. It seemed curious to him.

They drove along Main Street in Paterson and my mother turned down Grand Street and then up Spruce Street to avoid the traffic in the center of the city. They crossed the Spruce Street Bridge at the Falls and when they were across it, my grandfather asked my mother to stop the car. When she did, he placed the urn on the dashboard and walked over to the bluff above the falls. For a moment, my mother was afraid for her father's safety, but then she saw that he was merely inhaling deeply, and so she decided that he had simply felt a little dizzy and in need of fresh air.

My grandmother remained in the back of the Ford, where she stared out at the city in the distance. She could see, just to the right of the little urn, the clock tower of the city hall and a little further to the right, the post office and courthouse. Everything looked very quiet. It might have been a dead city. "Quiet today," she said.

"It's Saturday, Ma," my mother said. "Nobody works on Saturday anymore."

"We used to work on Saturdays."

"Not anymore, Ma. And there's not much work now—not even during the week."

"Bad times."

"Yes, Ma, I guess they are."

My grandfather came back to the Ford and got in. My mother drove the rest of the way to Haledon, and when they were back in the house, my grandfather unwrapped the urn of ashes and placed it in the front parlor opposite the piano.

How many times, in the years that followed, did he, I wonder, glance at it and say to himself, "I had a son, but they took him from me?" And did he think, I wondered as well, about who *they* were?

19   New Family

AFTER THE DEATH of his son, my grandfather spent even more time seated at the rolltop desk at the back of the store. He realized that he was getting old and began to worry about his health. Now, when he walked up the hill to look at the lots he had purchased at the top of Tilt Street, his heart beat faster, and he had difficulty catching his breath. The body runs down, he told himself. That's the way nature is: things come apart.

So many things had come apart. His son was dead. After ten years as mayor, he had lost an election. There was no future for him in politics now. He continued to vote the Socialist ticket each year, but he couldn't see much hope for the party. The whole country had fallen on bad times. People were out of work, many had lost their houses, and even more had lost their savings on Wall Street. What could a man do? Look sharp. Don't take any chances. That was it, he told himself. Keep your money safe. Watch the family. Keep the body running as long as possible. If you didn't, in times like these, everything would run through your fingers, everything you worked for, life itself.

Before long he lost Kitty too. She fell in love with my father, an Irish boy from Paterson whom she had met in high school. He was tall and handsome, a dark-haired, dark-eyed young man who had gone on after graduating from the high school to study engineering at Pratt Institute in New York. He doted upon her and followed her to the farm in Sussex County in the summers. It was a sure-fire strategy; she was used to being adored by a man. My grandfather tried to postpone the marriage. The times were so bad, he told Kitty, not right for starting a marriage. At night, when my father came to visit her in the front parlor, my grandfather would retire to his bedroom early and drop his shoes emphatically to send the message that the visit ought to end. But even that didn't discourage them. My mother wanted her adoring Irish boy and brought my grandfather around in no time. He had never really been able to deny her anything she had her heart set on. To please her, he even attended the wedding ceremony at St. Joseph's Catholic Church in Paterson, although it gave him some pain to see his daughter married by a Catholic priest. After the wedding, my grandmother threw a party at the house. As it drew to a close, my grandfather called my mother and father out onto the back porch and gave them two hundred dollars to help them through the bad times.

It was in many ways a most improbable union. My paternal grandparents were different from the Brueckmanns in every imaginable way. I had better try to explain them to you, those two other grandparental figures in my childhood, two astonishing figures about whom I might well have written another book, had they spoken more about themselves or had their acts been chronicled in the press as was the case with my German grandparents. My father's mother was a member of the Long family, Irish Catholics from Tipperary, who had come to America only a generation earlier and who resided, like many recent Irish immigrants, in the Dublin section of Paterson not far from the Catholic cathedral. They were people of high temperament and indomitable will. My grandmother Sadie had three imposing sisters—Bridget, Julia, and Margaret. Their brother, Johnnie, was for me nothing more than a legend, for he had, as a young man, wandered off for a walk along the Morris Canal one Sunday after dinner and had never been seen again. The girls, on the other hand, were always seen and always heard. Bridget was the most terrifying, an enormous woman with fiery eyes that menaced everyone they fell upon. She had survived three husbands, having withered their souls, I always imagined, simply by turning her gaze upon them. She confronted and provoked everyone the moment she entered a room. I remember that when I visited her, she would glower at me and pass her judgement. "You're just like your grandfather," she would say, meaning my Irish grandfather. "You know that, don't you?" Of course, I agreed and continued agreeing well into my twenties, knowing, since my grandfather had not had the good grace to die early in his married years, that her opinion of me was not positive. In some ways, now that I think of it, Julia, whom we had to address as Aunt Jewel—she insisted on that spelling—was even more dangerous, for although she appeared to be a frail and proper little Irish lady, she too was an iron-willed Irish virago. She soon dispelled any illusion of elderly gentility wherever she went. When we took her out for Sunday dinner, she would astonish condescending young waiters by demanding at once not a cup of tea, as they expected, but a cocktail.

"Give me a Mike Martin," she would say. She wanted a martini, you see, but refused to drink anything with an Italian name. She might have two or even three Mike Martins, pack away a solid dinner, and bring us back to her little house in South Paterson, where she would lead me into her bedroom and stand me before a photograph of Franklin Roosevelt. "That's Mr. Roosevelt," she would say. "He got us the Social Security." I am quite sure she thought he was Irish.

The Long girls had very little use for men unless they were priests. Witness the high mortality rate among Bridget's spouses and my own grandmother's separation from my grandfather just before I was born. And the men who actually remained married to the other two, Margaret and Julia, had been reduced to shadowy and mute figures who moved through their houses silently and with great caution. Even now I can scarcely picture them and am at a loss to recall their voices.

Priests, however, were another matter, for they were part of the church. The Long girls were relentlessly devout. There was no liturgy, no supererogatory devotion into which they did not plunge themselves. It was all magic to them, the statues, the candles, the Latin. They had no use whatever for the Church's teachings on morality and were horribly, indecently uncharitable to almost anyone who was not fortunate enough to be Irish, but they believed that all that would be purged by the rituals, the golden, incense-laden devotions that represented for them another realm of being, Plato's world, that had the power to lift them in spirit out of "this vale of tears" and transport them to a paradise of plaster saints. Within very recent memory, I sat in an attorney's office, calculating with Bridget's only daughter, Bernadette, how many Masses she would have to pay for to ensure that she and her mother would escape from purgatory in no time flat. Bernadette took no chances; she paid a considerable sum.

My father's father was quite another brand of Irishman. The Sheas had come to the United States earlier in the nineteenth century and were already flourishing, even prominent, in Paterson by the time the Longs and Brueckmanns and Ruhrens arrived. The first of the Sheas to come over, Michael, was a school janitor in the city around the middle of the century and was, incredibly, a deacon in Grace Methodist Church. My great-aunt Mabel, his granddaughter, told me stories of his performances in what was called the "Amen Corner" of that church, and I later read in ancient Paterson papers of the Bible classes he gave in his house on Clinton Street, where his wife, referred to as "the genial Mrs. Shea," served tea. She also, Aunt Mabel informed me, smoked a clay pipe. His son Maurice ran a saloon in Paterson for a time but then rose in Republican political circles to become the justice of the peace not long before the Paterson strike. They had great hopes for his son, my grandfather, the first Shea to bear the name George. They got him a commission in the National Guard and pushed him into the best clubs and lodges. I still have a picture of him on a very large white horse with a cavalry saber in his hand. He was an enormous man, imposing even off the horse, and throughout my life, I kept coming across older women whose eyes glazed over when I told them my name. They were remembering him, of course, and most would add something like, "If only I had had my chance." That was the problem, or part of it, I gather. He was something of a womanizer and, on top of that, a prodigious drinker, in spite of the Methodist upbringing. So the marriage to the youngest and perhaps the strongest willed of the Long girls was doomed, and the political career was not as glorious as the Sheas had hoped. He was a railroad detective for a time, then an investigator for the prestigious Paterson law firm of Ward and McGinness, and finally a member of the Passaic County Board of Elections. If the Church was the center of my grandmother's hopes, the Republican Party was beacon and bedrock for my grandfather. He lived his life for it, drank with Republican chieftains, probably slept with Republican women now and then, and took care to move in all the best circles, buying his clothes at Charles Elbow's establishment on Main Street and dining at the Elks Club. He dazzled me with his worldly and easy conversation. He spoke of Al Capone as of an old friend, and the infamous Joe Bozzo, Republican mover and shaker, whom my other grandfather had once rescued from jail, was one of his cronies.

What a coming together that must have been, those two German Socialists, who had conspired to end Republican hegemony in Paterson and who had spoken with Trotsky, and the Irish—a woman whose rosary was seldom out of reach and a man who had probably beaten up IWW strikers in his day and who had engaged in casual conversation with Al Capone. Amazingly they all came together at Thanksgiving and Christmas every year, taking dinner at our house and delighting children with extravagant gifts. You would have thought that the arguments would have been Homeric. Not so. They were sensible people. They retired to the kitchen after dinner and played pinochle. It appeared to be difficult to discuss either politics or theology over pinochle.

After they were married, my mother and father moved into the Granada Apartments on Broadway in Paterson. He worked for a company that manufactured aluminum furniture, and she continued to teach in Haledon, driving the Model A to Haledon each day and often dropping in to see her mother and father. Then, in 1934, I was born, and so my mother had to give up teaching. She and my father moved out of the apartment and into a house on East Thirty-fourth Street in Paterson, not far from where my grandfather had started his son in business. But this was a very temporary move. Before long we all came back to Haledon.

My grandfather continued to lay plans at his desk in the back of the store. My father was taking cuts in his salary because of the depression, and so my grandfather decided to offer my father a job in the store at a better wage. Billy's death and Emma's subsequent decision to move in with her own parents had thwarted my grandfather's plans for the house on Zabriskie Street, and so my grandfather had been forced to rent the house to a woman who took in boarders. He could see that the condition of the house was beginning to deteriorate and so, he decided to offer it to his daughter and son-in-law at a rent well below what they were paying for far less space in Paterson. Apparently my father balked at the idea of coming to live and work in Haledon at first, but when my grandfather offered to buy them a new car as well, he gave in. It was 1935, and the times were very bad.

So we came to live in the house on Zabriskie Street, next door to the Grundys. It would be the house of my childhood and of my children's childhood as well. It had a broad gambrel roof, high enough to permit a third story that remained, when I was a boy, an unfinished attic. The attic was a place of great mystery, for on one of its unfinished walls hung a toothbrush holder that was said to belong to one of the Martin children, who apparently lived in the attic while their father was working on the house. One little girl died of pneumonia in those days, sleeping through the winters, I suppose, in that cold attic, and her little body was laid out at the foot of the staircase in the house. As I slept, spoiled by quilts and central heating in my room on the second floor of the house my grandfather had taken from her family, I was convinced that I could hear her footsteps above me, pacing indignantly across the attic floor.

It was a wonderful family house, however, with a large living room and dining room on the first floor, a sun porch, and a double kitchen. Upstairs were four bedrooms and a bathroom that was remarkably up-to-date, for, since Martin had never finished it, my grandfather did so later. The house stood close to the street, but there was a small garden behind it with a grape arbor that ran to the large barn that Martin had changed into a garage with an attic loft of its own. Beyond that stretched Grundy's large garden, which was filled with fruit trees and beds of flowers. From April to September there were always blossoms outside our kitchen windows—lilac, forsythia, and apples early in spring, then hundreds of irises, roses, and tiger lilies and, late in the summer, phlox, marigolds, and poppies. And all summer long, the humming of honeybees filled the garden as they settled on the flowers and hovered above us among the eaves of the house and garage.

I believe that my grandfather and grandmother began to come alive again in those days. Whatever personal affection they had once felt for one another was almost gone, that was true, but I think that they began to find some small joy in life again when we came to Haledon. In those difficult times, they had provided the house that sheltered us, the income that fed us. I remember, as a very young child, in those days before the beginning of the Second World War, that they were often with us, my grandmother running errands for my mother, my grandfather dropping in whenever I was sick to take a quick look at me and to tell my mother that her worrying was "*Unsinn*" and my complaint nothing more than a bellyache.

My grandfather still gave a good deal of his attention to accumulating property and money, a pastime he continued to delight in until the end of his life. He rented out the new store he had built to one of the first supermarkets in Haledon and used that income to acquire even more property. He bought the small farm in North Haledon, where his son had once gone to buy bootleg liquor, and several acres of land at the top of Tilt Street on the hill near the county sanatorium, from which they had brought the voters to defeat him in his last election bid. When Grundy died and his widow put their house up for sale, he bought that too. Having to sell it to her husband's old enemy pained the poor woman, but he was the only one who had enough money, and so she had no choice. I can remember the morning that my grandfather came to our house with the purchase price, three thousand dollars, in a cardboard box. We brought it next door, and Mrs. Grundy was very polite as she signed the deed, but it was clear that she was thinking about how grieved her husband would have been to see the house going to that "damned Socialist Dutchman." When we crossed back to our house, I removed the row of stones that Mrs. Grundy had placed at the edge of her property to keep me out of her flowers. The garden was now ours. My grandfather had bought it for us.

These were the years in which I began to spend long hours with my grandparents. I often visited in my grandmother's kitchen, sometimes with my older cousin, Billy's boy. We played with my grandmother's fabulous button box (delivering the buttons down chutes like coal men), munched on her outrageously sweet fruit pancakes, and watched in fascination as she prepared and consumed her daily glass of Bromo Seltzer. "I would die without this," she would say, bringing up some gas, and we would believe her, never even suspecting the fruit pancakes. The Sunday morning walks with my grandfather began then as well, those antidotes to the attendance at Sunday Mass that my Irish grandmother insisted upon.

Sometimes we walked up to the lots he owned on the hill where we could sit and look out over the town, at Paterson beyond it and, in the far distance, at the skyline of New York. He would point out the landmarks in the town—the ivy-covered brick walls of the Columbia Ribbon Mill and the chimneys of the Harmon Color Works just beyond it, the bell tower of the Kossuth Street School and near it, Gaiz's farm, and beyond that the little pond in which people swam in the summer months. We could see the big gambrel roof of our house and the wooden steeple of the Cedar Cliff Methodist Church across the street from it. Past the old Cedar Cliff Hotel a tiny bus might be rolling. No trolleys now; they had been discontinued. Past the hotel the bus went and then between the old mills where he had stood to keep an eye on the strikers. "Down there," he would say, pointing, "we wanted to bring the railroad in, but they said there wouldn't be enough traffic. So I never got them to do it." I learned on those walks that, for a man who builds a place, there are a thousand unrealized structures. "There's no use talking," he would say then. It was the phrase he used to bring closure to useless speculations about the past and sometimes about the present.

The present could still bring disappointments. Not all his schemes for holding things together were successful. The Irish, who had intruded so suddenly on his orderly German world, were in part responsible. The Irish provoked him, not at family gatherings, certainly not over pinochle, but in the way they conducted their lives. It was not his way. The Long sisters' religion was, of course, unsettling, given his own very negative attitude to the Church and the clergy, but it went beyond anything that abstract or remote. He was troubled by the way they went about working and especially about how they conducted their politics. For him, work was getting up at five in the morning, doing all the things that had to be done—the hard physical labor and the tedious balancing of the accounts—and not getting any rest until nine o'clock at night perhaps. And politics was not much different. It meant walking the streets to make sure that the DPW was doing its job, testing the concrete being poured, and chairing stormy meetings with contentious councilmen. It meant listening to complaints from the residents of the borough all day long. It was not like that for the Irish. He saw that at once. My grandfather saw that my father hated working in the store, and my grandfather was not surprised when, after my father had been offered his old job again, he left the business. "They wanted life to be like the moving pictures," my grandfather once said to me. He saw that my father wanted to ride on Pullman cars and even fly in airplanes to cities halfway across the country. He wanted to go to lunch in hotel dining rooms and drink after work at the Astor Bar with a vice-president of his company, who made five times as much money as he did. And it was the same with politics. He knew how it went with the Republicans and with my other grandfather. Politics for them was standing at the bar in the Elks Club, buying one another drinks and scratching one another's backs. That's how the Republicans ran things as far as my grandfather could see.

20 Sunday Walks, Sunday Mass

ONE SUNDAY MORNING in 1941, I got my grandfather to walk up Snake Hill with me, past the house where years ago he had courted my grandmother and then past the Hobart's three-hundred-acre park. I was fascinated by the Hobarts, by the idea that one of them had actually been vice-president of the whole country and knew all the big shots and millionaires in New York and Washington. As it happened, I had powerful politicians on my mind because my father had just flown back from Washington the night before and had sat next to the president's wife, Eleanor, on the plane. The mechanics union had threatened a strike against the airlines over wages, and in the rush for seats on planes to New York, Mrs. Roosevelt had taken whatever she could find.

"My father sat next to Mrs. Roosevelt last night," I said to my grandfather as we climbed the hill.

"So I hear," my grandfather replied.

"He was real excited."

"*Ja, Junge*, I guess he was." My grandfather hummed a little to himself as we went.

I asked him what he thought of Roosevelt. I think I was looking for an antidote to Aunt Jewel's adulation of the man.

"Your grandfather doesn't think much of him," he said, meaning my father's father. "The Republicans think he's going to ruin the country."

"Will he?"

"No more than the Republicans, *Junge*." he said. "That's not to say I like Roosevelt very much either. They say that he's brought in a lot of things that we were fighting for years ago. *Unsinn*. The workers have a union now, and they get a minimum wage, but those poor mechanics still have to strike to get three thousand dollars a year, when Roosevelt makes seventy-five thousand, and that's on top of the millions his family has. And if things go bad, the way they did a few years back, where do the workers have to turn? To Roosevelt and his government in Washington. And who gives them their money to live on when they're too old to work? Same thing, *Junge*. Just look at all the out-of-work loafers we have working for the WPA now, standing around leaning on brooms all day and then taking Roosevelt's money. It's not what we had in mind years ago, *Junge*."

We walked over to the stone gates of the Hobart estate, and I peered through them, trying to get a look at the chimneys on the mansion that stood about a half mile up the drive, hoping that maybe one of the shiny convertibles or station wagons would roll by on its immaculate white-walled tires. "They're pretty rich people, I guess," I said.

"*Ja*," my grandfather replied. "Old Hobart made a pile of money in the railroads and in politics the way the Old Party men do. That's their politics—a way to get rich."

I couldn't resist putting an impertinent question to him. People had told me that he was probably one of the richest men in town and the stingiest. "You have a lot of money, Grandpa, don't you?" I asked.

"I have enough to take care of my family, *Junge*, enough." There was a small suggestion of apology in his voice. "You have to look sharp in this system, *Junge*, and no two ways about it. We had other ideas, but it didn't work out."

I knew I had hit a nerve, and so I quickly changed the topic of conversation. "Will Roosevelt get us into a war, do you think, Grandpa?"

My grandfather turned away from Hobart's gate and started down the hill again along the estate's tall black picket fence. "I wouldn't be surprised if we get another war, *Junge*," he replied, as I hurried along beside him. "Look what they did to the old country after the last war—bled it dry, the rich and their politicians." He cocked his head toward Hobart's invisible mansion in the woods. "And now we've got Hitler, a real no-good, to deal with. I think we get another war, *Junge*, we get another war all right. And they'll make a lot of money," he added, cocking his head again. "And quite some boys will die."

The war came, of course, just as he predicted that Sunday, and not long after it began, my mother and I, along with my two very small sisters, Helen and Catherine, joined my grandparents for lunch at my grandmother's large, round dining-room table. My grandfather had

had to sit me down in the dining room before lunch because he had learned that I had been inviting my friends to join me in his back garden where we would read comic books that I would fetch for them from the store. My grandfather gave me a serious lesson about the way business worked. "If you sell something, *Junge*," he said, "You can't give it away. Otherwise, no money comes in, and then there's no food on the table."

I nodded and told him I understood, and then my grandmother put the food on the table, her marvelous heavy German food, roast and potatoes and spinach, for lunch was their main meal. As we began to eat, I sensed some tension in the air and suspected some disagreement between my grandfather and my grandmother, who in her own way provoked him even more than the Irish in the family did. Still gentle with us, she had become, either from experience or from the example he himself set, harder and more stubborn than she had been in the early years of their marriage.

"So I think I'll give up the business soon," my grandfather said when he had finished eating, for he never spoke while eating.

"Give it up, Pa?" my mother said.

"Sell it. Wash my hands of it. We have enough money now."

"And what would you do, Pa?"

My grandfather did not reply at first. Then he said, "I told your mother we could move out of here."

"This is my house," my grandmother said.

"It's not what it was, Katie," he continued, "with all the building now and the machines on the avenue. You can't smell things growing in the summer anymore with all the gasoline and the smoke."

"It's all in your mind, Will."

"We used to enjoy nature in the old days, Katie," my grandfather said, forgetting our presence, perhaps even his daughter's. "We used to take walks up near your family's place. I can remember it so clear."

"We were young then."

"You still like the countryside, Katie. I still see you take walks up to the top of the hill with the boy here." He had not forgotten us entirely.

"A walk is good enough for me now, Will," my grandmother said, piling the empty plates in front of her. "This is my house."

"I've got the farm up in North Haledon," my grandfather said. "It has a little house on it and ten acres of nice land."

"I've seen that place, Will. A shack out in the woods. Nothing but chickens and trees. Is that a life for me?"

"We could fix it up nice," my grandfather persisted. "There's plenty of money in the bank. We could fix the house, put in new heating, plant a garden . . ."

My grandmother got up. "Nothing doing, Will," she said, clearly angry now. "I'm not going to live up there in the woods at the end of a dirt road. I don't care how you fix it up. Besides, you know it was a place where they made that bootleg liquor that—"

"I have the lots on the hill up there, Katie," my grandfather said, interrupting her. "It's nice up there too. A wonderful view . . ."

My grandmother set her mouth hard and fixed her eyes on my grandfather. "This is my house," she said.

"I could build a little house up there for us, Katie. You can look down over Paterson, see all the way to New York on a clear day."

"And what will I do, Will? Sit and look at the view all day long? Here at least I can see people, I can go out and talk to people in the stores, go over to Zabriskie Street to see the children. And you want to put me up there on the hill, so far up I wouldn't be able to climb down? Nothing doing, Will."

"Lots of nice lilac up there in the spring," my grandfather said, touching upon one of her favorite flowers.

To no avail. "I've got enough of nature, Will," my grandmother said, carrying the plates to the kitchen. "Just leave me in my house. I raised my family here. I want to stay here."

They never moved from the rooms over the store on Belmont Avenue, not to the farm in North Haledon, not to a house at the top of the hill west of Haledon. I sometimes felt that my grandmother would in fact have liked those places, but she had decided that she would never give in to my grandfather on anything he wanted. Next to her as she was then, the Irish were a pushover.

That's not to say that the Irish and their religion did not present problems. Constant compromises had to be worked out, and since I was the oldest and for a time the only grandchild, they inevitably centered on me. I went to Mass every Sunday with my father, but it was agreed that I would attend the local public school and receive religious instruction only at weekly catechism classes held in the basement of Father O'Sullivan's rectory. My grandfather never understood fully, I think, what a wonderful compromise this was from his point of view, for nothing could have more effectively set my mind against religion for life than those dreary catechism classes. They were taught by two stolid nuns, who were obliged, after a day of teaching enormous classes in a nearby parochial school, to deal with a hundred of us in a dusty, steamy cellar. I can hear the voices still, reciting the old Baltimore Catechism: "Why did God make you?" "God made me to know, love, and serve him in this world and be happy with him forever in the next." How true those words seemed to me then! Surely the next world would be better than this, this sitting in a horrible basement with dozens of restless, uncomprehending catechumens, badgered by the screeching voice of the angry nun who was clearly offering it up, offering us all up, for the salvation of what she called her "immor'al soul."

The altar boy affair stands out in my mind. The nun had obviously spotted me as one of the more promising of her late afternoon charges, and one day, as I fled as if from Plato's cave to the light above, the nun overtook me, an altar-boy outfit on her arm. "Have your mother wash and iron these," she said. "And next week Father will teach you the Latin."

I carried the costume home, knowing that I might just as well have been carrying a blazing torch into a barn full of dry straw. I even dared to give my mother the nun's command. Needless to say, Kitty was unused to receiving commands from nuns about washing and pressing religious garb. My grandfather was summoned from the store. The Irish were, of course, absent, but he still recalled his recent conversation with my Irish grandmother.

"He'll make a wonderful priest," Sadie Long had said of me.

"He's too smart for that," my grandfather had replied.

"Then he'll be a bishop," my grandmother insisted.

It was not surprising, therefore, that I was ordered to carry the altar-boy duds, unwashed and unpressed, back to the church. It was the end of my ecclesiastical career.

How surprised I was, then, in the middle of the war years when I was ten or eleven, to learn that my grandmother and grandfather were going to accompany us to Easter Sunday Mass. It was my mother's doing, of course. Not that she cared a fig for religion, but she loved to dress up at Easter, loved to dress her children up, and needed someone before whom to parade herself and us. Who better than the man she adored, her father? And so we went, leaving the baby, my youngest sister, Catherine, with my father's Aunt Mabel, one of the Methodists who happened to be into spiritualism and Ouija™ boards rather than churches in those days. We squeezed into the 1940 Oldsmobile to make our way, not to the little wooden church of Father O'Sullivan, in whose basement I had suffered for so long, but to the stone magnificence of Our Lady of Lourdes on River Street, the very church in front of which my grandmother had stood years earlier for the funeral of the Italian worker killed in the violence that accompanied the strike.

The church was very crowded, but we arrived early enough to find seats together in a pew about halfway along the center aisle. My mother pushed in first with my sister behind her. I followed them, and my grandfather and grandmother followed me. My father sat on the aisle with his own mother, Sadie, beside him. I could see that my mother was very nervous and that she was worrying about whether her father might do or say something that would embarrass her in front of her mother-in-law. She was especially afraid—I knew because she had confessed her fear to me—that her father would refuse to put any money in the collection basket, either out of atheistic rancor or parsimony and very possibly out of both. She watched him out of the corner of her eye as he sat stiffly in the pew, not kneeling for a prayer like the rest of the family.

Behind us in the loft, the choir began to sing as an altar boy appeared from the sacristy and, mounting the stairs of the altar, lit the candles, whose light fell upon banks of lilies, turning their petals from white to gold. The sight of the candles and the flowers had a deep effect upon my grandmother, upon Katie that is, for, as she told us afterwards, it evoked memories of her own childhood Easters. She remembered, she said, the strange feeling of new First Communion shoes being put on her feet, remembered how different they were from the clogs she wore to school every day. The new shoes seemed to be part of her, and she danced to church years and years ago, rejoicing in the new power of flight that the shoes seemed to have bestowed on her.

The choir stopped singing now, and a bell sounded in the sanctuary. Two altar boys appeared, followed by a young Irish priest. At the foot of the altar he stopped, bowed, and began to pray. My father gave my grandfather a missal, and he took it in his hand and scanned the English as the priest recited the Latin. Something about youth. Did it make him think of his youth, I wondered. He'd adored his mother, but the fond memories of her surely could not efface the memories of poverty and of his bitter disappointment at not being able to go to the university. The Creed now—"Conceived of the Holy Ghost and born of the Virgin Mary." *Not the way it is,* my grandfather was certainly thinking. *Life comes from life, blood from blood, and in the mingling, who could tell what would come from that wild hungering of flesh for flesh?* The priest was moving across the sanctuary now, and as the people rose, he began to read the Gospel. "You are looking for Jesus of Nazareth, who was crucified," I heard him say. "He has risen. He is not here." *The dead are dead,* my grandfather surely reflected as he heard it. *My mother is dead and my brother is dead and my son is dead.* Perhaps he thought of the urn that had stood for years on the mantelpiece and that, only days before, I had watched him scatter over the rose bed in the garden. *My son is dead,* he surely told himself then. *No angels. No stone rolled back. He was a man like any man, made out of our blood, and now he's gone.*

The young Irish priest was in the pulpit now, addressing the people. I looked at my grandfather out of the corner of my eye and could see that he wasn't listening. He had often complained about how the priests, who he insisted knew nothing of life, presumed to tell other people how to live. "Work hard and don't ask for much, and you'll go to heaven. That's what they preach," he had once said on a Sunday morning walk. "No wonder the mill owners and the politicians love them." When the sermon was finished, the choir began to sing again and the ushers walked to the front of the church with the collection baskets under their arms. I could see my mother watching my grandfather as the usher approached our pew. She had pressed a dime into my hand and the hand of my sister and had a dollar bill ready herself. She saw her mother shuffling through her own pocketbook, looking for the emergency dollar bill they had agreed she would stuff in the basket if my grandfather refused to contribute. Now she saw my grandfather reach into the breast pocket of his blue suit and remove his wallet. A few seconds later she was astonished, as I was, to see my grandfather's ten-dollar bill lying beneath our dimes in the basket. My mother's only regret was, I could see, that her father had slipped the money into the basket so furtively that her mother-in-law had not seen it.

"Holy, Holy, Holy," the choir sang, and more images surged up in my grandmother's memory. She remembered her First Communion day, she told us as we drove home, the white dress and stockings, the rosary she had clutched, the voices of children filling the old stone church in Krefeld. She even remembered the feeling of the host, wet in her mouth. Life had seemed incomprehensibly good then, in spite of poverty, and now, for a moment, it seemed so again. Dreadful things had happened to her, and her expectation of joy had proved again and again false. Two of her children had died, joy had fled, and nature had turned to her a cruel face, but that Sunday, for an instant, life seemed to her good again. She was happy as we drove back to Haledon.

"Hoc est enim corpus meum," the consecration, and my grandfather was still following the text. Did he say *"Unsinn"* to himself then? Can you make flesh and blood by magic? He knew blood, like the red blood painted on the life-size crucifix beside the altar, salty blood, like the blood he had sucked from his son's finger one day when the boy cut himself with a knife in the store. How often had he recalled the incident as a warning to me? People were filing up to the altar now to receive Communion. He knew what this meant. He had grown up in the Catholic Rhineland, after all. And now they would consume, destroy the very blood, the very life they believed they had made. He must have found that a childish fancy. I saw him look away from the line of communicants and let his eyes fall on the bleeding life-size Christ on the cross that hung above one of the side altars. His eyes rested on it for a long time, and then I saw him lean forward and clutch the back of the next pew.

"Will," my grandmother whispered, "what's wrong?

He gathered himself together. "Nothing," he said, "Just a little close in here. A little hard to breathe."

As the communicants prayed, the choir sang the "Ave Maria," and it made my grandmother, Katie, not Sadie, weep. It was not the way of nature, she knew that. Nature made children in pain and sorrow, and sometimes, she knew well, nature turned against them. Nevertheless she loved the image of the Virgin Mother and the sound of the children's voices in the choir, and even knowing that some of the joy she felt might be counterfeit, she allowed that joy to grow and flourish until the Mass was over. Then the young Irish priest came down to the foot of the altar and prayed, mentioning the devil and his roaming around the world seeking the ruin of souls. That troubled her, I could see. Did it, I wonder now, take her back to the porch in Haledon, the nights when she had stood there watching the black presence moving closer and closer to her, so close that she felt that it would reach out and extinguish her life? She sighed as the priest finished his prayers, and then, as he left the sanctuary, we rose and left Our Lady of Lourdes.

As we got back into the Oldsmobile, my mother said, "Wasn't it nice, Pa? Wasn't the singing nice?"

"It was pretty fair singing," he admitted.

"It was beautiful," my grandmother said, settling herself beside him. "It made me cry."

2 1   Retired Now

....

WHEN THE WAR CAME TO AN END, my grandfather sold the store, and Brueckmann's, which had become a Haledon landmark by then, was no more. He spent more and more of his time in his own garden now and in the garden behind our house on Zabriskie Street, which had once belonged to Grundy. And he was always ready to work for the town he had helped to build. I can remember that when a flood struck Haledon and the communities around it, he arrived at our house early the next morning, clothed in overalls, announcing that he and I would have to go out and help the fire department pump out the basements of neighbors whose houses had been swamped by the rising waters of Molly Ann's Brook. They also asked him to serve on the newly formed zoning commission, which he did, playing Solomon in disputes over who could build what and where, a role for which he was now well suited. People respected him and enjoyed seeing him on the avenue, twisting the ends of his mustache as he talked politics. The fiercer the discussion, the sharper the mustache.

In some ways, he was disappointed in Haledon. There were too many saloons, for one thing. As a member of the zoning commission, he knew the list by heart and sometimes recited it, grumbling as he went along. The Cedar Cliff Hotel was on that list, of course. He had run it once, he had to admit. Now it was run by an Italian family named Cartotta. They were related to the popular comedian, Lou Costello, another product of Louis Ginsberg and high school classmate of my parents. When he came to visit, the old hotel became again the site of prolonged revelry and celebration. My grandfather never went back there, but in time, when the food store moved out of the building he had built for his ice-cream parlor, he himself was forced to rent the property to yet another saloon. No one else wanted to rent it.

And so now he had to listen to the noise of a jukebox every night. Did the songs recall "Alexander's Ragtime Band," I wonder? Did the noise of the patrons, abandoning their revels at one or two in the morning, recall other early mornings when Billy would come home after those nights that he claimed brought him more fun than his

father had had in his whole life? My grandparents must have argued
in those later years over getting away from the noise on the avenue,
the smell of gasoline and liquor, and the noise of the music. But she
never gave in. I remember one morning that she came to our house
and told my mother the dreadful story of how my grandfather had
lost his temper and actually placed his hands around her throat. It
was a momentary aberration, I think, but symptomatic of his desperation and of the tenuous bonds that held them together.

Not long afterward, perhaps in part out of shame, he took my
grandmother to New York to the Metropolitan Opera House. As a
boy in high school in Germany, he had lived with a family that often
attended the opera, and he had long dreamed of having the same
experience. When he learned the Metropolitan was going to perform
the entire Ring Cycle of Wagner, he purchased tickets for each production and took my grandmother to see them—*Das Rheingold and
Die Walküre, Siegfried and Götterdämmerung.* Lauritz Melchior
and Helen Traubel sang the leading roles in German, of course, and
so my grandparents followed the story with ease. Watching and listening, my grandfather was moved by the music and astonished by
the spectacle.

He told me the story of the Ring, episode by episode, in the days
after his attendance—the birth of Siegfried, the forging of the sword,
the love of brother and sister, the slaying of the dragon Fafner, then
the casting of Gutrune's spell, and the deaths of Siegfried and Brun-
hild, and finally the destruction of Valhalla and the annihilation of the
gods themselves. I knew from the way he told the story that he had
been deeply moved by it, by the sweeping storm of the violins and
cellos, by the trumpets' blasts, by the clashing of the cymbals and
tympani, and no less by the play of light and color on the stage, by
the monstrous shapes of rocks and trees, by dark crypts and lightning-
swept promontories.

He had bad dreams in the weeks that followed the performances,
and once my grandmother had to come into his room. "What's
wrong, Will?" she asked. He kept saying something in German over
and over. It sounded like *"Macht"* and then *"Mann."* My grandmother couldn't quite make it out. When he awoke, he muttered,
"Unsinn," and sent her away. In the end, in fear of the dreams, I
think, he dismissed opera, dismissed all storytelling as something for
women, not men. It was imaginary, like religion, and he had never

trusted his imagination. Soon, he told me once, they will run out of stories, and a good thing it will be too. For him, storytelling kept you from seeing things as they are. Later when I was studying German myself, I asked him to read *Faust* with me, but he refused.

He found a less disturbing pastime. Baseball came to Haledon. We had had little experience of baseball as children, living in a place remote from Ebbet's Field, the Polo Grounds, and Yankee Stadium. I didn't know any players by name, and if I played a ball game, it was stickball in the street. But then, not long after the end of the war, the local volunteer firemen announced that they were going to build a baseball field. The borough gave them a dreary stretch of land down near the Paterson city line, which we had referred to simply as "the Lots." The Lots were reputed to be infested with rats, and no one ventured into them except a few old Italian men who searched for mushrooms in the hidden recesses of the place. We children had little faith in the firemen's ability to produce a baseball field on such unpromising terrain, but the firemen persisted, tearing up the lush vegetation and, with great effort, making the muddy expanse level. They were not quite able, however, to finish the job by the date set for the opening. No grass had been planted, no trees along the street. Only a single temporary grandstand graced that unlovely patch of mud, but plans went forward, and we were appalled to learn that they had actually invited a former professional baseball player to help open the field. My grandfather took me to the new baseball field that day. Had it not been built for the boys in the borough? We both stood looking out over the moist and muddy landscape, hoping that the baseball player might not come to look upon Haledon's pathetic tribute to the national pastime.

But he came. Mr. Siebert, the local manufacturer of roadside diners, a man who had dotted the eastern seaboard with his shiny structures, drove him in his new Cadillac convertible through the center of Haledon and, finally, to the ugliness that had been the Lots and was now the Roe Street Field. The baseball player, a bit long in the tooth, got down off the back of the Cadillac and walked carefully to the pitcher's mound. The police commissioner, my friend Henry Vitz's father, picked up a bat and strode, courageously, given the state of the grounds, to the batter's box. If the field was an embarrassment, Henry's father was even worse. No matter how slowly the professional baseball player pitched the baseball, Henry's father was unable to come even close to it. It must have taken at least fifteen pitches, the professional baseball player throwing underhand now, contemplating bouncing the ball before the plate, I think, before the commissioner was able to chop a ball weakly toward the morass that was first base. The Roe Street Field was open.

The mayor spoke. Henry's father spoke. And then the baseball player rose to speak. He did a remarkable thing. He called to the boys who were gathered around the little grandstand and asked us to come and stand in front of him. When we had taken our places, he talked to us, not to the crowd, about baseball and how important it was and why we should play it. He looked at the field and said that he knew it was just a beginning but that he was looking forward to coming back to see us play when the grass had grown and the permanent grandstands were built. He didn't talk for a long time, because his throat seemed to be giving him trouble, but I was impressed by what he said, and so was my grandfather. I could see my grandfather was sad, a few months later, when he showed me a newspaper that announced the man's death. His picture was on the front page of all the papers, of course. He was Babe Ruth.

My grandfather was no doubt the oldest spectator touched by Babe Ruth that day and became a baseball fan in his seventies. After that, on Sunday afternoons, my father and grandfather and I would climb into the Oldsmobile and drive down to Eastside Park in Paterson to watch the Paterson Silk Socks play. They may have been, I'm not sure, the descendants of that infamous baseball team that the mill owner Doherty had begun back in the teens. They weren't all that good, I think, but my grandfather grew to love the game as he watched them play. From what he said, I think that he liked the idea that it was game in which you had, as he always put it, to "look sharp," in which winning often came down to taking advantage of your opponents' mistakes. Whatever the reason, he became a serious fan and spent much of his final years watching the major league teams playing on television.

Ironically, the Paterson Silk Socks also played a role in shaping my future. The question of my education arose at the end of the forties when I graduated from the old school on Kossuth Street, Grundy's school, where my mother had both studied and taught. My grandmother Sadie Long was determined that I would attend a Catholic high school, of course. She still dreamed of a bishop or a monsignor in the family, and since her sister Margaret's grandson had gone to a Jesuit school in New York, that school was her choice for me. The Brueckmanns, in spite of my grandfather's insistence that I have the best possible education, had misgivings. They respected the Jesuits as teachers, but my grandparents' anticlerical views made them uneasy. In the end, astonishingly, my Irish grandfather cast the deciding vote. He too had been a baseball fan in his earlier years, and a close friend of his had been a star pitcher for the Paterson Silk Socks, one Zeke Duffy. Zeke Duffy was so good that he had been offered a contract with the New York Giants. This he had turned down, however, signing up instead with the New York Jesuits. And where was Zeke Duffy at that fateful moment? Teaching Greek at Xavier High School on West Sixteenth Street in Manhattan, the very school Sadie Long had her heart set on. My fate was sealed. The Germans caved in. Off to Xavier and the Jesuits I went.

Around the time that I went off to Xavier, my grandfather's health took a turn for the worse. His doctors told him that they would have to operate on his enlarged prostate gland. He had never had much respect for physicians, and so the news troubled him, and he spent more and more time brooding about the future, now seated in his old chair in the dining room, now bent over his roses in the garden behind the house. One afternoon, after reading some German with him, I sat out on my grandparent's back porch in the sun while he went down to the garden to tend to the roses. At the end of the garden, one of his neighbors, Joe Hamer, was cutting deadwood from the privet that marked the boundary of their properties.

"How are you, Bill?" Hamer called. They were good friends; my grandfather had helped him with the mortgage on his house.

"So-so, Joe."

"We all felt better twenty years ago, Bill."

My grandfather stood up. "We all get old," he said. I could see he didn't mind talking to Joe Hamer. It didn't require much effort; Hamer talked most of the time. He was a verbose and impulsive man, given to sudden and strange enthusiasms. My grandfather once told me about how Joe Hamer had brought home an artillery shell that they had found after a fire at the Picitinny Arsenal where he worked. He asked my grandfather to display it in the front window of his store, in spite of the fact that nobody was quite sure whether it contained explosives and had a fuse. My grandfather had had to throw him out of the store, and Joe Hamer had carried the shell home, where he terrified his wife by announcing that he was going to keep it in the cellar.

". . . the things we did in the old days," Joe Hamer was saying. "Some hot times here in Haledon, Bill. I can remember standing right over on the corner there arguing with Pat Quinlan. Do you remember it, Bill, the meetings we had, the people?"

"Pretty near all of them dead now," my grandfather said.

"They wanted to turn the country into another Russia."

"*Ja*, they had quite some ideas about what they wanted to do all right."

"I guess we all have big ideas when we're young, Bill. Life trims them down to size as easy as trimming this hedge. It gets them trimmed down nice and low and manageable."

My grandfather nodded.

"The roses look like they need a little cutting back, Bill." Joe Hamer bent over and began clipping at the bottom of his privet.

"What I had in mind," my grandfather said. You could just see the outline of Joe Hamer's body through the privet now, but his open face and bright menacing eyes were gone. My grandfather turned away from the privet and crossed the garden to another rosebush where he began to cut off the flowers whose petals had turned brown and fallen to the ground. Then he began to loosen the soil around the bottom of the plants, working with his fingers in the dirt, so that the roots would get enough moisture. The soil was deep and rich there because he had covered the beds with leaves every autumn. It was just there, I knew, that he had scattered his son's ashes after taking them from the mantelpiece in the front parlor. He had confided that to me, packing the soil down firmly around the plants. "You've got to keep things in order, *Junge*, or everything blows away."

"Loosen them up good, Bill." Joe Hamer's head appeared above the top of the hedge again.

"I do my best," my grandfather replied, and I could see that he didn't have his mind on Joe Hamer and his talk anymore. Cohen, the junk man, drove down Norwood Street, the string of cowbells swinging above his wagon, making their sad sound. My grandfather looked up at him, saying nothing, until the wagon disappeared around the

corner. "Enough for today, Joe," he said, getting up, but Joe Hamer
was gone. No bright face appeared, smiling over the privet, no dim
outline through its leaves. My grandfather turned, still hearing the
bells on Cohen's wagon and walked across the garden toward the
stairs. The sun was going down, and it had turned suddenly cold.

My grandfather's surgery was successful, but when he returned from
the hospital, he found himself more and more confined to the chair
in the dining room. I visited him frequently there, and whenever I
did, he encouraged me to go to college when I finished at Xavier.
One day he produced his report cards from the high school in Germany and read off the grades: "*Religionslehre: gut; Deutsch: gut;
Französisch: gut; Geographie: gut; Geschichte: gut; Naturbeschrei-
bung: gut; Schreiben: genügend; Gesang: mangelhaft.*" He had never
had an especially good voice, he explained, but he had been, in spite
of the grade in singing, the first in his class. He read aloud the citation
at the bottom of the report card: *Er ist unter 39 Schülern der Klasse
der Erste,* (Of thirty-nine students in the class, he is first) and then
beneath it, his teacher's name—*Branscheid.* "He wanted me to go to
the university," my grandfather said, "offered to pay my way, but it
was no good. Father came and took me home. Things were bad then
in the old country, and we needed the money. So I went to work with
the others." He paused. "You go to it, *Junge.* What you put in your
head they can't take away from you." He patted his sweater pocket.
"I've got the money."
    So I went to university, staying with the Jesuits at Fordham in the
Bronx and going in my junior year to study at the University of Paris.
My grandfather was elated and paid all the bills, but my stay in Paris
was also the cause of what was probably his last great political worry.
Like all U.S. citizens in Europe in those days, my friends and I found
ourselves outrageously affluent by European standards and so were
able, even then, to travel extensively. I spent time travelling with the
actor Bob Alda and with his son, Alan, a classmate, who would go on
to be a fine actor himself. We studied French in the Pyrenees and
motored on to the Riviera and to Venice and Florence and Rome.
They were days of incredible happiness and discovery, and I fell in
love with travel then. The more exotic the destination, the more excited I would be. I traveled across North Africa in the middle of the
civil war, and then conceived what was a very foolish idea. I decided

that I would visit what was then the most exotic place—the Soviet Union. I had studied Russian at Fordham, but I had little idea how unwise it was to petition the State Department for permission to visit the Soviet Union in the early 1950s. An agent from the FBI appeared at the doorstep of the house on Zabriskie Street within weeks after my request was made.

Even this grim reminder of the troubled times we lived in in those days had its lighter side, however, for when the agent arrived, my grandmother was alone in the house. My mother had begun to teach again as a substitute teacher, and my sisters were both in school. My grandmother never tired of telling us about her only meeting with the FBI, and so I know the interview almost word for word.

My grandmother found a big, round-faced man at the front door when the bell rang that afternoon. He looked quite respectable, and so my grandmother did not hesitate to let him in. For some reason, perhaps it was the business suit, she assumed that he was one of my father's associates, someone she had met before at our house. From this misapprehension, the farce that followed sprang to life.

My grandmother invited the agent into the living room and explained that her son-in-law was not yet back from work.

"I have come about George," the agent said. (Both my father and I were named George.)

"Oh, yes, I know," my grandmother said. "I remember you from the last time you came."

The agent looked puzzled. "I'm with the FBI, ma'am," he said. "I'm an investigator."

My grandmother laughed at his little joke. "I know you," she said. "You work for George's company."

"No, ma'am, I don't," he said. He tried to show my grandmother his identification card, but she paid no attention to it.

"You were here with your wife," my grandmother said, enjoying seeing through his pretence. "You all went out to dinner."

The agent tried to get my grandmother to read his identification card again, but she pushed it away. "Not without my glasses," she said. He put it back in his wallet. "How is your wife?" my grandmother asked. "Ma'am—" he tried to begin again.

"I remember that she had arthritis, and I told her that I had it too, in this shoulder—"

"Ma'am, you don't—"

"Would you like some coffee while you wait?" my grandmother asked. "I've got some on the stove."

The agent agreed to have some coffee, and my grandmother got up to get it for him. When she returned from the kitchen with the cup in her hand, she asked, "Do you have children?"

"I have three children," the agent said, and taking his wallet out again, he showed my grandmother their pictures. "The boy is in college," he said. "He goes to Holy Cross. That's in Massachusetts."

"My daughter's boy goes to college," my grandmother said. "He goes to Fordham in the Bronx but he's in Paris now, at the university there. He studied with the Jesuits in high school too. They're wonderful teachers, the Jesuits."

The agent agreed. He had gone, he explained to St. Peter's in Jersey City.

"Before you moved to California?" my grandmother asked. My father's company was located in California and almost all his colleagues lived there.

"No," the agent insisted, "I don't live in California, ma'am. I live here in New Jersey, and I work with the FBI. I swear it."

My grandmother laughed again. She had been delighted to learn that he had studied with the Jesuits and began to reminisce about her own Catholic childhood. "I made my First Communion," she said, "and went to Mass every Sunday, but we gave it up. My husband was—" she stopped. "I always say you don't have to be religious to lead a good life."

"That's certainly true," the agent said. He had pretty much given up. My grandmother had foisted a new identity on him, and he accepted it.

"Can I get you another cup of coffee?" my grandmother asked.

The agent looked at his watch. "No, ma'am," he said, "I think I'd better go now. Could I ask you to give my card to your son-in-law and ask him to call me? I just have a few questions." My grandmother took the card, whose fine print she could not decipher, and led him to the door. "I will," she said. "Say hello to your wife for me. I hope her arthritis is better."

The agent went down the front steps looking confused.

Thus my grandmother, in the final political confrontation of her life, achieved what hundreds of others, struggling before interrogations and congressional hearings, had failed to do. She convinced the forces of darkness that they were a joke and endeared herself to them in the process. My father wrote to me in Paris, of course, and I, in turn, had to write to the FBI explaining that I had no sympathy with the Communist regime in the Soviet Union, that I had just wanted to see the place. We never heard from them again, but who knows what file may be stashed away somewhere, and what report of an agent's bizarre visit to Haledon, that fabled hotbed of sedition, it may contain?

For my grandfather, however, the visit was far from a joke. After the troubles he had had years ago, the appearance of the FBI was a serious matter. Did they know, he wondered, that the student they were investigating was his grandson, that he himself had once been called the "Red Mayor," that he had known Trotsky, that his cousin Karl in St. Louis had joined the party and gone to visit Moscow? He was relieved when he learned that my letter seemed to have put an end to the matter, but it didn't keep him from giving me a long lecture about political reality when I got home. "Just as well you couldn't go, *Junge*," he said, "It's not the paradise Karl said it was. But look sharp. It's not paradise yet here either. What kind of country is it where they're afraid of a boy like you going to Russia?"

22 Things Run Down

THE POLITICS of the fifties were troubling to my grandfather, but neither they nor I brought the final crisis in his life. He did worry about my marriage at the tender age of twenty-one. He may have worried about the great-grandchildren it would produce, those strange creatures who would arise from a new mingling, perhaps to make new tragedies in that time to come that was as strange and frightening to him as the United States had been on that first night, when he had drifted to sleep, listening to the rumbling of trolleys bound for places he had never seen. No, his health brought on the last crisis. The doctors had warned him when he had had his first operation that his blood sugar level was dangerously high, but he had paid them no heed. Now he learned that he was suffering from diabetes and, worse still, that one of his legs would have to be amputated. He was devastated. His trust in the power of his own will to be healthy was shaken. Nature had turned against him, and he saw himself in years to come an incomplete man, confined to a chair, visited by long-faced friends who would view him as an object of pity. But there was nothing to be done. He went into the hospital again, and the amputation was performed.

The day after the operation, I went to Paterson with my grandmother to visit him in the old General Hospital. Since my father needed the car for work, we had to take the bus down to Paterson. On Market Street, across from the city hall, we waited for a second bus. The clock in the city hall tower struck three, and flocks of starlings and pigeons rose from their perches on the cornices and sills of the bank buildings and shops around us. My grandmother watched them as they drifted back to earth again, some settling indecorously on the statues of old Hobart the vice-president and Mayor McBride, my grandfather's old enemy. It made her think of the strike, and she reminisced about the funeral procession she had walked in years ago and about how they had marched by city hall that day. McBride, she recalled, had not come out.

We arrived at the hospital at about half past three, entered the old redbrick building, and followed one of the nurses down a corridor to my grandfather's room. We found him lying on a high bed just inside the door, covered by a hospital gown, his arms bare, revealing the marks on the skin where they had given him injections. I could see that plastic tubes ran from under the sheets carrying an amber fluid to bottles under the bed. On the other side of the bed, another bottle hung above him, and a tube ran from it to his arm.

My grandmother sat down quietly beside the bed. She stared at her husband, who looked very pale and somehow surprised. He seemed unable to open his eyes all the way, and his hair was uncombed. "Hello, Will," my grandmother said at last. "I came down on the bus to see you."

"You came all the way on the bus, Katie?" he asked.

"It's not so far," she said. "Young George came with me."

My grandfather nodded.

"I was afraid you would be lonesome, Will," my grandmother explained.

"It was nice of you to come, Katie."

"Have you seen anybody else?" my grandmother asked.

"This morning a priest came," he said, having trouble speaking clearly, pausing between sentences. "He asked me if I was Catholic, and I told him that I was brought up Catholic but that I didn't go to church anymore."

A nurse came to the door and then went away again.

"He was a nice boy," my grandfather said, "and so when he said that he would come back to see me, I didn't make a fuss, Katie."

The nurse came back into the room. "Time for your temperature, Pop," she said, sticking the thermometer into my grandfather's mouth. "He's a good boy, doesn't give us any trouble," she said, tapping her rubber-soled shoe on the floor. My grandmother said nothing. The nurse took the thermometer out of my grandfather's mouth, looked at it, and then shook it, causing the bracelet on her wrist to jingle. She went to the end of the bed, noted the temperature reading on the chart there, and then left the room, her shoes squeaking as she went.

My grandfather went to sleep then, and when a mill whistle blew somewhere nearby, my grandmother began talking about the sound of the mill whistles in the old days in Haledon, when they ran the hotel. She talked about her forty dinner boarders, one of her favorite topics, and described for me the lunchtimes then—the way she brought in the platters of free potato salad, her husband behind the bar, washing glasses, tapping a new keg of beer, arranging bottles in front of the mirror behind the bar. When they got really busy, he would have to run from one end of the bar to the other, his sleeves rolled up, drawing glass after glass of beer from the taps. "And if anybody misbehaved," she said, "he took out the nightstick from under the bar. He always insisted on respect."

A little later, after my grandfather woke up, the young priest came back. My grandmother asked him to come in and sit down. He thanked her and then turned to my grandfather. The priest told him that he knew that he was troubled and frightened by the loss of his leg, and then he reminded him that it was God's will and that we had to accept whatever God sent us.

My grandfather stared at him, clawing with his fingers at the sheets. Then, very slowly, he said, "I don't believe in God."

The young priest nodded and looked at the window. "What is it then, Mr. Brueckmann, that you believe in?"

My grandfather did not reply at once. Then he whispered, "I believe in myself and in hard work and in nature."

The priest nodded again. He sat in silence for several minutes and then he rose and said, "I will pray then, Mr. Brueckmann, that nature will be good to you and that you will be at peace with it."

"And I thank you," my grandfather replied.

My grandmother walked to the door with the priest. In the corridor she said, "Don't mind him. He's afraid."

"I understand," the priest said, "and I will pray for him and for you."

The last visitor that afternoon was, astonishingly, Joe Ruhren. He came into the hospital room suddenly, his old brown overcoat nearly touching the floor now because he was bent with age, his thinning, curly hair ruffled by the wind.

"Here's Joe," my grandmother said hopefully, wanting his visit to go well but worrying about how her husband would react.

Joe himself looked ill at ease, I could see. "How are you, Will?" he asked.

"Pretty fair," my grandfather said, pulling himself up a little in the bed. "They had to cut the leg off. I guess Katie told you."

Joe Ruhren nodded. "Do you remember, Katie," he said, as he took a seat, "the way we used to tease the children at New Year's about the man with as many noses as there are days in the year? Well, now we'll be able to tell them to watch for Will with as many legs as there are days in the year."

My grandmother laughed. "What a thing to say, Joe," she said, and then, to change the subject, she asked him about his children. They talked about children and grandchildren for a while, and then the nurse came back into the room and gave my grandfather a pill. When she was gone, Joe Ruhren asked, "Will you get a wooden leg, Will?"

My grandfather explained that they made artificial legs of aluminum now and that he was going to buy one and learn to walk on it.

Joe Ruhren thought for a moment. Then he said, "Maybe, Will, you should do what we used to do with the furniture. If one leg was too short, we cut the others down to match. It might be cheaper."

My grandfather smiled. "Joe," my grandmother protested, "Don't you take anything serious?"

Joe Ruhren got up to leave and pulled his frayed overcoat around him. "Only the way I dress, Katie," he said. "Only the way I dress."

After Joe Ruhren left, my grandmother got up and said that it was time for us to go too. Then she stepped over to the bed and looked down at my grandfather. "Will," she said, "you ought to ask them to keep your hair straight." She reached over the bed and straightened the loose strands of hair. She saw that her gesture had embarrassed her husband and that his face was flushed, and so she explained herself. "I want you to look right, Will." Then, a little embarrassed herself, she hurried from the room.

23   The Last Walk

....

ABOUT A MONTH after his operation, my grandfather began to walk again, using the aluminum walker the family had purchased. He would go out twice a day, pushing himself further each time he used it. On the day he had gone to be measured for his artificial limb, he insisted on taking the walker out late in the afternoon. He was excited by the idea of soon being able to walk without it and so decided to walk around the entire block in preparation for the more strenuous exercise to come.

With my grandmother beside him, he lowered himself down the front steps of our house on Zabriskie Street where he was staying, leaning on the bricks of the porch with his left hand. Then he grasped the walker firmly and made his way along the picket fence that extended from the side of the house to Grundy's old wall, picking the walker up and putting it down with each step he took. Concentrating on the uneven pavement and on the patterns that the fallen leaves made on the sidewalk, he went along the wall in front of the Grundy house, stopping to wave to Abe Joffe, who ran his father's drugstore now and had come out of the front door to shout "Hello."

When he reached the avenue, my grandfather stopped and examined the basins of the storm sewer. They were clogged with fallen leaves, and it angered him. "Those loafers who work for Bernascone," he said to my grandmother. "All they do is lean on their brooms all day, WPA style."

"Don't get yourself worked up, Will," my grandmother warned.

My grandfather turned the corner and started along the flats that occupied the long building that had once been the Masonic hall. Looking at it, he recalled having joined the Masons years ago and having contributed to the building of their temple in Paterson. He was, after all, a weaver and a builder, he told himself; and Katie and Kitty had liked the ceremonies of the Order of the Eastern Star.

He made his way past Oropallo's shoe repair shop. The sound of the shoemaker's machinery drifted out of the small store, and with it came the smells of his trade, the scent of raw leather and the acrid odors of stains and polishes and of harsh carbolic acid. Oropallo himself, his face as leathery as the boots and shoes that lay in the window, smiled at my grandfather and waved. My grandfather waved back to him, in spite of the fact that the two of them had had an argument just a few years ago about a small corner of land behind the Grundy property. Oropallo had gone out one night and knocked down a piece of the wall that had stood between their properties for over a hundred years and built a ramshackle shed on the little plot of land.

They pushed on past Gionti's toy shop, and my grandmother made my grandfather stop to rest for a while. Together they gazed at the stacks of games and the array of tiny objects in the window of the store, dolls and masks, a gaudy display of drums and horns, and a fleet of small boats, a battleship, and several destroyers. When he saw the toy destroyers, he turned away quickly. It was like the picture of the destroyer that still hung in the front parlor, placed there as a reminder but never spoken of. Turning from the store, he waved to the town gossip, Helen Hassler, who sat with her husband in front of her house every night in the summer, watching the Haledon parade, collecting news, and dispensing some herself when the opportunity arose. She shouted something to my grandparents, but they couldn't make it out. There was too much traffic on the avenue; it was nearly five o'clock and most of the mill whistles had already blown.

My grandmother tried to convince her husband that he ought to turn around and go back to the house. She could see that his face was red and that he was breathing very hard. But he wouldn't listen to her. He struggled along the short stretch of Clinton Street and turned the corner of East Barbour. When he reached Coda's house, he stopped to admire the roses, the finest in Haledon. These would be the last roses of the year, he knew, and their bushes now stood almost as high as a man's shoulders and carried dozens of late blossoms, deep red and pink, flaming orange and white. My grandmother tried to engage him in conversation about the roses, but he refused to stop for long and set off again at the same pace. Across from the small mill on East Barbour Street, he had trouble with the walker after placing it unevenly in the small hollow in the sidewalk that carried off rainwater. He complained about that too, insisting that if the job had been done properly, a pipe would have been run beneath the sidewalk. After he had straightened the walker out again, he made his way along the old flats across from Barbero's house to the corner of Roe Street where the Italians had a club that everybody called the

Cold Feet Club. Many members were sitting outside the front door, enjoying the fine weather. Mrs. Barbero's father, who was a kind of caretaker of the club, was there as was a little round-faced man named Louie, who had for years passed my grandfather's store, pulling two jars of water down from the Tilt Street Spring on a little cart he had made. Now they sat on the stone step in front of the door of the Cold Feet Club, talking politics and families and remembering their old country. They all knew my grandfather and remembered that he had helped the Italian workers years ago during the strike. And so he had to stop and talk to them and tell them about the artificial leg he was going to get. They told him that they were glad to see him walking again, some struggling a little to say it properly in English, and they wished him luck, in their courtly way, with his new leg. My grandmother pushed him along then, because she didn't like the strong smell of the Italian wine.

They turned up Roe Street, my grandfather's face very red now, my grandmother afraid. The sun was low in the sky, just above the hills to the west of Haledon. Its dusty rays fell through the trees along Roe Street, forming irregular patches of light on the pavement. The shadows of the peaked roofs stretched across the street and fell on the aging automobiles that were parked along the curb. It was a street like an old dusty attic, containing an odd assortment of objects, many about to lose their usefulness forever. As he passed the frame houses and made his way beneath the oaks and maples, my grandfather must have thought of the people who lived on the street—the Ciolettis, the Vergas, the Quagliettas, the Finnamores, he knew them all. How many years had it been? Not far to go now. Chambers' old house across the street and that woman with the yellow hair and the voice like a stevedore, sending him a greeting. There stood Lena Duroche and Mary Gallina talking together, Lena animated as ever, Mary long-suffering and patient. Mary, whose name was Anspach now, was the daughter of Gallina, who had worked on the DPW when my grandfather was mayor. "Hello, Mrs. Mary," my grandfather said, stopping. He always addressed her that way. "Hello, Mrs. Mary." And they stopped and talked awhile, to my grandmother's great relief, about their children and grandchildren.

Then my grandfather moved his walker past our garage and along the wall to our back steps. He left the walker there and pulled himself up the stairs, holding the wall with his left hand. He made his way to the back door, after my grandmother handed the walker up to him, and paused there to look at the grape arbor. Most of the grapes had fallen to the ground and been eaten by the birds, and he complained about that too, pointing out to his wife that it was a waste and that she should have made some jam.

Once inside the house, my grandfather watched the evening news broadcast and smoked the one cigar that he was permitted each day. When the broadcast was over, my grandmother wheeled him in his chair to the dining-room table, where the two of them had supper. My sisters had already eaten and had gone out for the evening with boyfriends, and my parents were having drinks before their own dinner. My grandmother could see that her husband was troubled. The noisy car the girls had driven off in annoyed him and so did the sound of the cocktails being stirred. He was worried about me, for he had seen me leave for the Army just days earlier, and he kept swallowing hard in a way that told my grandmother that he was suffering from indigestion. When he finished his food, he stared down at his plate humming and rubbing one hand with the other the way he often did.

My grandmother realized then that he was more troubled than usual and perhaps in pain. She could see from the large vein at his temple that his heart was beating very fast, and his face was flushed now and marked by small spasmodic twitches. "Are you all right, Will?" she asked.

My grandfather did not reply. He seemed to be listening to something far away, seemed to be trying to make out what distant voices were saying. As if in a trance now, he stared across the table, his eyes growing watery, the blood draining from his cheeks. He turned very pale and the expression on his faced changed to one of confusion. His humming became a kind of low moan now, and it frightened and paralyzed my grandmother. Unable to rise, she watched as her husband raised one hand to his chest. Then, amazed, disbelieving, he threw both arms into the air and fell back in his chair. My grandmother knew at once that he was dead.

Many people came to the funeral. The fire company, of which he had been a member and which he had once threatened to disband, attended in uniform. Cona, who was the mayor, and all the councilmen brought and read a resolution they had passed. When Cona read it in front of the casket, it occurred to my grandmother that her husband might not have liked the way it began: "Whereas Almighty God in His infinite wisdom has seen fit to remove from our midst William Brueckmann. . . . " But he would have approved of the end, she admitted to herself, for it referred to him as "a highly respected resident and a devoted public servant," and he would have been especially pleased, she knew, because it had been written by Republicans.

After the funeral, my mother tried to convince my grandmother to leave the rooms over the store and move in with us, but my grandmother refused even then to leave her own house. I was not surprised by her firmness. I had watched her at my grandfather's funeral, for which, of course, I had returned. I watched as Aunt Bridget, ever ready for a funeral, entered the funeral parlor, glowering, putting people in their places. I watched in astonishment as she looked my grandmother in the eye and then, incredibly, flinched and looked away. No, my grandmother was not moving out of her house to please anyone. She continued to look after herself, did her own cooking and washing and went shopping each morning. In the bad weather, she sat in a rocker at her kitchen window and watched the people passing along the avenue. And when it was fine, she would stand out on the porch and look up the hills to the west of Haledon, boasting that even at ninety, she could see clearly the figures of people walking along the crest of the hill. "This is my house," she said to my mother, to Kitty. "I want to stay in it and live a while yet." Which is what she did, until in 1970, at the age of ninety-four, she died quite suddenly but peacefully of a stroke.

INDEX
....

The two main figures, William and Katherine Brueckmann, and the narrator himself, who appear throughout the book, are not included in this index.

Abrams (Haledon councilman), 42, 48

Adams (Haledon councilman), 116

Alda, Alan, 190

Alda, Robert, 190

Belcher (Haledon councilman), 42

Bernascone, George, 162

Bimson (chief of the Paterson Police Department), 51, 60, 68, 79, 89

Bottos family, 64, 76

Boyd (speaker at the strike meetings), 76

Bozzo, Joe, 65, 149, 170

Brauch, Emma (Brueckmann), 122, 148, 165

Brueckmann, Frieda (Meyer), 12, 23, 31, 59, 123, 124, 128

Brueckmann, Karl, 43, 127, 134, 193

Brueckmann, Paul, 3, 128

Brueckmann, William (William Brueckmann's grandson), 140, 154, 165, 173

Brueckmann, William Jr., 23, 24, 44, 61, 72, 82, 102, 109, 120, 124, 129, 138, 141, 144, 148, 152, 155, 159, 160, 173

Buckley (New Jersey Assemblyman), 40

Cartottas family, 184

Christener (Haledon councilman), 38, 76

Cohen (trash collector), 139, 189

Cona, Charles, 201

Conboy (A. F. of L. speaker), 68

Coon (Haledon Borough clerk), 39

Costello, Lou, 22, 184

Dean, Bernadette, 169

Debs, Eugene, 37, 62, 134

De Yoe, J. Willard, 43, 98

Doherty (Paterson mill owner), 49, 187

Duffy, Zeke, 187

Dunn (Passaic County prosecutor), 74

Duroche, Lena, 200

Flynn, Elizabeth Gurley, 51, 57, 60, 67, 68, 70, 73, 77, 87, 89

Force (Passaic County assistant prosecutor), 96

Fordyce (mayor of Paterson), 102

Frignoca, H., 162

Gallina, Mary, 200

Gallina (member of the Haledon Department of Public Works), 41, 138

Garbaccio, Laurence, 144, 149
Ginsberg, Allen, 111
Ginsberg, Louis, 111, 184
Gish, Lillian, 126
Gloor, Mrs., 165
Golden (A. F. of L. speaker), 68
Gompers, Samuel, 75, 135
Goodbody family: 21, 44, 139
Grossgebauer, John, 91
Grundy, Absolom, 44, 109, 154
Grundy, Phoebe, 172

Hamer, Joe, 188
Hassler, Helen, 199
Haywood, William (Big Bill), ix, 53,
    60, 65, 68, 70, 73, 75, 78, 87, 134
Heller, Andrew, 123
Hillquit, Morris, 62, 134
Hitler, Adolph: 176
Hobart, Garrett A. Jr., 139, 148, 175
Hobart, Garrett A. Sr., 21, 194
Hovenberg (local magistrate), 65
Hueck, Paul, 38, 47, 48, 65, 118
Hughs, William (Billy), 75

Joffe, Abram, 120, 198
Joffe, Leo, 66

Kapp (Haledon councilman), 39, 42,
    46, 79, 106
Katz (leader of the Socialist Party in
    Paterson), 49
Keaton, Buster, 126
Keyes (Paterson justice of the
    peace), 95
Killingbeck, Wilson, 51, 60, 65, 99
Klenert (Passaic County Court
    judge), 95
Koettgen (one of the original orga-
    nizers of the I.W.W. Paterson
    strike), 50, 51, 59, 68, 72

LaFollette, Robert, 67
Lessig (one of the original organiz-
    ers of the I.W.W. Paterson strike),
    50, 60, 75
Lischer, John, 24, 110, 124
Lohr, Ludwig, 114, 117
Long, Bridget, 168, 202
Long, Johnnie, 168
Long, Julia, 168
Long, Margaret, 168
Long, Sadie, 168, 180, 187

Marelli (I.W.W. lawyer), 67
Martin, Otto, 139, 163
Marx, Karl, 19
McBride, Andrew, 51, 64, 65, 68, 75,
    79, 89, 194
Melchior, Lauritz, 185
Meyer, Louis, 123, 128
Mohl, Frederick, 76
Morgan, J. P., 76
Morris family, 105
Murner, Sargent, 94

Orapallo (local shoemaker and
    Brueckmann neighbor), 198

Paterson, Captain, 94
Pickering, Fred, 36
Pries, Edward, 38, 42

Quinlan, Patrick, 51, 57, 60, 64, 68,
    70, 73, 74, 77, 87, 89, 95, 189

Radcliffe (sheriff of Passaic County),
    81, 89, 92
Reed, John, ix
Ritchie, Bill, 36, 41, 94, 114, 151
Rockefeller, John D., 76
Rolando (Haledon councilman), 76,
    92, 136
Roosevelt, Eleanor, 175

Roosevelt, Franklin D., 169, 175
Roosevelt, Theodore, 32, 37
Ruhren, Anna, 1, 13
Ruhren, August, xi, 1, 11, 13, 18, 110
Ruhren, Christine, 1, 13, 24, 34, 110, 124
Ruhren, Joe, 1, 110, 133, 155, 196
Ruhren (Katie's father), 15
Ruth, George Hermann ("Babe"), 187

Saner (Haledon police officer), 38, 55, 58, 66, 90
Scott, Alexander, 59, 89
Seibert (owner of the Paramount Diner Co., Haledon), 186
Shea, Catherine A., 176, 180
Shea, George A. (author's father), 167, 174, 180
Shea, George Sr., (author's grandfather), 169, 188
Shea, Helen Brueckmann (Kitty), 28, 61, 103, 122, 124, 129, 137, 152, 155, 163, 165, 167, 177, 179, 198
Shea, Helen C. (Baldasarre), 176
Shea, Mabel (Morrison), 169, 180

Shea, Maurice, 170
Shea, Michael, 169
Silvermann, Hannah, 84
Sinclair, Upton, 76
Spangenmacher (Haledon superintendent of Public Works), 41
Stein, Father, 66
Stewart, John, 43, 47

Taft, William Howard, 37
Toohey, Father, 109
Traubel, Helen, 185
Tresca, Carlo, 51, 58, 60, 65, 70, 71, 73, 77, 87
Triquart, John, 43, 47
Trotsky, Leon, 114 117, 193
Turner, William, 38, 42, 46, 92, 105, 106, 115, 119, 134, 136

Urban (right-wing agitator), 107, 137

Valentino, Modesto, 67
Vitz, J. Henry, 186

Watts, Rev., 44, 118
Wilson, Woodrow, 37, 75
Wuentsch (Haledon socialist), 95